CHARLOTTE HORNETS

Sharpening the Stinger

Rick Bonnell

SAGAMORE PUBLISHING
Champaign, IL

Production Manager: Susan M. McKinney
Dustjacket and photo insert design: Michelle R. Dressen
Editors: Susan M. McKinney, Russ Lake
Proofreader: Phyllis L. Bannon

Library of Congress Catalog Card Number:93-84955
ISBN: 0-915611-82-1

Printed in the United States.

To Ruth and Claire, who taught me that
life is what happens after deadline.

———————————

Contents

Acknowledgments vii

Introduction ix

1   *"They can't afford to have theirs chopped up."* 1

2   *"Hey, I'm not a Larry Johnson. . . . What I say is my word."* 13

3   *"You trade Gatt, you trade me."* 31

4   *"Do I strangle him if he takes another*
     shot from the outside?" 39

5   *"Guess Grandmama didn't wanna play no more."* 59

6   *"I don't think anyone was turning back flips*
     over Sidney Green." 77

7   *"He won't admit it because he's Napoleon."* 99

8   *"Everybody wants to be shooting stars, superstars."* 115

9   *"There's no place like road."* 127

10 *"It ain't Godzilla versus the X-monster."* 141

11 *"I'll have 80 on 'em next time. Eighty!"* 153

12 *"Hope I see you guys Thursday."* 159

13 *"This is a cocky team, those Charlotte Hornets."* 177

14 *"If Allan Bristow's an NBA coach, I'm an astronaut."* 185

15 *"I'll walk out of here with a Honey Bee under each arm."* 199

16 *"They've got the slowest front line in the*
     history of the game!" 217

17 *"Now it's a team you can almost root for."* 241

18 *"If he's here the first day of camp, one of you won't be."* 257

Acknowledgments

John Feinstein once tried to talk me out of accepting the assignment of covering the Charlotte Hornets. He compared it to covering the Washington Redskins for the newspaper where he then worked, the *Washington Post*. Feinstein warned me I would be so consumed by minutia in following Charlotte's first major-league team that I'd hate my work.

Feinstein, as smart as any sports writer I've met, was half-right. The job was filled with minutia. But I didn't hate it, I thrived on it. It was all so new, all so fascinating.

The problem was I couldn't cover it entirely by myself for the *Charlotte Observer*. There were just too many things to monitor, too many twists and turns. Fortunately, I work with a great group at the *Observer* who cheerfully jumped in when I needed help. Those people — Tom Sorensen, Charles Chandler, Leonard Laye, Liz Clarke and Ron Green — will all notice bits and pieces of their thoughts woven through this book. In some cases, they will see quotes they reported. In those cases involving one-on-one interviews, I tried to credit the reporter on the scene.

I have also worked throughout the five seasons with two excellent editors in David Scott and Gary Schwab. They are good bosses and good friends. And I owe a thanks to Frank Barrows, Rich Oppel and Jane Shoemaker, who gave their blessing to this project.

There's a rule somewhere that any sports writer doing a book needs to thank the team's public relations office for its cooperation. In this case, that thank-you is far more than obligatory. Harold Kaufman, Jason Brannon and Keith Kroehler are total pros. The Hornets are lucky to have them.

There are many others in the Hornets organization who made my job easier. Thanks in particular to Spencer Stolpen,

Allan Bristow, Dave Twardzik and George Shinn. Also to Dr. Glenn Perry, who can fix my shoulder anytime, and to John Delong of the *Winston-Salem Journal* and Mike Smith of the *Gaston Gazette*, nice guys to share a ride to and from a road game.

When I changed beats from covering colleges to the NBA, several veteran reporters were particularly giving with their advice and knowledge. Thanks to Bob Ryan, Terry Pluto, Phil Jasner , Sam Smith and Fred Kerber.

Three close friends — Jim Naughton, Blaise Ferrandino and Bud Poliquin — have helped shape how I look at life and sports. If this book is any good, credit them. The lousy parts are all me. I'm also indebted to Mark Wallinger, who, as always, was a dear friend, particularly during a mid-season anxiety attack.

And finally, thanks Dad, for giving me my first taste of sports journalism. Twenty years later, I still love this business. I guess passing on law school wasn't such a bad idea after all.

Introduction

This might have been the slowest Kendall Gill ever moved from one baseline to the other on a basketball court. The other 17,338 who filled Chicago Stadium that night to watch the Bulls win their second straight NBA championship had all departed long ago, scared off by the warnings of celebratory violence in the ghetto that surrounds the Bulls' ancient home.

The only ones left at courtside as Gill sauntered up the court were a hundred or so sportswriters, trying frantically to meet deadline and jump on the buses back to the press hotel before the shooting began.

But Gill dawdled, as if his body could somehow sponge up whatever it was that made the Bulls a great team and Michael Jordan the definitive player if his time. He stopped momentarily to shake hands with a writer there from Charlotte, but the reporter still had half a story to write and no time to chat. So Gill pushed on into the night to dream of what a championship is like, thinking of how Jordan and his teammates had just danced on tables and sloshed around champagne bottles and chewed on fat, expensive cigars.

This was not the first time Gill fantasized about being, as Gatorade's commercial suggested, "like Mike." It also wouldn't be the last.

Just as Chicago police had warned, the streets were full of violence after the Bulls put away the Portland Trail Blazers. It wasn't like Los Angeles a month earlier, when outrage over the Rodney King verdict had touched off days of burning and looting, sending the Lakers off to Las Vegas for one playoff game and the Clippers into the suburban bosom of Orange County for another. But there was violence; shots from an automatic weapon could be heard in the distance as reporters left the arena. And unlike what the rich yuppies who fill Chicago Stadium would like to think, the violence wasn't contained to poor, black neighborhoods. Thousands who spilled onto Rush Street, Chicago's upscale bar district, rocked and destroyed cars like there was no law. Because on that night, there was none.

As Chicago awoke from its collective hangover the next day, sweeping up the thousands of broken beer bottles and reading endless retellings of the game in the *Tribune* and *Sun-Times*, all-sports radio station WSCR — "The SCORE!" as the station reminds before and after each commercial break — was naturally presiding over an orgy of basketball gab. Having run out of Bulls officials to interview (hey, you can only talk to a ticket manager so long, right?), The SCORE coaxed Chicago-born Gill onto the air to talk about these Charlotte Hornets, an expansion team that no longer looked like an expansion team.

Just days earlier, with two weeks still to go until the draft, the Hornets had made it clear that they would take Georgetown center Alonzo Mourning with the second overall pick. Finally, the Hornets would have their center, someone to make Charlotte fans forget about such doomed experiments as Dave Hoppen and Stuart Gray. Finally, someone to block shots and draw the double-team away from Gill and Larry Johnson.

And best yet, Mourning was known primarily for his defense. He was basketball's equivalent of a soccer goalie in college, so there'd still be plenty of shots for Gill and Johnson. Gill was going to be a star on a great team — just like his buddy Mike. This thing was going to work out after all.

So when the announcer on The SCORE asked Gill if he'll be disappointed if the Hornets fail to qualify for the playoffs next season, Gill responded with a typically brash prediction.

"I'll be disappointed," Gill said, "if we don't make the second round."

Eleven months later, the Hornets were in the second round, trying to stay in a series with the New York Knicks. Gill was there, too, only his presence on the team was nearly as big an upset as the Hornets reaching the second round.

CHAPTER ONE

"They can't afford to have theirs chopped up."

It's not often that manure deliveries make the 6 o'clock news. However, this was an event.

George Shinn, owner of the Charlotte Hornets, had just accepted delivery of a truckload of processed dung purchased by Tampa Bay radio station WBTV. The station's original intention was a rather cruel practical joke. Two disk jockeys wanted the manure company to drop a "fresh" load of excrement on Shinn's lawn unannounced. The station was pulling a publicity stunt in protest of Shinn's efforts to keep the San Francisco Giants from moving to St. Petersburg, Florida.

Shinn caught wind of the stunt, so to speak, and originally stationed Roger Schweikert, a former FBI agent who works for Shinn, at the house to head off the delivery.

"I've had a lot of shitty jobs," Schweikert joked. "But this was the shittiest." The radio station's plans were far from secret. *The Charlotte Observer* and WBTV each had a photographer and reporter stake out Shinn's house, anticipating the delivery a day before it actually arrived.

Shinn had the good sense to accept the fertilizer graciously and contribute it to a local country club. For once, he had turned bad publicity into good press. That doesn't happen often. The Hornets, and particularly their owner, have a long track record of public relations disasters.

Shinn always wanted to buy a baseball team, and the Giants looked like a good match, at least temporarily. The Giants had already been tentatively sold to Florida businessmen looking to provide the Suncoast Dome with a tenant. But major league owners preferred that the Giants stay in San Francisco, and that city's government lobbied Shinn to serve as an alternative buyer.

Shinn loves playing white knight; to whip a town into civic frenzy, then replenish his year-round suntan in the glow of community affection. But St. Petersburg didn't play nice. The boys from Florida paid a five-figure retainer to a New York public relations firm to dig up dirt on Shinn.

Actually, calling this a public relations firm is too kind. These guys were propaganda ministers and character assassins, and Shinn was an easy target. He's done a lot of questionable things in his five years as the Hornets' owner. He once threatened to move the team out of the Charlotte Coliseum to blackmail the city into a better lease. He fired his first coach, Dick Harter, on the day Harter's brother died of cancer. He hired as his right-hand man a former lawyer who was once charged in Florida with conspiracy to smuggle marijuana.

George Shinn is a guy with liabilities, and that's no secret. Many former employees think Shinn demands total loyalty and provides little loyalty in return. But these New York p.r. types were vultures. When they called *The Observer* sports department, looking for more dirt, they got only a lecture on ethics. No matter what mistakes George Shinn had made, he didn't deserve the treatment of these jokers.

As it turned out, Shinn pulled out of the deal to buy the Giants. The numbers didn't add up to viable profitability. Besides, Shinn Enterprises needed to devote all its energy to what proved to be the biggest season in Hornets history.

The best and the worst of George Shinn is defined by his childhood. He may be the owner of a $100 million business, but Shinn knows all about poverty.

Shinn grew up in Kannapolis, North Carolina, a mill town where his father was owner-operator of a convenience store until he suddenly died of a stroke at age 51. (George Shinn eventually suffered a stroke in the same vein of the right frontal lobe as his father). Shinn was just eight when his father died, and learned quickly about credit and liability. The debt on the store's operation was heavy. Most of the Shinn family possessions had to be sold at a public auction to pay off the creditors after the father died.

Shinn says the memory of that auction is still vivid four decades later. His mother managed to save the house, but that was about it. She went on to work in various jobs to support the family. One year she was a telephone operator, another year the manager of a small motel.

The Shinn family had to accept some public assistance to make ends meet. "I got free lunches, and a lot of that inspired my later drive to succeed," Shinn recalled. "Kids can be cruel when they'd hear you get free lunches. Word always gets out about those things.

"I had a mother who really loved me, who really busted her chops for me," Shinn said. "I didn't have a steak until I was a sophomore at a high school football banquet. I remember asking mom why the neighbors had steak and we always had hamburger. She'd say, 'They can't afford to have theirs chopped up.'"

Shinn is a most unlikely candidate for the great success he's achieved, and that's not just because of his impoverished youth. Shinn wasn't a particularly disciplined student — he freely admits to finishing last in his high school class at A. L. Brown in Kannapolis.

"I'm sure people who've been to high school with me are as puzzled as I was," Shinn said of his achievements. "But I had a burning desire to succeed and a knack for surrounding myself with good people and motivating them to do a good job. People with no experience and no real direction, but I got them turned around."

Actually, Shinn might as well have been discussing himself as a young man. He was working part time as a janitor in a small for-profit college when somewhat by accident he recruited some prospective students to the school. He really was what bosses like to call a born salesman. Shinn rose through the organization until he owned the school, and then a chain of schools. Later he diversified, investing in car dealerships and land development, and made himself a millionaire many times over. By 1986, a personal-worth statement listed Shinn's assets at $50 million.

In that rise, Shinn demonstrated that his real gift in life is making others like him — self-made men with a love of wealth

— believe in him. That gift served him particularly well in pursuing an NBA team for Charlotte. Shinn loved sports and clearly was attracted to the high-profile status of being a major league owner. Hey, the average Joe doesn't know who the president of IBM is, but everyone's heard of George Steinbrenner.

A columnist from Phoenix once wrote that the only franchise Charlotte would get was one with golden arches, a catchy turn of phrase even without a kickback from McDonald's. Fortunately for Shinn, he was just too focused or perhaps too naive to understand that many in the league turned up their noses at the thought of expanding to Charlotte.

"He doesn't know how to take no for an answer," NBA commissioner David Stern said of Shinn. "We didn't know if Charlotte was in West Virginia or the Carolinas, but we knew pretty fast when he started selling. He convinced us that Charlotte's not so small. Actually, it's very large when you consider the extended area — then it's five million."

Actually, the NBA was the logical league to accept Shinn's sales pitch. First, basketball is a virtual religion in Charlotte, the largest city in the Carolinas. The Atlantic Coast Conference, which regularly holds its tournament in Charlotte, sends three or four first-round picks to the NBA every year. Second, the NBA has a tradition of success in mid-sized markets like Phoenix, Salt Lake City, and Portland. Third, Charlotte was building a trendy new arena that could seat nearly 24,000 for basketball.

Actually, the new arena was attractive, but its capacity was not. Stern and others in the league thought the building was far too large to create demand. In pursuing the franchise, Shinn agreed to curtain off the upper half of Charlotte Coliseum if that became a problem. To everyone's surprise, just the opposite was true — the largest arena in the NBA could not service all the demand from Hornets fans seeking tickets.

Almost from the first game, the Hornets became an obsession in Charlotte. *Chicago Tribune* reporter Sam Smith, who wrote *The Jordan Rules,* often jokes that the Hornets' astounding success proves just one thing — there's nothing else to do in Charlotte.

While facetious, Smith's point bears some truth. There's an incredible supply of yuppie money in Charlotte, one of the country's primary banking centers. However, unless you are a fan of stock-car racing, the Hornets represent the only major league sport in the immediate area.

The whole town acted like teenagers experiencing their first love the winter of 1988 — a giddy, floating feeling. The Hornets could do no wrong. Players who came from more established, more cynical towns found the atmosphere amazingly appealing.

"What I found so interesting was the way the fans cared about you," said Kurt Rambis, who played for the Hornets the first one and a half seasons. "It didn't matter if you won the night before. In other towns, they didn't talk to you if you didn't win."

Rambis, his wife, and another player, Tim Kempton, went to a local Italian restaurant after the team's first home game. The Hornets had just lost to the Cleveland Cavaliers by 40 points, yet the crowd at Villa Antonio stood and clapped when Rambis and Kempton walked in.

"We almost felt embarrassed by the response," said Kempton. "They wouldn't let us get down. If you drank every drink they bought, you couldn't have walked out of the place.

"You knew they wouldn't accept it when we lost, but they understood."

In the first season alone, the Hornets netted $11 million in profit, according to an informed source. That's particularly incredible considering the NBA's expansion fee was $32.5 million.

"It was too little, and I'm thrilled," Stern said, laughing at how the league underestimated the Hornets' immediate value. "It's great to make a deal that turns out good for everybody."

Really, all the Hornets had to do to remain a colossal success was to stay out of their own way. However, that was asking far too much. The team in general and Shinn in particular went through the most public of growing pains. It certainly appears Shinn's impoverished past played a role in those growing pains.

Shinn loves being a big shot and hates spending money. No one likes spending money, but Shinn hates it. Or at least fears it. A former close associate says Shinn's hand would visibly quiver whenever he signed checks. The compulsion to keep expenses to a minimum colored the Hornets' early years.

Take marketing director Tom Ward, for instance. Carl Scheer, the team's first general manager, needed Ward, then with the Washington Bullets, to run the team's marketing. Shinn said he'd do his own marketing rather than buy Ward away from the Bullets. Finally, Shinn relented after an outside marketing firm doing business with the Hornets offered to foot part of Ward's $75,000 salary.

Or take the team's first public relations director, Andy Warfield. Shinn had two conditions for filling this position. He wanted someone local and he wanted the salary no higher than $25,000. Warfield accepted both those terms, but he was badly out of his element in sport public relations. Within a season, Warfield was moved to another job in the organization and Harold Kaufman, a former intern with the Dallas Mavericks, was promoted to public relations director, a position he should have had from the start.

Marketing and public relations directors don't make or break sports franchises. But coaches can, and Scheer wanted one of the best, Larry Brown, who had just won a national championship at Kansas. Shinn didn't want to pay Brown's asking price, so the team eventually turned to Dick Harter. The Shinn-Harter marriage turned into one of the franchise's earliest and biggest mistakes.

Harter impressed Shinn by showing up in a white starched shirt (a Shinn preoccupation) and talking with passion about all the fight in his persona. Nearly as important, Harter was willing to work cheap, as NBA coaches go. But Shinn and Harter were destined to repel each other, which made it impossible for Harter to succeed. They had absolutely nothing in common. Harter is an urban Yankee; Shinn is a mill-town Southerner. Harter is an Ivy Leaguer; Shinn graduated last in his high school class. Harter is the ultimate worry-wart; Shinn is a perpetual optimist. Harter is a technocrat; Shinn believes in that version of the Golden Rule that says he who has the gold makes the rules.

They fought constantly over trivial issues. Harter won't comment on Shinn, in part because he has filed a lawsuit over lost income involving his firing halfway through the team's second year in existence. Shinn is happy to discuss Harter's faults.

"I think his biggest problem is Dick is a pessimist instead of an optimist," said Shinn. "He's a good coach — he's one of the best defensive assistants in the NBA. But he's not a people specialist. He's not good at dealing with people."

The handling of Harter's firing also helped break up the Shinn-Scheer relationship, according to current team president Spencer Stolpen. About a week before Harter was fired — the morning of Super Bowl Sunday — Scheer confirmed for a *Char-*

lotte Observer reporter (this author) that Harter's job was in jeopardy. Stolpen now claims that by answering the reporter's questions, Scheer was trying to make Shinn look like the bad guy.

"Carl set (Shinn) up by giving you that interview," Stolpen said. "There was a power struggle between George and Carl as to who really owned the team."

Scheer's description of the Hornets' early days is very different. Shinn had suffered a stroke early in the first season and was essentially incapacitated for several months. Scheer ran things, as was appropriate in his role as the team's general manager and president. When Shinn began to recover, he decided to buy out his partners and consolidate control of the team. Shinn began depending more on Stolpen, less on Scheer for input.

Scheer now resists the temptation to suggest Stolpen was in fact the one making the power play.

"(Stolpen) always tried to tell me he had no interest in basketball, that his job was to be George's right-hand man," said Scheer. "I don't think he had any master plan. Many people thought it was his plan to become Hornets president all along. I don't."

Scheer left for the Denver Nuggets when Shinn wouldn't sign him to an employment contract, a customary practice in hiring a major league general manager. Scheer became furious later upon discovering Shinn offered a contract, first to NBA vice president Rod Thorn, then to Nuggets assistant coach Allan Bristow, to replace Scheer as general manager.

Stolpen wound up in the president's seat, which raised some eyebrows in Charlotte. *The Observer* uncovered that Stolpen gave up his law license in Florida rather than turn over records involving some of his clients to the Florida Bar Association. Stolpen had a criminal law practice in Florida, and represented at least one client with reputed ties to the Mafia. Stolpen once called his refusal to turn over those records "noble." What wasn't so noble was his getting indicted for allegedly sending money to a client in South America that authorities claimed was meant to buy and smuggle marijuana.

The charges were thrown out when it was determined that wiretaps used to acquire some evidence were inappropriate. Stolpen admitted in an interview with *Observer* reporter Elizabeth Leland that he withdrew $5,000 from his client trust account for Louis Ippolito. Stolpen told Leland he didn't know how Ippolito spent it. He also helped Ippolito find a large boat that authorities suspect Ippolito wanted for smuggling purposes. Stolpen told Leland "it was fair for me to assume" Ippolito was involved with illegal drugs. However, Stolpen maintains he did nothing illegal.

Ippolito was later convicted in another case of racketeering and possession with intent to sell cocaine.

Stolpen later burned some records rather than provide them to the Florida bar. That cost him his law license. Stolpen claims he feared for his safety if those records became part of a proceeding, even a private one involving the state bar.

Stolpen ended up teaching business and paralegal courses at one of Shinn's schools. Stolpen advanced to president of that school, and kept on impressing Shinn from afar until Shinn brought him to Charlotte.

Today, he is president of the Hornets.

The information above illustrates that Stolpen is ambitious, pragmatic, and made some colossally bad decisions as a young adult. What it doesn't convey is that Stolpen is also a brilliant organizer. Stolpen filled a void for the Hornets, particularly in the area of long-range planning. The NBA salary cap is an impossibly complicated document that strings up most teams. Stolpen knows the cap, knows the team's cap responsibility to the length of every player's contract, and has helped bring order to a sometimes chaotic franchise.

As one Hornets employee put it, "Spencer's thing is information." Translation: He's a sponge for gossip and minutia, and that's what makes him a good negotiator.

Stolpen also acts as a buffer between Shinn and the players and staff.

"Fifty percent of my job is translating George to the world and the world to George," Stolpen said.

Shinn loved being the highest-profile millionaire in town. That is, until the headaches of being an owner started. After years of insisting male employees wear white shirts, Shinn wasn't ready for strong-headed, sometimes rebellious basketball players making millions.

"He didn't understand why Rex (Chapman) wasn't his buddy, why he wasn't enthusiastic about working here," Stolpen said of the Hornets' first negotiation with a first-round pick.

Worse yet, Shinn didn't understand the difference between marketing and press coverage. He took no real heat from the local media or Charlotteans in general back when he was chasing the franchise. But within two years of the team's existence, fans and local reporters were asking tough questions about this franchise's progress toward a playoff berth.

"We're in a business where 400,000 people in this town can do a better job than us and are quick to vocalize it," Stolpen said. "But without them, we wouldn't be in business."

There was much to criticize. The first two first-round picks — Chapman and J. R. Reid — were mediocre at best. The team's front office couldn't service the various autograph requests, so they forged various players' signatures on balls, caps, and pictures and eventually were caught by *The Observer*. Worst of all, when Shinn decided he had a poor lease deal with Charlotte Coliseum, he threatened to bolt and build his own arena across the South Carolina border.

"If there's a flaw in George, it's that he's too naive, too open," Stolpen said. "There's a difference between being a public figure and baring your soul to the media every day.

"George says, 'I still owe that to the reporters who helped me get the team, through exposure.'" That description by Stolpen might be a bit too kind. Actually, Shinn is addicted to microphones. He gets his kicks discussing the team's latest triumph or failure whenever the television cameras show up.

Shinn's popularity around Charlotte dropped markedly by late in the second season, when some local novelty stores stocked "Shinn Happens" T-shirts.

"It's plagued us from Day 1 — people not always in a position to talk, do [talk]— George, Allan, Carl," said Stolpen. "Carl shouldn't have said what he said to you (about Harter). George shouldn't have said what he did to WBTV (about the Coliseum lease). Allan shouldn't have gone off during the Mourning negotiations."

However, the biggest indiscretion in Hornets history occurred when Coach Gene Littles was critical of the team's decision to draft Larry Johnson. Littles was promoted to interim coach when Harter was fired. The other assistant at the time, Ed Badger, was Harter's buddy, so he was eliminated from consideration. Littles wasn't soiled by Harter's firing. In fact, the two didn't like each other at all, and Harter suspected that Littles helped turn the players against him.

Littles's strongest qualifications for the job were his loyalty to Shinn and an initial impression among some players that Littles was more sensitive to their feelings. In fact, Littles was no easier to get along with. At least Harter was consistently critical. Littles would suddenly turn on players, as he did the night he ripped into J. R. Reid in a postgame interview in Dallas. Reid was furious, not because Littles criticized him, but because he did so through the media rather than face-to-face. Littles made a grand show, when he took over, of telling the players to keep their problems in the locker room rather than running to the press.

Littles clearly didn't practice what he preached. It became apparent several days before the 1991 draft that the Hornets would select Johnson, primarily at the urging of Bristow, then team vice president.

Littles first wanted Syracuse's Billy Owens, then Georgetown's Dikembe Mutombo. So he second-guessed the team's decision in a rambling diatribe to the *Gaston Gazette*. Then, attempting to shield himself from the fallout, he told different stories to different people. Bristow said Littles denied making those comments to the *Gazette*. But when asked five different times by an *Observer* reporter, Littles wouldn't say he was mis-quoted, only that his comments to the *Gazette* posed questions rather than made statements, whatever that meant.

Bristow was steaming, and Stolpen knew he had a problem.

"We were concerned about Gene talking off the cuff," said Stolpen, again citing the franchise's chronic problem.

Yet Stolpen says the incident with the *Gazette* wasn't what got Littles kicked off the bench before the start of the next season. Rather, it was Littles's inability to communicate with players — particularly Reid — combined with Bristow's burning desire to return to coaching.

"We couldn't get (Littles) to take a look at what our plan was for development. We wanted him to sit down with J. R. and try to work it out," Stolpen said. "Allan *really* wanted to get back on the bench. Allan was the one who approached me with the idea."

Bristow's move to the bench consolidated power in his hands. Bristow's close friend, Dave Twardzik, rose to director of player personnel, a job that made him responsible for the draft and trades but left the major contract negotiations to Stolpen. That's how Twardzik preferred it. Bristow also hired as his assistants Bill Hanzlik and T. R. Dunn, cronies from Bristow's Denver days. Neither had any previous coaching experience.

Bristow and Twardzik disagree occasionally, but their relationship is not the coach-general manager rivalry it is on many teams. Shinn admits Bristow has more influence over the roster than anyone else in the organization. In other words, if Bristow were to fail as coach, he'd have no one to blame but himself.

Essentially, it comes down to personal trust and respect. Shinn just believes in Bristow in ways he never believed in Harter or Littles, and that isn't necessarily a judgment on Bristow's basketball knowledge. It's more a testament to how Bristow finesses Shinn's personality and approach.

Harter openly revolted against Shinn's hands-on management style. Littles tolerated it better, but never really played to it. Bristow is more patient with Shinn's questions and ideas. For instance, when he was team vice president, Bristow traveled to Sacramento on a fact-finding mission to discover whether Ralph Sampson, a Shinn favorite, could still play. Bristow came back saying Sampson was washed up, and that satisfied Shinn, who at least wanted to be taken seriously by his employees.

Shinn has, to some degree, learned from his previous mistakes. He says he isn't as quick to second-guess the basketball people on his staff as he once was. But he also feels Bristow and Twardzik listen to his input more than their predecessors.

Maybe Shinn and Bristow work well together because of their similarities. Like Shinn, Bristow is Southern and frugal. Bristow is probably tighter with Shinn's money than Shinn is, which only complicated the negotiations over Alonzo Mourning's contract.

CHAPTER TWO

"Hey, I'm not a Larry Johnson. . . . What I say is my word."

George Shinn beamed at the press conference, one day after the 1992 draft, and it wasn't just because Shinn had gotten his man at center. It was the man behind the man who so pleased Shinn.

To no one's surprise, Georgetown center Alonzo Mourning had hired David Falk to be his agent. Or to be more precise, Nike, the multinational sneaker company — the "Just Do It!" guys from Beaverton, Oregon — had hired Falk to negotiate Mourning's contract on Nike's behalf. Mourning had signed an agreement with Nike that went far beyond the normal sneaker deal. Mourning wouldn't just wear Nike's Force series of shoes, he would actually let Nike manage his career. It was a novel idea that left some wondering if this was the first step in the shoe companies taking over major league sports.

Forbes magazine reported that Nike had guaranteed Mourning he would make $16 million over five years off his first NBA contract, his sneaker endorsement, and any other endorsement deals Nike could round up. Nike's radical deal was inspired, in part, by Chicago Bulls star Michael Jordan doing an underwear commercial that some at Nike thought clashed with the image in the sneaker ads. Nike worried that Jordan's hawking everything from soda pop to bikini briefs might leave him overexposed. The sneaker company was willing to pay a huge fee to have a say in how the next generation of Nike-wearing NBA superstars would be marketed. Mourning and Southern California guard Harold Miner would be the well-compensated guinea pigs in Nike's experiment in sports agentry.

It was ironic that Falk, the man who negotiated that underwear endorsement deal for Jordan, would be Nike's hired gun in contract talks with the Hornets. Ironic, but far from surprising. You see, Mourning's coach at Georgetown, John Thompson, is on Nike's board of directors. Thompson is also represented by Falk. In fact, Falk calls Thompson his "mentor," and every Hoya of consequence in the past few years — centers Patrick Ewing of the New York Knicks, Dikembe Mutombo of the Denver Nuggets and Mourning — have been represented by Falk.

(Falk, by the way, earned his law degree from Syracuse, the bitterest of Big East rivals with Georgetown. It could be said without too much exaggeration that Falk is the first Syracuse graduate ever to have anything nice to say about Thompson, known as Darth Vader around Syracuse's upstate New York campus.)

Though several other agents tried to compete with Falk to represent Mourning, their sentiments were summed up by Arn Tellem, a friend of Falk's, who represents Hornets guard Kendall Gill. In Chicago for the 1992 predraft camp in June, Tellem was asked if he had any chance at Mourning. Tellem shrugged with a look of resignation, saying, "Trust me, he'll be David's guy."

And so Mourning was "David's guy," which made Shinn very, very happy. The winter before, one of Falk's other clients, Rex Chapman, was one miserable Charlotte Hornet. Gill had outplayed Chapman to be the starting shooting guard, and Dell Curry, one of the NBA's best sixth men, was also well suited for the off-guard spot. Chapman was not used to sitting and was far from pleased about it. He moped when Hornets coach Allan Bristow benched him, following a particularly putrid night of defense against the Milwaukee Bucks. Chapman was a gifted leaper and daring passer, but his shot selection was inexcusable, and his defense lacked fundamentals and a willingness to be physical. Worse yet, Chapman had signed a contract extension the summer before that would pay him about $2 million each of the next five seasons.

Chapman wanted out of Charlotte and the Hornets wanted him out. But where to go? Who would trade for a player making so much who had done so little? Enter Falk, the dealmaker. Falk might have the fattest Roladex in major league sports. He is so well connected that some in the NBA think he could succeed as a general manager without knowing much about who can play. Falk just might be able to bluff his way through as a GM, because he knows all the men who know who can play and has a fine track record convincing them to do as he wishes.

Falk set out to play matchmaker between Chapman and a new team. He found the Washington Bullets, one of the few in the league with enough salary-cap room to fit Chapman's contract. Plus, the Bullets had a glaring need for a shooting guard. Chapman was a show pony, if a flawed one, and the Bullets' shooting guards belonged in a dog pound. With Falk guiding the teams to each other, the Bullets and Hornets made the deal. Chapman went to Washington, while Tom Hammonds, a forward of marginal skill signed to a cheap contract, moved to Charlotte.

After this little bit of alchemy, Shinn thought Falk was the next best thing to Elvis. Imagine, an agent who could get something done to help a team! And best yet, Falk had a reputation for setting the market on rookies each summer instead of waiting for some other agent to do so. Falk hated holdouts almost as much as teams did.

Most agents resist signing a client early out of fear they might misread the market and undercut a player's value. The consequences of such an act can be professional suicide. Though the extra hundred thousand or so per year difference doesn't mean much relative to the entire contract, an agent's ability to recruit clients this year can hinge on how much he whittled out of a team's salary cap last year.

Falk knows all that, but frankly, he has more faith in his own reading of the market than anyone else's, so he is not afraid to sign a client early if he gets what he wants. Falk's brilliance is obvious, but his arrogance is just as apparent. In his book, *Taking to the Air, The Rise of Michael Jordan*, Jim Naughton accurately compared Falk to Pete Rose for the way Falk sifts his own statistics of achievement into just about any conversation. Falk's right — he's a brilliant agent — but no one will ever accuse Falk of being humble about it.

Shinn, rather arrogant himself for a guy who admits to finishing last in his high school class, wasn't put off by Falk's manner. Shinn loved Falk's can-do style.

"Obviously, we feel very good, based on David Falk's history," Shinn said just after the draft. "David likes to set the pace, as opposed to following it.

"We'll make him a fair offer — not low-ball him, not high-ball him. They want him signed, we want him signed. I think it can happen quickly."

In typical Shinn overstatement, he announced, "If (Falk) had been Larry Johnson's agent, Larry would have been in camp." Johnson, the previous season's No. 1 overall pick, missed all but the last day of the 1991 preseason before signing a six-year contract worth a dollar under $20 million. The problems in signing Johnson really rankled the Hornets, who took to treating Johnson's agents like hillbillies.

It was true that Johnson's representatives — Steve Endicott and the somewhat shadowy Sherwood Blount — were Johnson's agents primarily because of their connections to Southern Methodist, the scandal-ridden Dallas university where Johnson first signed before attending Nevada-Las Vegas. Endicott doesn't know a tenth of what Falk does about the salary cap. However, it's also true that Endicott bargained in good faith with the Hornets, who manipulated the cap to have available exactly what they wanted to offer Johnson and not a dollar more.

Endicott was accurate when he said the cap, as the Hornets used it, served as a "vise" around the Johnson negotiations. A similar ploy by the Hornets in these negotiations would eventually blow up in the team's face.

But for now, everyone was smiles, particularly Mourning, who got a kick out of the 5-9 Shinn standing on a chair to greet him eye-to-eye. Mourning said for weeks before the draft that he would be signed by the start of training camp. He even offered to show up for the team's midsummer mini-camp, something elite rookies seldom even consider attending. Only an extraction of wisdom teeth kept him away when the veterans got together for what Bristow called a "summer workshop" in July.

Bristow laughed when Mourning repeatedly promised to be signed on time. Bristow reminded Mourning that Johnson said all the same things, then signed barely in time for the team's first regular-season game. Mourning replied, "Hey, I'm not a Larry Johnson. . . . What I say is my word."

Bad choice of words, Alonzo. *Very* bad choice of words. Mourning would be reminded again and again of what he said as he remained unsigned through the first four games of the regular season.

The Alonzo Mourning contract negotiations made the Larry Johnson negotiations look no more painful than paying a parking ticket. What started in June in that press conference full of handshakes and backslaps deteriorated into a series of threats and counter-threats, name-calling, and grandstanding. Falk likes to keep things quiet during negotiations, and both sides were mum at first. But once the Hornets started hurling mud, Falk retaliated. Falk would later call this episode the ugliest negotiation he'd ever been in, comparing it to the divisive arbitration hearing he forced on the Knicks to try to get Ewing declared an unrestricted free agent.

The Hornets' sentiments on the matter were summed up by one member of the front office, who once joked he wouldn't mind Falk contracting a slow and painful disease. Fun stuff, these negotiations.

The pressures on the talks were varied. Bristow didn't want the Hornets paying Mourning more than Johnson made, figuring that could be a real threat to team chemistry. Johnson emerged quickly as a future superstar, and paying a No. 2 pick more than the previous year's No. 1 pick could cause immediate problems.

"I had a difficult time convincing Allan what the market was," said team president Spencer Stolpen. "Allan for a long time said Zo should *never* make more money than Larry."

Also, Shinn was still adjusting to the cost of doing business in the NBA. His team had netted more than $11 million that first season in 1988-89, but that was back when the players the Hornets inherited from other teams' benches were low paid. Now, the lottery was supplying them with great college talent who — *surprise!* — expected great compensation.

That was particularly true of Gill, who had the option to become a restricted free agent at the end of the 1992-93 season. The Hornets knew that whatever they paid Mourning would help Gill and Tellem establish an asking price down the road. As Tellem said of the Mourning talks, "Obviously, Kendall is watching it very closely. He's following it with great interest."

At the other end, Falk had his own problems. A friend of Falk's repeatedly called the Mourning negotiations crucial to Falk's ongoing status as an elite sports agent. Falk was the agent to the stars, all right — his stable included Jordan, Ewing,

Atlanta's Dominique Wilkins, and Utah's John Stockton. Add Mutombo or Mourning as an oversized power forward, and you'd have a virtual Dream Team starting five.

"David is very strong-minded, very assertive, and probably the best in the history of his business," said Orlando Magic general manager Pat Williams. "He certainly has the best stable of players."

But Jordan, Ewing, Stockton, and Wilkins are all closer to the end of their careers than the beginning. Frankly, except for the players acquired through his Georgetown connections, much of Falk's NBA client base was graying. In five years, most of his top clients would be playing golf instead of basketball in the winter.

"David had a history of getting players in early, but we didn't realize this was his last big shot," Shinn would later say.

Falk went about stirring up new business with a passion his friends hadn't seen in some time. It was rather like watching North Carolina coach Dean Smith go back out on the recruiting trail to land a top class. If Mourning was a virtual lock, then Duke's Christian Laettner, the third-best player in the draft behind Mourning and Shaquille O'Neal, was the longshot for Falk.

Laettner isn't very popular among anyone but 16-year-old girls, and with good reason. He's petulant almost beyond description. He thinks he's a cross between Luke Perry and James Dean (long sideburns, soulful pout, baby-blue eyes), a pretty boy blessed with an equally pretty outside jump shot and a post-up game belying his good looks. He has a face that makes advertisers swoon, and talent and toughness and. . . an attitude problem.

According to a third party with knowledge of the incident, Laettner once talked down to Falk in Jordan's presence. Essentially, Laettner asked Jordan, with Falk nearby, why he needed Falk. As if Falk, who has 10 or 15 basketball and football clients of Laettner's stature, needed to come begging for Laettner's services. It was an insult, and typical of Laettner's know-it-all, self-important manner. Laettner eventually hired a group of ex-Duke football players in law practice in Durham as his representatives. That group — "the Durham bunch," as Falk later described them — ended up subcontracting the actual negotiation of Laettner's contract with the Minnesota Timberwolves to Tellem.

Protecting his client base wasn't the only pressure on Falk. He also wanted Nike to walk away happy. This could have been considered somewhat of a tryout. Nike planned to sign other athletes to management contracts, so why couldn't Falk end up as their gunslinger on a permanent basis? After all, it was Falk who was credited with coining the phrase "Air Jordan," which helped sell millions of Nike sneakers.

"He had a lot of pressure," Stolpen said of Falk. "It was not a pleasant situation, from what I hear. The negotiations amounted to him auditioning for Nike."

Of course Falk denies that he was any more concerned with getting Mourning a good deal than any other client. And it's certainly true that Falk is one intense negotiator, armed with every graph, chart, or turn of phrase necessary to talk the other side into a concession. Those who have negotiated with Falk all say they go hoarse before Falk does.

Ex-Hornets general manager Carl Scheer said Falk's great strength is convincing himself that his client — whoever that client is — is the greatest, then setting out to convince the team of that, regardless of the statement's validity.

"He's a competitor," Jordan said of Falk. "He researches his numbers, he prepares his positions very well. He's always trying to learn about the sport. He's very versatile and he's enhanced his knowledge, his expertise, the whole way."

Finally, there was pressure from the Hornets' fans, who filled the 23,698 seats in the Charlotte Coliseum for every home game. At first, public opinion was squarely against that "greedy" Mourning and his henchman, Falk. "How dare they ask for more than our Larry Johnson was getting?" fans thought. But as time went by, and particularly after Laettner landed a $21.6 million contract from the Timberwolves, fans came to the conclusion that it was time for Shinn to open the vault and get the center in here while the Hornets were still in the playoff hunt.

One fan, Viki Lagle of Davidson, even wrote *The Charlotte Observer* to say fans should take up a collection to help Shinn pay what the market on starting centers demanded. In fact, it was an effort to shame Shinn into resolving the situation.

Lagle, who went so far as to open an account at a local bank, wrote: "Since the Hornets' management would just as soon sit back and risk losing Mourning over $340,000 (the difference in first-year salary between Falk's demand and Charlotte's offer) . . . I will put up $20 and challenge 17,000 others to do the same. If I am going to have to pay $50 per game again this year, then I would just as soon pay $20 now and hopefully see a winning team."

One thing neither side expected to be a problem was comparison to O'Neal's deal with Orlando. Falk took it for granted that the Magic and O'Neal couldn't agree on terms before Mourning signed with Charlotte. After all, O'Neal was the best prospect to emerge from college ball since David Robinson, so establishing his compensation would take forever. Plus, the Magic had even bigger salary-cap problems than the Hornets. So, Stolpen and Falk agreed immediately to think of O'Neal as an aberration.

Or at least they thought they agreed. Stolpen considered Orlando's negotiations with O'Neal moot. Falk said fine to that, as long as the Hornets then consider Mourning the de facto No. 1 pick in any discussion of his contract. It all seemed rather moot since O'Neal would never sign before Mourning, right?

Wrong. In late July, about a month after the draft, the Dallas Mavericks launched a sneak attack on the Magic, signing Orlando restricted free agent Stanley Roberts to a five-year, $14.7 million offer sheet. The Magic had 15 days to decide whether to match the offer sheet or let Roberts go to Dallas without any compensation.

It was a good gamble by Dallas. After all, O'Neal would replace Roberts as Orlando's starting center the second O'Neal was signed. Also, since the Magic couldn't exceed the cap to sign rookie O'Neal, but could to sign Roberts, the offer sheet essentially gave Orlando a two-week deadline to sign O'Neal or lose Roberts.

However, Orlando's Williams was determined not to lose Roberts without compensation. So he went about restructuring four contracts on the team, traded one player and cut another with unguaranteed money. Williams made the deadline by just four hours, signing Shaq to a seven-year, $39.9 million contract in time to match the offer sheet on Roberts.

The rest of the NBA was startled, not just because Williams had worked so fast but because O'Neal's contract was so rich. Suddenly, that moot point wasn't moot anymore. Falk, just back from a trip to Europe, reemphasized his stance that either the

Hornets treat Mourning like the de facto No. 1 (which meant he had to make more than Johnson) or pay him No. 2 money relative to what O'Neal got (which again meant Mourning had to make more than Johnson).

As logical as that reasoning was, it made Bristow cringe. Usually, anything that comes out of an agent's mouth makes Bristow cringe. He once said newspaper sports editors around the country should all agree to limit any references to agents to the business pages. More likely, Bristow probably thought, references to agents all belonged in the obituaries.

"Allan can't deal with agents because he hates them personally," said Stolpen. "That's why he's not (negotiating contracts) anymore."

Bristow had once done that, as Charlotte's vice president of basketball operations, a fancy name for general manager. The year before he became coach, replacing Gene Littles, Bristow lost his temper at Tellem and grabbed him in a much-publicized choke-hold. Tellem is a bookish sort who weighs perhaps 170 pounds and might be 5-9 (he's a dead ringer for the character "Miles" on "Murphy Brown"). Tellem was obviously no match for 6-7 ex-player Bristow. After seeking treatment for a sprained neck, Tellem sent a letter of complaint to the league. Eventually, Bristow apologized and paid Tellem's medical bills.

Shinn laughed the whole episode off at the press conference announcing Gill's signing, referring to Bristow as "Rocky." The crowd at the press conference broke up over that one, though Tellem was clearly unamused.

That might have been the only time Bristow roughed up an agent, but there are other examples of his loathing of the agent profession. One such story involving Falk refers back to Chapman.

At the end of Chapman's stay in Charlotte, he suffered from plantar fascia, essentially a serious inflammation of the arch of the foot. Bristow wondered whether Chapman was just brooding over not starting, and using the foot as an excuse not to play. Shortly after Chapman was traded to Washington, Bristow found himself seated near Falk at a Duke home game. Bristow was there to scout Laettner; Falk was there looking to be Laettner's agent. But it was Bobby Hurley, Duke's point guard, who proved to be the point of contention.

Hurley had just recovered from a broken foot, yet was playing superbly. So Bristow wondered loud enough for Falk to hear how a college kid like Hurley could play so hard after a serious injury, while Chapman hobbled along with a seemingly less serious ailment (hint-hint, nudge-nudge).

Falk isn't prone to pick fights, but he's happy to joust when challenged. First, he suggested that perhaps the Hornets' medical staff wasn't up to Duke's standards. Then came the real jab.

"Coaches ought to stay out of scouting," Falk told Bristow.

It made Bristow's week that he had gotten so far under Falk's skin.

Any personal friction between Falk and Bristow was minimal compared to the issue of compensation. The Hornets built their initial offers around a first-year salary of $2.2 million. First-year salary is crucial to any offer to a rookie because no year-to-year raise in a player's initial contract can exceed 30 percent of the first-year salary.

In other words, if Falk wanted to get Mourning a deal averaging $4 million over six years, he had to get the Hornets up to $2.4 million in first-year compensation. An average of $4 million always seemed in the back of Falk's mind in his discussions with the Hornets. Stolpen and Hornets director of player personnel Dave Twardzik strongly suspect Nike had some sort of target clause in its agreement with Falk that gave him a bonus for reaching that average.

Nothing much had happened before September. Falk had helped restructure the contract of another client, Charlotte point guard Muggsy Bogues, to help free up some room under the team's salary cap. Despite the slow pace, neither side seemed concerned. In fact, Stolpen went so far as to bet *Winston-Salem Journal* beat writer John Delong dinner that Mourning would be signed before the start of camp in October.

That confidence sagged following a meeting between Falk and Stolpen in late September. The Hornets had $1.6 million available to sign Mourning, and Stolpen said he thought there were some options that could raise that amount to about $2.2 million. Stolpen added that Kenny Gattison's contract of about $600,000 was unguaranteed, so as a last resort the team could trade or cut Gattison to get the available cap room to where it needed to be. Falk said he wanted $2.4 million in first-year salary (which just happened to get him to the magic $4 million over six years). Stolpen recalls the rest of the conversation this way:

"That's not necessarily an unreasonable number," Stolpen told Falk. "I'll make a deal with you. I won't artificially hold the number below the range (between $2.3 million and $2.5 million). In exchange, if we get close, you'll work with us to find a way to get this done."

Falk remembers that conversation somewhat differently — as a commitment to get to the $2.4 million range. He essentially thinks Stolpen offered one thing, then yanked it back when the coaches convinced Stolpen that losing Gattison was unpalatable.

Things simmered to the point that it was obvious Mourning wouldn't be signed for the start of camp. Then one Friday night, as most Charlotteans watched the Atlanta Braves in the World Series, Falk went off, telling *The Charlotte Observer* he was prepared to "drop a bomb" on the Hornets.

"I think they're sitting on a time bomb," Falk warned the night of October 9. "I'm sure there will be a point, some point in time, when he takes all this in and says he just does not want to play" in Charlotte. Then Falk made it clear the Hornets couldn't paint him and Mourning into a corner with the salary cap, as they had Endicott and Johnson.

"I'm not Steve Endicott, and this isn't Larry Johnson. He's got the leverage, the resolve and the financial security. He doesn't have to play (to make a living) and if he didn't have that, I still wouldn't recommend anything that suggests he be intimidated."

The implication was clear — Falk was threatening to hold Mourning out the entire season and reenter the draft. Falk even threw the reasoning of player-personnel director Dave Twardzik back at the team. Twardzik had repeatedly said the 1993 senior class was particularly weak. So the master debater that he is, Falk made sure to mention regularly that, on the basis of Twardzik's assessment of the next draft, Mourning's value could only rise by sitting out a year and reentering the draft.

The Hornets were a bit flustered, in part because Falk put out the word that Mourning would make a living off his Nike deal regardless of whether he signed with the Hornets. That gave Mourning leverage most rookies can't match. Shinn said he was taking Falk's threat seriously, and others around the league agreed — Falk was not prone to false bravado.

"I've never known him to pontificate or bluster," said Orlando's Williams. "Some (agents) are on the phone to the press every day. That's not David's style. He must be really upset.

"He's very knowledgeable about what he does. Strong willed but realistic. Some (agents) just don't know what they're talking about."

Falk was in total agreement with Williams on that. He hated being called an "agent" — he called himself Jordan's or Ewing's attorney — and felt there was a terribly negative connotation in the term "sports agent."

To Falk, players and agents were never going to be popular in these situations; it was just the nature of his business.

"The public just doesn't have a lot of sympathy for players making millions, even if they're underpaid relative to what owners make," Falk said. "So you're never going to win, especially when the economy is bad and jobs are hard to find."

Also, Falk wondered whether he was getting an even shake from all the Charlotte media.

"The local media, the ones covering the team day in and day out, need access and friendly relations with the coaches and general manager. So they're not quick to give the agent's side," Falk said.

One example of Falk's point: WBT-AM 1110, the flagship station for Hornets broadcasts, gave over most of an hour of its "Sports Huddle" talk show to Stolpen one night, to give his side of the debate. When asked if he planned to have Falk on the next night, "Sports Huddle" moderator and Hornets play-by-play announcer Matt Pinto said he wasn't about to give Falk an open forum for his view of the negotiations.

Well, why not? Isn't that what Stolpen got the night before? In fairness to Pinto, a good journalist who aggressively covers the Hornets when wearing his reporter's hat, this was typical of how television and radio stations treat agents. Not right, but typical.

Not that agents don't contribute to their own bad image.

"The whole profession of being an agent has a bad reputation," Falk said, "because there are so many unqualified people doing it. You don't even need a high school diploma to be certified" by the NBA Players Association.

At first the Hornets thought, somewhat hopefully, that Nike's presence would help speed a settlement of the negotiations. After all, why would Nike want all that bad press? Nasty letters to the editor were flowing into *The Observer*, blaming Nike for the impasse. Once printed, those letters were being faxed back to Nike's Beaverton, Oregon, headquarters, and there was some concern over why a mass-appeal company like Nike should be involved with a business as unpopular as sports agentry.

"I read enough of the letters. David Falk, and to some extent Nike, didn't look very good to the people of North Carolina," said Nike director of sports management Fred Schreyer. "But I think that the big bucks are here to stay. Negotiations of that level are not just lay-downs. It would be easier to just stay out of it. But we feel it's really important."

Schreyer, a former Los Angeles attorney who helped represent several athletes in negotiations, didn't take it well when the Hornets put pressure on Nike to get Mourning signed. With endorsers like Charles Barkley, John McEnroe, and Andre Agassi, Nike rather revels in a rebel image.

"At first, Hornets management thought we'd force him in," Schreyer said. "Then they thought the opposite, and all of a sudden we were bad guys."

Schreyer clearly enjoyed turning the tables after wrestling with sports teams over contracts in his previous job as an agent.

"I don't think that's something Nike should apologize for. If us working with an athlete gives him more leverage, that's a positive. The salary cap has become a tool to turn a crank on an athlete.

"I don't know if we went looking to create more leverage, but that was a by-product. Alonzo's such a principled, strong-willed guy. And he had the right guy representing him. David can do the job."

As training camp opened, Bristow came around to the realization that the Hornets had to pay Mourning more than Johnson to get him into camp. But how much more? One of the things that bothered Bristow about Falk was that Falk was nebulous about what it would take to reach an agreement.

"He knows three words: 'That's not enough!'" Bristow shouted in one of his many tirades against Falk.

But the Hornets were getting closer, after restructuring contracts for Mike Gminski and J. R. Reid. Reid signed a deal on his wedding day that would pay him $200,000 less this season, but would end up paying him an average of about $1.7 million over the next four years. Gminski reshifted his money so that he would make about $435,000 less this season, but would get an extra $1 million guaranteed in two seasons.

The Hornets regretted not accepting one of the trade offers for Reid around the time of the draft. Nothing was very firm, but both the Los Angeles Lakers and Minnesota Timberwolves probably would have exchanged a first-round pick for Reid. A low first-rounder (Minnesota would have acquired one from Golden State late in the round) wasn't much in return for a player taken fifth overall in 1989. But Reid had been a disappointment, and Gattison had shown last season he was a better, and cheaper, version of the same power forward-center player.

Gattison was glad for Reid, but wondered aloud why Reid's extension would average about three times as much as Gattison's current deal, when Gattison had demonstrated he was the superior player.

"That baffles me," Gattison said. "You just don't know what management is thinking."

Then again, perhaps Gattison, a distributive education major at Old Dominion, did know what Hornets management was thinking. "What I'm worth and what they're going to pay me are two entirely different things," Gattison added. "I've learned that."

It was right about then that Falk started pressuring the Hornets to do something — even if that meant dealing away Gattison for little — to get this thing resolved. The Hornets must blame themselves for that pressure. Over the summer they had invited Falk to search out a deal that would help clear the cap room for Mourning's contract. Heck, it had worked once before with the Chapman deal, so why not let Falk scout around for some options?

Unfortunately for the Hornets, that invitation let the genie out of the bottle. Falk felt this "partnership" with the Hornets meant he could advocate just about anything that would get Mourning his money. During one particularly frustrating day, in which Falk reminded the Hornets that "it's not the player's responsibility to wiggle into the (cap) space available," Falk explained just how easily he could end the impasse.

"I could free up cap room for the Hornets in 30 to 40 minutes with three or four different situations," Falk said. "I know that because they asked me to check."

Falk never said so publicly, but it was obvious to Bristow and Stolpen that any such quick fix would mean losing Gattison.

"We really felt there was a breach on his part when he said we need to cut Gattison to make the deal," Stolpen would later say.

Somewhere along the line, tempers cooled. Bristow asked former Hornets general manager Carl Scheer, a friend of Falk's, to act as an informal go-between, someone to smooth the waters. Also, the Hornets appealed to Georgetown coach John Thompson.

Thompson was somewhat of a silent partner in all this. Thompson helped set up the Nike deal for Mourning, assuring that Mourning would never want for money. Also, he pretty much shoved Falk onto Nike, as one company official confirmed.

Thompson wanted to stay in the background, as far as the public and media were concerned, but Stolpen knew Thompson's influence over these negotiations was great.

"I'll use David's words: 'You don't have to convince me, you have to convince John Thompson. He's a father figure to (Mourning),'" Stolpen recalled.

A meeting was arranged in Washington, D.C., involving Stolpen, Shinn, Twardzik, Thompson, and Falk. The Hornets were constantly pushing Falk to get Mourning more involved personally. It was an old Shinn trick — get the player to smell the gym, see his future teammates, and he'll sign anything to start playing.

Falk wasn't falling for it. Besides, players tend to take negotiations over their value too personally.

"Players hire representatives to keep them out of the ebb and flow of negotiations," Falk said. "If a player is involved, it tends to hurt the relationship with the team."

Tellem once described that relationship more colorfully, saying his job was to be the attack dog, and it was the client's role to decide when to pull him off.

The attack dogs from both sides assembled in Washington, agreeing beforehand to set aside past differences and work fresh toward a solution. Late in another long session of useless debate, Falk suggested an offbeat compromise he said he concocted the previous evening. Falk proposed a 10-year deal, nearly twice as long a contract as any previous Hornet had received.

Twardzik, a former point guard for the Portland Trail Blazers and ABA Virginia Squires, sometimes has a hard time maintaining a poker face. He cracked a sarcastic smile over the thought of signing Mourning, guaranteed, through the year 2003. Falk, a man of great pride, became immediately offended at Twardzik's expression, and the meeting quickly broke up.

Meanwhile, the players were screaming for the help Mourning could provide. The most vocal on the subject was Gill. After the Hornets were clobbered on the boards by the Utah Jazz in a preseason game in Winston-Salem October 25, Gill said, "You put Larry and Alonzo in there, and that will take care of itself. That's why we've got to get him into camp."

Gattison was more to the point, after wrestling with O'Neal throughout the third game of the regular season. Gattison, a 6-8 power forward, was not placed on this earth to contain the 7-1, 300-pound monster O'Neal. After "holding" O'Neal to 35 points in a 112-108 Hornets victory in Orlando, an exhausted Gattison said, "They'd better get the big guy in here, and quick!"

The stalemate might have continued indefinitely had Laettner not been signed to his six-year, $21.6 million deal Oct. 14. Stolpen made much of the fact that Laettner's contract had no escape clause. However, Laettner's number demonstrated what Falk had been saying all along — that the Hornets' bargaining position could only deteriorate once Laettner signed.

Falk accurately projected months earlier that the Timberwolves' available funds, combined with their need for a star with Laettner's marketability, meant Minnesota was a prime candidate to open the vault. Any reasonable draft observer would say Mourning was a far better prospect than Laettner. In fact, Bristow had said that if the Hornets ended up with the No. 3 pick, they'd try to trade away the rights to Laettner, since he probably couldn't play beside Johnson.

So as the regular season approached, the Hornets came around to Falk's number. They worked out a deal with a first-year salary of $2.4 million. Mourning would get six years guaranteed at that magical average of $4 million, plus an escape clause granting him the option of becoming a restricted free agent after four seasons.

But even then, there were problems.

"It almost fell apart at the last minute," said Stolpen, explaining that Falk came back looking for a little more money. "We came to a number and you accepted that number," Stolpen said. Falk backed off.

The Hornets had an agreement, but still not enough room under the salary cap to exercise that deal. The Hornets and Falk agreed to give the team about a week of the regular season to work something out to create the room. Announcement of an agreement without a contract would have alerted the other teams in the league that the Hornets were having a fire sale. So the Hornets secretly signed a contract, giving it to Falk for safekeeping, awaiting Mourning's signature once the cap room was found.

The secret deal was made several days before Gattison told the Hornets to "get the big guy in here." Strangely enough, the man asking for the help was nearly the one shipped out to ship Mourning in.

CHAPTER THREE

"You trade Gatt, you trade me."

The night of November 11, 1992, was a fateful one in Hornets history, not because of what happened during the game — hey, the Boston Celtics beat the Hornets all the time — but because of what preceded and followed that 109-99 Boston victory.

Hornets president Spencer Stolpen chatted with reporters outside the team locker room at Charlotte Coliseum about one and a half hours before game time. Suddenly, Larry Johnson marched up to Stolpen and demanded a meeting. Now! Johnson wanted to know about these rumors that the team might trade away Kenny Gattison to create the cap room to sign Alonzo Mourning.

Gattison was probably Johnson's best friend on the team at the time, but this wasn't about friendship. Gattison had also been Johnson's tutor the past season, but this wasn't about losing a mentor. It was about Gattison's leadership and the way Johnson felt management underestimated Gattison's importance to this team. The summer before, Gattison had turned down the Hornets' offer of a four-year contract extension that would have guaranteed him an average annual salary of about $1 million. Gattison was making just more than half that this season, and was far from financially secure by NBA standards. Somewhat out of desperation, Hornets coach Allan Bristow had started the

6-8 Gattison at center the season before and Gattison had played surprisingly well. He averaged 12.7 points, 7.1 rebounds, and was willing to get himself beaten up nightly in an effort to guard the likes of Patrick Ewing and Hakeem Olajuwon.

To play center at his size in the NBA, Gattison had to accept these beatings as central to the job description. His calling left him with a surgically repaired knee and a chronically sore back. As one Hornets official described, Gattison often looked 50 as he gingerly left the Charlotte Coliseum following home games. That scared the Hornets. Gattison wanted four years, not three, guaranteed beyond the current season to sign an extension, and he wanted more than a $1 million average. The Hornets worried that all the pounding Gattison took would greatly diminish his abilities in three to four years. So guaranteeing four years meant the Hornets would still be paying him at a time when he'd be of little use as a player.

But Gattison, one of the brighter Hornets, had a mind for business. He understood that the market for a free agent center-power forward the summer of 1993 would be better than $1 million per season. And he knew there was nothing the Hornets could do to keep him from leaving if they didn't up their offer.

"The key word is *unrestricted* free agent," Gattison would say with a smirk whenever the contract issue came up.

A Western Conference general manager agreed in the 1992 preseason, saying Gattison could easily get $1.2 to $1.3 million per season on the open market. If Gattison chose to move, the money was definitely out there if he just put in another good season.

But Gattison wanted to stay in Charlotte — he grew up in Wilmington, North Carolina, and loves the Virginia Beach area, a five-hour drive from Charlotte. So he was glad Coach Allan Bristow was lobbying for the team to keep him.

However, some in management had other thoughts, including trading away Gattison's $600,000 contract to create the room under the salary cap to sign Mourning.

The Hornets were running out of options. They had already extended the contracts of Mike Gminski, J. R. Reid, and Muggsy Bogues to create short-term room in the cap. They had convinced Johnny Newman to push money from this season to next without an extension. And they had also talked trade with the Detroit

Pistons, who were looking to get younger and were willing to unload mercurial forward Dennis Rodman.

Rodman had become a huge distraction to the Pistons. Some thought he literally went crazy after Chuck Daly resigned as Pistons coach and was replaced by former Miami coach Ron Rothstein. Rodman all but worshiped Daly, who was pressured out. Rothstein, an ex-Pistons assistant, was taken in as television commentator and consultant by the Pistons. It was a poor disguise for what amounted to a coach-in-waiting.

Rodman's life in Detroit was falling apart. There was also a messy divorce and an ensuing separation from his daughter. So by skipping practices, shootarounds, and even some games, Rodman went about forcing a trade.

The Hornets suggested a swap of Reid and Newman for Rodman. Since Rodman was willing to rework his contract, such a 2-for-1 deal would solve the Hornets' cap problem and give Charlotte the elite defender Bristow craved. That is, assuming Rodman could regather himself emotionally and the Pistons would take Reid and Newman as compensation. Hornets director of player personnel Dave Twardzik scouted Rodman against the Indiana Pacers and quizzed *Flint Journal* beat writer Dean Howe about Rodman's emotional state. The next night, Rothstein and Detroit director of player personnel Billy McKinney showed up in Richfield, Ohio, to scout the Hornets against the Cleveland Cavaliers.

The Pistons wanted Dell Curry and Gattison, not Reid and Newman. That deal wasn't acceptable to Charlotte under any circumstances, so Rothstein and McKinney agreed to scout Reid and Newman with an open mind. Reid was awful in a 19-point loss to the Cavaliers, shooting 0-of-3 and grabbing one rebound. Rothstein wouldn't specify what he was doing in Richfield, but he told Detroit beat writers he didn't like what he saw. Trade talk with the Pistons was over.

The Hornets only had two options left — extend Curry's contract by several years or move Gattison. Management resisted extending Curry, so Gattison's departure looked increasingly likely. And that's where management and Charlotte's players had the first major confrontation in franchise history.

The night before the Boston game, Gattison had played hard and well against rookie sensation Shaquille O'Neal of Orlando, helping to squeeze out a four-point road victory. But against the Celtics, the Hornets' heads were everywhere but on the court. They all expected an announcement that Gattison had been traded to New Jersey or somewhere. And they were furious about it.

Johnson and Kendall Gill, then the two most influential Hornets, weren't about to let management trade away Gattison, whom Johnson described as "the guy who holds this locker room together."

"You trade Gatt, you trade me," Johnson warned after the game. "He's like a father figure. He, Dell, Muggsy, and the rest of these guys are who made me rookie of the year.

"How can you trade Gatt? For one thing, you're underpaying the guy. I understand it's business and all, but you've got guys busting their rears and you gotta accommodate those guys. If you don't, you'll have attitude problems on this team."

To which Gill added, "Kenny Gattison has got to be with this team. He's one of our core guys. He's a lot of our heart and soul. He's what drives us. He helped me break into this league when I was a rookie and he helped Larry last year, and he'll help Alonzo, too."

What Gill and Johnson were saying, and owner George Shinn and team president Spencer Stolpen had such a hard time initially understanding, was that Gattison's value to the Hornets goes far beyond the statistics sheet. He's probably the one person in Charlotte's locker room, beyond Johnson, who is universally respected and liked by his teammates. He is utterly without pretense or agendas, and is willing to say the things that need to be said to keep this team from imploding by the sheer force of combined ego and insecurity.

"When you say 'leader,' you're not necessarily talking about a stat sheet," Gattison said later in the season. "I'm not a real loud, talkative guy (actually, he's as articulate as any Hornet), but when things need to be addressed, I'm a guy who can get it across without pointing a finger at players or coaches or management. You've got to have a mediator — it's an 82-game season, so you're sure to have some friction.

"Players get frustrated, coaches get frustrated, and you see a fuse is about to get lit. I'm the one who tells everyone to relax, to take it easy."

No one took it easy that night following the Boston game. To listen to the players speak, there was a virtual mutiny brewing over the possibility Gattison would be traded.

"It meant a lot," Gattison later said of the way his teammates forced the issue. "Most professional athletes don't want to ruffle management's feathers. We worked for years, trying to get people together here. You can't pull pieces out of the foundation."

If the players were the ones flustered during the game, then management was clearly rattled after the loss to Boston. Bristow didn't want Gattison to leave — he might have been Gattison's biggest fan — but whatever Stolpen, Twardzik, and Shinn had to do, Bristow wanted it done quickly so the team could return its focus to basketball.

Not that management was dragging its feet. The Hornets were nearing a self-imposed deadline to clear the salary-cap room and get Mourning into the house. Mourning had already missed the entire preseason and four games of the regular season. The Hornets were 2-2 in those games, right on target for the .500 record probably necessary to make the first playoff appearance in franchise history. But how long could that record last without Mourning's presence in the middle?

It was settled. The Hornets would make their decision the next day, even if it meant sacrificing Gattison.

"It's getting to the point where our meetings are not as cordial as they usually are," Shinn said that night. "We are all ready to get this thing done."

The next morning was more like London than Charlotte. The rain was constant, the skies hanging heavy with slate-gray clouds. If this was to be a goodbye to Gattison, the climate was appropriately gloomy.

The Hornets public relations department called local reporters first thing in the morning, not to announce a press conference, but rather to inform the media that for the first time in franchise history, practice was closed to reporters. It was a strange move for a team that prides itself on availability to the press. In particular, Bristow generally treats reporters as welcome guests, not vultures or parasites, as many coaches do.

But Stolpen wanted to address the players about airing their grievances to reporters. *The Charlotte Observer* printed four stories on the players' annoyance with the possibility of losing Gattison. Stolpen went so far as to tell the media, through publicist Harold Kaufman, that players would not be available after practice for comment.

Now, it's one thing to close practice —about half of all NBA teams do — but it's quite another to tell the media they can't talk to players afterward. Kaufman, a savvy public relations operative, should have known that barring the media from anything is the surest way to get them to storm the place. *The Observer* went so far as to consult its lawyer about reporters' rights on public property. The Hornets leased their practice facility, Grady Cole Center, from the city of Charlotte, so surely the media could at least stand at the doorway to the building and wait for players to emerge.

By 11 a.m., two *Observer* reporters had set up camp under an awning outside Grady Cole, trying to stay dry. Reporter-cameraman Jay Squires from WCNC-TV had already been dismissed, which caused a little argument between Kaufman and Squires. Kaufman, normally even tempered, had had enough of Squires long before this incident. Squires was constantly shoving a camera into the players' faces at odd times and asking bizarre questions. Kaufman picked this day to blow up at Squires for several past incidents.

Just as the assembled media prepared to engage Kaufman in a first-amendment debate, Kaufman announced that a settlement had been reached and Mourning would be signed that day. Instead of trading away Gattison, the Hornets extended Curry's contract three years to pick up $450,000 in additional room under the salary cap. After four months of debate, the Hornets had arrived at a solution that made everyone happy.

It also showed Johnson and Gill how much influence star players in the NBA can have over management decisions. Shinn didn't like being told by Johnson what to do, but he was careful at the press conference that afternoon not to scold Johnson for the outburst.

"I could have gotten mad and told Larry we had to run the business, that we wouldn't criticize the players for having a bad game, and they shouldn't criticize in public what we're doing," Shinn said. "But that wouldn't have helped anything."

It was clear the players felt their little revolt made a difference in management's thinking.

"I think it had a lot to do with it," Gill said. "(Johnson) came straight to the point."

Though Johnson didn't say so, it was clear he also felt he'd made a difference. Later in the season, he tried the same parlor trick, attempting to get David Wingate a quick contract extension. But Wingate isn't Gattison in general affection or importance, and Johnson's lobbying effort grew quiet after a few days of working the beat writers.

Still, this incident cemented Johnson's role as a team leader. The season before, he was the team's best player, but as a rookie he could hardly tell others what to do and how to act. Johnson taking on management showed he had the personality, as well as the skills, to be the centerpiece of a championship team.

The press conference to announce Mourning's signing had a noteworthy absence. Agent David Falk, who normally revels in such occasions, was nowhere to be found. He said he didn't want to take attention away from Mourning, but that never stopped Falk from attending press conferences for his other prominent clients. More likely, Falk didn't dare tempt himself to go off to the Charlotte media about the runaround Hornets management had given him. Shinn, Stolpen, Bristow, and Twardzik apparently thought they could manipulate and intimidate Falk like they did Steve Endicott the year before.

To Falk, the four months of negotiation and the preseason camp Mourning missed amounted to a silly waste of everyone's time. Falk had correctly predicted long ago what Mourning would sign for within about $200,000 over a six-year deal. Falk was still complaining at February's All-Star game in Salt Lake City about how ridiculous the whole affair was. And he was right, this whole thing was a waste of good minds and effort.

Fortunately for Falk, he had a client with the will to stand up for his value in the NBA marketplace.

"I sat back and took notes," Mourning said of the holdout. "I had one of the best people in negotiating experience in David Falk and one of the best advisers who's sent a lot of players to the NBA, and that's (Georgetown coach) John Thompson."

Mourning's press conference lasted only about 20 minutes, because the Hornets had to fly to Indianapolis for a game the next night against the Pacers. Mourning joined his new teammates just as they were boarding the Hornets' charter flight. Mourning walked on the plane behind Johnson, who was wearing a custom-made leather jacket Coca-Cola gave him for being the previous season's NBA Rookie of the Year.

Turning to see Mourning stare at the gaudy red, purple, and teal jacket, Johnson flashed his smile with the gold tooth and told Mourning:

"You work hard, you get one of these."

Mourning didn't know whether to laugh. A few feet away, assistant coach Bill Hanzlik howled.

CHAPTER FOUR

"Do I strangle him if he takes another shot from the outside?"

For the first day or so, Alonzo Mourning's new teammates wondered if he ever smiled or laughed. Did he sleep wearing that constant frown?

At shootaround at Indianapolis' Market Square Arena the morning of Mourning's first game as a Hornet, Larry Johnson finally ambled over to say, "Hey, Zo, relax. You gotta smile once in a while. It's a long season."

Initially, Mourning had all the bubbly charm and personality of RoboCop. Which, if you think about it, was pretty much what the Hornets needed in a center. Mourning was brought in to clean up the town, to finally stand up to the Patrick Ewings, the Hakeem Olajuwons, and, yes, the Bill Laimbeers.

The Hornets' game-operations staff, always looking to choreograph the arrival of a new star, started playing the first few bars of Darth Vader's theme music from "Star Wars" whenever Mourning entered the game. If Mourning got the joke, he never let on. The beat writers were waiting for him to say something glib, like "Luke . . . I'm your father!" as he checked in at the scorer's table.

The Hornets blew one chance at drafting a fine, young center their first year of existence when they chose Kentucky guard Rex Chapman over Syracuse's Rony Seikaly in 1988. A rich Lebanese kid who grew up in Greece, Seikaly successfully bluffed the Hornets into believing he'd play in Europe if they drafted him. Seikaly's goal was to go to the Miami Heat with the pick just after Charlotte's. He did go to Miami, with a climate and culture that suited him, but Seikaly pays a price for that bluff every time he plays in Charlotte. He can't touch the basketball without hearing thousands of boos from the Coliseum crowd. Shinn called passing up Seikaly as big a mistake as any the Hornets have made.

The Hornets passed on another center in 1991, when they took Nevada-Las Vegas power forward Johnson with the No. 1 overall pick, rather than Georgetown's Dikembe Mutombo. Johnson was a personal favorite of coach Allan Bristow, and Johnson earning rookie of the year over Mutombo justified the Hornets' decision. But how many times could Charlotte afford to pass up pivots?

Marty Blake, who heads the NBA's scouting service, once did a study showing that the average team gets the chance to draft a center in the first round once every 20 years. So by all rights, the Hornets had 60 years to wait for their big man, after turning up their noses at Seikaly and Mutombo.

However, luck, the factor that always seems to keep the Hornets out of serious trouble, popped up again in May 1992, when the Hornets won the No. 2 pick in the draft lottery. It was exactly where Bristow wanted to select. He thought Louisiana State center Shaquille O'Neal, the consensus No. 1 pick, would have trouble sharing the lane with Johnson. Mourning, 6-10 and an exceptional shot blocker, coexisted in the pivot with Mutombo at Georgetown. He would complement Johnson ideally.

One glance at the stats shows how Mourning could help the Hornets most. He averaged as many blocks in his college career (3.7 per game) as the Hornets averaged as a team the season previous to Mourning's arrival. The Hornets had been awful in the area of shot blocking, finishing last in the league each of the previous four seasons.

Mourning just had this knack for rejections, and he joined the league leaders in shots blocked almost immediately. To him, shot blocking was more an art than a science, an instinctual ability to anticipate when an opponent would shoot.

"A lot of it is just God-given talent — long arms and being tall. But timing really helps and so does being a quick jumper,"

Mourning said. "A lot of it is getting into the other guy's mind. You block a shot, the other players see that, and they know they can't put up something weak. A lot of times, I'm not trying to block a shot, I'm trying to alter it . . . 'Don't go to the hole!' that's all I need to say with a block."

Almost immediately following Mourning's arrival, opponents started thinking twice about how and when to shoot when Mourning was in the game. Most importantly, Mourning demonstrated an exceptional gift for making a big block at the end of a close game. A particularly good example was how the Hornets won at Washington in mid-December. Tom Gugliotta, another fine rookie who played at N.C. State, was out near the three-point line with an open shot midway through the fourth quarter. Charlotte had led most of the way but the Bullets were edging back into the game. Mourning streaked out at Gugliotta, rejected the shot from well outside the lane, and the Hornets pulled away for a 126-117 victory.

"You can have about 10 blocks in the first half, but when the game is on the line, that is when you should have blocks," Mourning said. "If you don't, then the other 10 don't mean anything."

Mourning's gift for shot blocking gave him a reputation as basketball's version of a soccer goalie — someone who would happily take care of the defensive end and politely leave the scoring to others. That's a common misconception about Georgetown centers, starting with Ewing and running through Mutombo. Hoya coach John Thompson's ability to teach defense to pivots and Thompson's restrictive offensive system make fans think Georgetown centers don't want to score.

In fact, Ewing has proven to be a better scorer than a defender at the pro level, primarily due to a feathery fadeaway jump shot that complements his post moves. Mutombo fell so in love with offense as a Denver Nuggets rookie that he led the league in turnovers with 252.

So it was somewhat predictable that Mourning would consider scoring a bigger priority in the pros than in college ball. A rival coach once said the biggest crime in college basketball was how Thompson kept Mourning's offensive skills under wraps. In fact, Mourning was developing those offensive skills while attending Georgetown, he just did so in summer workouts with Ewing and Mutombo at the campus' McDonough Gymnasium.

Thompson would later say Mourning and Ewing "beat the hell" out of each other in those summer workouts. Often the noise from the gym would get so loud that Thompson would have to come by to tell them to calm down.

Thompson also encouraged Mourning to experiment offensively in the summer, to tune an outside jump shot and learn to dribble and shoot with his left hand as well as his right. Only Thompson told Mourning to stick to his low-post game during the college season, if he expected to go high in the NBA draft.

"There were no referees, so we'd definitely go at it," Mourning recalled of his workouts with Ewing and Mutombo. "We were playing so hard in the summertime. Our games would improve each of us. I owe them a lot. It was somewhat of a brother situation."

To some degree, it was the family Mourning never had. After Mourning's parents divorced when he was 10, Mourning went to live with a foster parent, Fannie Threet, the daughter of a Baptist minister who raised eight other children along with Mourning in a four-bedroom house near Virginia Beach. Mourning and his parents have reunited — he calls his father, Alonzo, Sr., one of his best friends. But clearly Thompson was a surrogate father during Mourning's years at Georgetown.

Mourning chose Georgetown because of Ewing. More precisely, Mourning chose Georgetown because of the way Ewing played in the 1982 national championship game against North Carolina. Ewing swatted at everything that night, drawing several goal-tending calls but also changing plenty of Tar Heels shots. The Hoyas lost the game but won Mourning's affection. The next day Mourning ran out with his grass-cutting money to buy a Georgetown T-shirt.

A few years later, when Ewing showed up at Nike's summer camp to introduce himself to Mourning, the deal was sealed. Mourning would be a Hoya.

Thompson guarded Mourning from the fast life of Washington, once warding off a known drug dealer who started hanging out with Mourning. In a more technical sense, he harped on Mourning to develop his "off" hand — his left — if he ever expected to be a great NBA scorer.

So when Mourning entered his first NBA game, against the Indiana Pacers November 13, he gave Thompson what amounted to a tip of the cap. The first time he touched the ball, Mourning lofted a wild lefty hook. It careened high off the backboard and missed, but Mourning was letting the world, and Thompson, know he now possessed a left hand.

"Coach Thompson used to say, 'Boy, if you had a mosquito biting the left cheek of your ass, you'd reach around and swat it with your right hand,'" Mourning once recalled.

Not anymore, coach.

Bristow and the other Hornets expected a certain wildness from Mourning in his first game. Bristow chose to start him immediately, just as he had started Larry Johnson the season before directly following a long holdout. It was like how the Navy teaches swabbies to swim — throw them overboard and see if they avoid drowning. Bristow felt that if there were growing pains to overcome, why not get through them quickly?

But this was more than growing pains, Mourning ran amok. He did not pass the first 12 times he touched the ball, each time shooting or turning it over. Someone must have told Mourning that scoring was the most valued skill in the NBA, because he sure made that his immediate priority.

To describe just what Mourning looked like that night, think of how a kid straight out of military school might react to his first college keg party. Mourning was intoxicated by freedom. He needed a reminder that Charlotte's offense was called the passing game, not the shooting game.

"He can pass. . . I think," Bristow said with a sly smile after the game.

At the other end, Mourning fouled constantly, looking to shut down Pacers center Rik Smits. Ewing and Mutombo had told Mourning that NBA referees are more lenient with what a player could do defensively. But Mourning's tactics initially belonged in an alley fight. Atlantic Coast Conference fans back in Charlotte, who always thought of the Big East as the conference of thugs, must have nodded their heads with satisfaction as Georgetown's Mourning got in immediate foul trouble against the Pacers.

Mourning ended up shooting four of 16. Johnson drove to the basket in both of Charlotte's last two possessions, running "Dallas," the isolation play named after Johnson's home town. Neither possession resulted in a basket or free throws (Johnson thought he got clobbered at least once), and the Hornets lost, 110-109, to drop to 2-3 for the season.

This wouldn't be the last time the Hornets would lose to the Pacers, a team they needed to pass in the standings to feel good about their playoff chances.

Bristow was left afterward wondering what to do. The coaches and players were shocked by Mourning's desire to shoot so much. Bristow would later call Mourning's offensive appetite the biggest surprise of the season. Friends and colleagues all told Bristow to rein Mourning in, but how far?

It goes against Bristow's whole philosophy to tell players they can take this shot, but can't take that one. Bristow is a student of the passing game, what college coaches generally call the motion offense. The artsy crowd would call the passing game the less-is-more offense because there's very little formal structure to what a team does to score. Like modern art, the passing game's mission is to foster creativity.

Essentially, each player is told to continually pass and cut. Set a screen here. Spot up for a jump shot there. Keep moving because sooner or later your man is going to tire of chasing you through screens and you'll be open for a jump shot or a backdoor layup.

It sounds a lot like street ball, and it is when run poorly. Players have to account for their own spacing on the floor. If they keep their feet moving constantly, players don't get bunched up together where they're easier to guard.

The gimmick is unpredictability. Opponents can't scout your plays if you don't run plays. In fact, when Michael Adams played point guard for the Denver Nuggets, he used to shout out, "Three!" or "Blue!" as he was dribbling downcourt, then go into the passing game the Nuggets always ran. Adams's signals were just a ruse to make the other team think the Nuggets ran plays when, of course, they didn't. It was a wonderful inside joke among Denver's players.

Teaching the passing game is a lot like parenting — you remind your players, just like you would your kids, that with new freedom comes new responsibility. Hornets veteran center Mike Gminski says players have it all wrong when they assume the passing game is easier than set plays. The passing game is more challenging, Gminski says, because players must anticipate where their teammates will go, rather than just fall back on blocked-out movements.

Smart players, like Charlotte shooting guard Dell Curry, love the passing game because it allows them to naturally float to open spots on the floor. Not-so-sharp players — sadly, J. R. Reid comes to mind — just get lost in the passing game because no one is telling them where to stand and when to cut.

"Once you learn it, there's really no secret to it," said Doug Moe, probably the passing game's biggest advocate on the NBA level. "It takes a while to see it and feel it out there on the court. But once you do, there's really nothing to it."

Bristow uses the passing game because, frankly, it's what he knows best. He played for Moe in San Antonio, then coached with him there and in Denver.

The knock on the passing game has always been that, while it quickly turns a bad team into a good team, it has never made a good team into a champion. But the passing game is a great equalizer, throwing off defenses the same way the run-and-shoot offense can in football. It sets the defense on its heels, rather than its toes.

Wes Unseld immediately installed the passing game as the Washington Bullets' offense when he took over as coach there in 1987. Unseld wasn't expecting miracles, he just thought the Bullets looked plodding and mechanical in the plays they were running. Unseld hoped the passing game would make the Bullets look crisp and restore their confidence. Unseld is still waiting. The Bullets have reached the playoffs only once in Unseld's six seasons as coach. For the most part, Unseld has returned to running primarily plays.

The passing game isn't for everyone and it sure isn't a cureall. Bristow's experience with the passing game was his primary motive in installing it in Charlotte, but this offense, and the trapping defense that complements it, made sense for Charlotte's players. You don't need great size or rebounding skills to succeed in the passing game. You don't even need great shooters because the object is to get more layups than the other team.

You do have to be versatile because big men have to handle the ball inside and outside the lane. And you have to be in better shape than the other team.

The trapping, scrambling defense that goes hand in hand with the passing game maximizes what several Hornets do well and minimizes what they do poorly. Curry and 5-3 point guard Muggsy Bogues were of little use guarding players in a conventional defense. But in Charlotte's trap and press, Bogues was first on the team in steals with 161, and Curry was third with 87. That made both players into viable weapons in Charlotte's defense.

The key on defense in this style is to force more turnovers than you commit. Speed the game's tempo into a tornado, get a slew of easy transition baskets off the other team's turnovers, and win, 115-105 — that is an ideal passing-game performance at the NBA level.

In this type of offense, Bristow couldn't very well tell Mourning to go stand under the basket and wait for an offensive rebound until he showed better judgment. So Bristow showed patience, even when Mourning would throw up hurried shots from the top of the key.

"There was a point along the line when I'd say, 'Do I strangle him if he takes another shot from the outside?'" Bristow recalled late in the season.

Considering Bristow's famous choke hold on agent Arn Tellem, "strangle" probably wasn't Bristow's best choice of words. Then again, it accurately described the frustration everyone felt, particularly Larry Johnson. Johnson was the Hornets' anointed "go-to" guy, and there were many times early in the season when he called for the ball and Mourning just wouldn't give it up.

Mourning's second game as a Hornet was a home date the next night against Miami. Hornets-Heat has always been a big rivalry to Charlotte fans, in part because the two teams entered the NBA together in 1988, in part because of Seikaly's effort to avoid being a Hornet. It annoyed Hornets fans to no end that Miami became the first of the four expansion teams to qualify for the playoffs, in 1992. Hornets fans, and the Charlotte coaches, took a perverse joy in watching the Heat be swept by the Chicago Bulls 3-0 in the first round.

Despite being swept, Miami thought it was established as a playoff team. In the off-season, the Heat traded its 1993 first-round pick to the Detroit Pistons for center-forward John Salley. Salley was a better comedian than basketball player — he does a semiprofessional stand-up act at various comedy clubs — but Miami thought the experience represented by Salley's two Pistons championship rings might lift the Heat to the next level.

Salley did more whining than leading in Miami, and the Heat was hurting at the 1992-93 season's outset. Oversized point guard Steve Smith, arguably the Heat's best player, was out for months with a knee injury.

Charlotteans gave Seikaly a typical reaction, booing him at the hotel. Ex-Heat coach Ron Rothstein used to boo Seikaly at practice before Hornets games, just to prepare Seikaly for the experience.

With Kendall Gill scoring 23 points, the Hornets built a 19-point lead in the first half and the crowd went nuts. But Seikaly brought the Heat back with 27 points and 13 rebounds for a 104-95 Miami victory.

Following Seikaly's big game, Miami coach Kevin Loughery had a suggestion on how Charlotte fans might contain Seikaly in the future: "Maybe they should cheer him, instead."

The 19-point choke was the start of a troubling trend that lasted the entire season; the Hornets were consistently lousy at protecting leads. Granted, every team in the NBA loses double-digit leads. It's almost expected that trailing teams will make a run and get the game close. But good teams shift back into gear after the opposition makes a run, to reassert the lead. The Hornets would end up in free-fall and lose.

There were various theories as to why the Hornets lacked a killer instinct. Most of those theories touched one way or another on the team's lack of experience. One hypothesis that made loads of sense was that past Hornets teams seldom had big leads, so how would the players know what to do once they got one?

The Hornets had a remarkable record in close games their first season. Dick Harter, the team's first coach, suspected the Hornets won those nailbiters because his players had to treat any fourth-quarter lead as precious.

For the first time in franchise history, the Hornets had the firepower to continuously build big leads. But no one regularly playing on this team knew how to protect them. Whether they kept running or slowed the tempo to milk the clock didn't make much difference; the Hornets struggled all season to win comfortably.

"We never handled leads," Bristow admitted at the season's conclusion. "What we've got to do (next season) is do a better job of understanding what a 15-point lead is, what a 10-point lead is.

"You're going to have a tendency with young or inexperienced players to slow down with a lead."

The coaches, too, had to take some blame for this trend, and Bristow did. He was always quick to take responsibility for any mistakes in game management. If the Hornets didn't have a needed timeout late in the game, he blamed himself.

Rather than noble, those admissions were simply accurate. Bristow was young and was inexperienced. When he replaced Gene Littles as coach at the start of the 1991-92 season, Bristow had never been a head coach at any level. He certainly knew the NBA after 11 seasons as a player and assistant coach. But his approach to running things — his minimal scouting of opponents, his sometimes erratic behavior during games — left some Hornets veterans questioning their coach's qualifications.

Fortunately for Bristow, he had a contract through the 1996-97 season, so owner George Shinn was prepared to give him the time to learn on the job. Team president Spencer Stolpen knew Bristow was a bright guy who understood who could play. The rest, Shinn and Stolpen hoped, would come with time.

The collapse against the Heat was the Hornets' third straight loss, so a visit by the Dallas Mavericks could not have come at a more opportune time. Through a series of injuries, drug suspensions, and free-agent departures, the Mavericks had regressed from a Western Conference finalist in 1988 to the worst team in the NBA. Many thought the Mavericks would replace the 1972-73 Philadelphia 76ers as the all-time worst team in NBA history. To do so, the Mavericks would have to finish 8-74 or worse.

The Mavericks didn't sign their first-round pick, Jimmy Jackson, until February. Dallas started lottery bust Randy White at forward and former Continental Basketball Association player Walter Bond at shooting guard. It's hard to imagine White or Bond starting on any of the other 26 teams in the NBA.

Dallas would manage to finish 11-71. While stranded in Chicago's O'Hare Airport by a blizzard in March, Dallas general manager Norm Sonju admitted the team's awful record wasn't misleading; the Mavericks really were as bad as any team in NBA history.

Carl Scheer, the Hornets' first general manager and president, took a certain satisfaction in Dallas' decline, not because he meant the Mavericks any ill will, but because Shinn had been so obsessive once in following the Mavericks' game plan for success.

Shinn has this compulsive way of latching onto a concept and then inflicting it on everyone around him. For several years Shinn Enterprises had a firm, if unwritten, dress code that all male employees had to wear freshly starched white shirts with ties. No pastels, no stripes. God forbid someone should wear a checkered dress shirt.

Shinn was nearly as compulsive in his attempt to mimic whatever the Mavericks had done to succeed initially. The way Shinn saw it, Scheer, former general manager of the ABA Carolina Cougars and the Denver Nuggets and commissioner of the CBA, needed lessons from Sonju on sports management.

"When I got to Charlotte, George sat down and said Norm Sonju would allow us to come there as a staff for a lecture on how to function as an expansion franchise. It was so patronizing in so many ways!" said Scheer, who now runs an independent sports marketing firm. "It was like a college professor lecturing on running a team."

Five years later those revered Mavericks were the league's worst, playing home games to a half-empty Reunion Arena.

"And that tells you that with all the vision, all the planning, you still have these problems," Scheer said. "After 13 years, the prototype for expansion is now the laughingstock of professional sports."

They sure were a laughingstock in Charlotte. Point guard Derek Harper, the only above-average player left on Dallas' roster, shot one of 14 as the Hornets scored a season-high 134 points to win by 23. Afterward, Charlotte's players talked about how gratified they were, not just to break their losing streak, but to have taken care of business against a bad team.

That was one of the big goals the players set for themselves — to start taking care of business against the league's dogs. In winning 31 games the previous season, the Hornets were terribly uneven; they'd beat the 57-win Cleveland Cavaliers one night, then lose to the 35-win Philadelphia 76ers the next. The coaches and players talked often in the preseason about making sure to put away the teams headed to the draft lottery.

That's how the better teams operate in the NBA. Phil Jackson, coach of the three-time champion Chicago Bulls, has it down to a formula: If the Bulls win every game in a season against the 11 lottery teams and then split the rest of the games against the 15 other playoff teams, then Chicago will always be in contention for the best record in the Eastern Conference and accompanying top seed in the playoffs.

The Hornets had another highly winnable home game next against the Golden State Warriors. The season before, the Warriors were everything the Hornets aspired to be — an opportunistic, trapping/running team that won 55 games. Last season's Warriors gave up more points (114.8) than any other team in the league, but that didn't mean they were bad defensively. They scored more than any other team (118.7) and led the league in opponent turnovers forced. That spin-'em-outta-control defense was just the style Bristow wanted the Hornets to emulate.

Unfortunately for Golden State coach Don Nelson, injuries crippled the Warriors throughout the 1992-93 season. It started when guard Sarunas Marciulionis broke his foot while jogging in his native Lithuania, and never stopped. The top five players on Golden State's roster played a total of three minutes together the entire season.

With several of his key players sidelined, Nelson resorted to a gimmick offense to try to win games. It's against the rules in the NBA to play a zone defense. You can double-team an opponent once he has the ball, but otherwise each defender has to guard a different opposing player, rather than defend a key spot on the floor. So on most possessions, Nelson would have three of his players stand still near either sideline while the others played one-on-one or two-on-two.

Every NBA team has isolation plays — the Hornets end quarters regularly by having Johnson "iso" in the "Dallas" play — but this went beyond an isolation. Warriors point guard Tim Hardaway was essentially trying to bait opposing teams into zone violations that would result in technical fouls.

Bristow hated the tactic, not because his players couldn't adjust their defense to it, but because watching a game like that was incredibly boring to the 23,000-plus fans in attendance. The

NBA, more than the other major leagues, is conscious of supplying an entertaining product, and in Bristow's mind, this was far from entertaining.

So after the Hornets won, 117-110, Bristow took a shot at Nelson for skewing the game.

"I don't think people pay $25 a game to see that kind of basketball — to isolate a player just to (force) an illegal zone," Bristow griped. "Why don't we just play (Iowa) girls' basketball — three on offense and the other two downcourt?"

This wouldn't be the last time Nelson would be criticized for the tactic. Later in the season he slowed a game against the Boston Celtics to a crawl to try to keep it close, running even more extreme isolation plays. After Boston won, 87-82, Celtics CEO Dave Gavitt put out a statement, saying the league should consider legislation to ban such tactics. Strangely enough, Nelson said he agreed that what he'd done was boring and was bad for pro basketball. But it was also the only way Nelson thought he had a chance of winning, considering his depleted roster.

The Hornets had won two in a row and were feeling awfully good about themselves. They felt even better after knocking off the Heat in Miami, 123-111. Sometimes Bristow gets carried away after a big win, and this was a classic example. He engaged in some revisionist history worthy of past Kremlin bureaucrats.

Bristow tried to convince a circle of reporters that drafting Chapman rather than Seikaly actually helped the Hornets because getting a franchise center too quickly would have improved Charlotte's record the first few years, thus lowering the quality of the team's later draft picks.

So, in other words, using the No. 8 overall pick on Chapman, a player whom the Hornets later traded away for virtually nothing, was actually a brilliant move on the Hornets' part, right?

Bristow just laughed at that sarcasm, shook his head at the memory of Chapman's out-of-control jump shots, and tried to change the subject before he further embarrassed himself.

The only down side of the night was Gill missing the game with a sprained left ankle. He would miss six straight games with the injury and never entirely recover. The same ligament would sprain two more times by the season's end.

Gill shot just 43 percent from the field in the season's first eight games, and eventually his average would dip to 41 percent.

That's an unacceptable percentage for any NBA player, particularly one who fancies himself as a future all-star. Gill is more a power player than a jump shooter. He muscles his way into the lane and often gets his attempts sent back into his face. In fact, Gill's shot was blocked 123 times the previous season, more times than any other player's in the NBA.

If Gill was going to become the great player he aspired to be (he often said he wanted to be top five in the league), he had to improve his jump shot, particularly his range. Gill took just 62 three-pointers the previous season and made only 17 (27 percent). Opponents knew to back off Gill, keeping him from driving and daring him to make his jumper.

The next game was a tough one for Bristow because it meant coaching against his mentor, Doug Moe, who had emerged from semiretirement to take the head job with the 76ers. Moe might be the least pretentious person on the planet. He's blunt sometimes to the point of cruelty, but he has no hidden agendas. Bristow worked for Moe for seven years in San Antonio and Denver. They have known each other since Bristow was a camp counselor in North Carolina while attending Virginia Tech.

In many ways, Bristow and Moe are complete opposites. Bristow is Southern and outdoorsy. Moe grew up in Brooklyn. Bristow is frugal; Moe is a free spender. Bristow is conservative, probably a straight-ticket Republican; Moe is . . . well, he might not be liberal, but he definitely thinks people should be left to their vices as long as they don't hurt anybody else. You could see Moe walk into that voting booth every November and cast a protest vote for the Libertarian candidate.

Moe does exactly what he wants and says exactly what he wants whenever he wants. Bristow's wife, Etoila, once made the mistake of telling Moe's wife that Bristow fretted so much about his job security the previous season that he took to sleeping curled up in the fetal position. Moe took great joy in relating that story to a circle of reporters in Charlotte.

Moe is prone to calling his own players "stiffs." (He once called Hornets assistant coach Bill Hanzlik, a former Nugget, the ultimate stiff). The only thing below a stiff on the Moe scale is a "no-hoper."

When Moe first started coaching the Spurs, his college coach, Dean Smith, used to subscribe to a San Antonio newspaper just to critique Moe's colorful postgame comments. Smith would cut out a story, circle a particularly nasty quote in red ink, then write in the margins, "Don't say this!" Finally, Smith gave up on the diplomacy lessons because Moe wouldn't change.

Bristow learned three things from Moe — how to teach the passing game, how to laugh at himself, and how to play craps. Moe loves Las Vegas, and now so does Bristow. There's a running joke around the Hornets that the real reason the team has had so many UNLV players (Larry Johnson, Armon Gilliam, Sidney Green) is so Bristow, Shinn, and the rest of team management can always count on a preseason trip to Vegas.

Moe's favorite way to needle Bristow is to call him cheap. Bristow isn't cheap; in fact, he's the first person to pick up a tab at a bar or a check at lunch. But he's definitely frugal, particularly compared to live-for-today Doug Moe.

"Allan was always so cheap. I sure couldn't have hurt him," Moe said. "The man was about dead when I met him. He was squeaking, he was so tight."

That was Moe's smart-aleck way of expressing affection. Bristow hired two former Nuggets players, Hanzlik and T. R. Dunn, as his assistant coaches in Charlotte, though neither had any coaching experience. Bristow said he needed to surround himself with assistants who knew the passing game. But over the next two seasons, there was a suspicion around the team that Bristow was primarily interested in loyalty among his assistants. Considering Shinn's track record, it didn't make much sense to hire an experienced, ambitious coach-in-waiting to sit next to Bristow on the bench.

Charlotte's passing game beat Philadelphia's passing game, 127-119, raising the winning streak to four games. The 6-4 Hornets were headed to Detroit, where they had never won, yet they were full of confidence.

Actually, you don't go to Detroit to play the Pistons, you go to Auburn Hills, Michigan, about 30 miles to the north. In fact, Auburn Hills is so removed from inner-city Detroit that you can drive from downtown to the Canadian border faster than you can drive from downtown to the Palace of Auburn Hills.

The Pistons are the NBA's prime example of white flight from the inner city, though far from the only one. First, the Pistons moved to the Silverdome, a football stadium a few miles from Auburn Hills, then they built their own arena, modestly christening it "The Palace!"

It's strange how a game so nurtured by inner-city playgrounds often ends up being played professionally in lily-white suburbs. But as a marketing ploy it's brilliant — bring the product to the rich suburbanites most able to pay for it. Also, by becoming their own landlords, the Pistons squeezed all the profit out of the venture, as long as they could book enough circuses, rock concerts, and pro wrestling cards to fill the open dates on the Palace's calendar.

Shinn was so impressed with the Pistons' ingenuity that he once threatened to build a similar arena in South Carolina and move the Hornets out of a still-glistening Charlotte Coliseum. This little bit of blackmail helped the Hornets get a better lease on the coliseum but devastated Shinn's popularity with the taxpayers of Charlotte.

The Hornets were on a four-game winning streak and Thanksgiving was a day away, yet not everyone was happy. Tommy Hammonds, a little-used forward acquired in the Rex Chapman trade, was sick of sitting on the bench.

Now, this is hardly out of the ordinary. Bristow often says that if he has only three of 12 players mad at him over playing time at any single moment, then he's doing his job well.

"I'd rather be released and weigh my options," Hammonds said before the Detroit game. "I'd still be getting paid (his contract was guaranteed), and maybe I'd find a place where I'm needed somewhere else. It's a good thing I've saved my money. I may never play again. I might do something else."

Hammonds was a pawn of the salary cap. He was in Charlotte because the Hornets needed to get out from under Chapman's $2 million-per-season contract, not because the Hornets wanted him. Hammonds, who made $850,000 in the last year of his deal, had fallen into disfavor with the Bullets. They had no particular problem with him; they just didn't want him or his salary. So to make the deal, the Hornets took on Hammonds' contract.

The Hornets' lukewarm attitude toward him came as quite a surprise to Hammonds, who initially thought he'd been released from prison the day of the trade.

In fairness to Bristow, he did try to find Hammonds a role. He told Hammonds that if he could become a defensive specialist, then there was plenty of playing time available. Hammonds was tagged with the nickname "The Terminator" back at Georgia Tech, though you would never call him that, based on the defense he played for the Hornets. He wasn't big or strong enough to wrestle with the power forwards, nor quick enough to guard small forwards. He was what coaches call a "tweener," for between positions. The term "tweener" is no compliment.

Johnson tried to toughen Hammonds up by occasionally pushing him around in practice.

Tom Hammonds was just too good a guy to be a nasty defender. You'd love to have him as a next-door neighbor, but you didn't want him as your backup small forward, guarding Dominique Wilkins.

In late January, the Hornets granted Hammonds' wish, and released him. He signed for the rest of the season with the Nuggets, where he got a little playing time as a scorer. Months later, Hammonds was still deluding himself as to why things didn't work out with the Hornets. "It seemed like no matter whether I scored 20 points in 30 seconds, I wasn't going to stay in," Hammonds said after catching on with the Nuggets.

After all that time, Hammonds still didn't get it that his defense was his liability. The Hornets didn't need his scoring, particularly off the bench.

"At the end I was just going through the motions," Hammonds said. "And that's something a professional athlete should *never* do."

The Hornets got a break against the Pistons when Joe Dumars, who would make second-team all-NBA, missed the game with a stomach virus. The deliberate Pistons offered a stark contrast to the Hornets' run-and-gun style. If the Hornets wanted to win a game, 115-110, then the Pistons wanted to grind one out, 98-90. The Pistons had four prominent holdovers from their back-to-back championship years — all-star guards Dumars and Isiah Thomas, disgruntled rebounding champ Dennis Rodman and a sneaky, malevolent center named Bill Laimbeer.

Laimbeer is basketball's answer to a hockey goon, though he has genuine basketball skills, including 20-foot shooting range. Laimbeer's range allows the Pistons to run a vicious screen-and-roll. One of Detroit's guards would lose his defender off a Laimbeer screen (he's a master at sticking his hip into the opposing player's groin or stepping on his foot). When Laimbeer's defender stepped over to help, Laimbeer would float outside the lane, take a pass, and hit a 20-footer.

The only thing Laimbeer does better than this is flop to the floor following any contact with an opposing player, attempting to draw a cheap charge.

Whenever Laimbeer would try something particularly dangerous or sneaky against a Hornet, Hanzlik, a teammate of Laimbeer's at Notre Dame, would walk over, shake his head and ask, "Bill, why do you do those things?"

On this night, Hanzlik had his own problems. Hanzlik rides the officials about as much as any assistant coach in the league. Referees will give head coaches more latitude than assistants. On this night, Hanzlik got mouthy with the wrong official, one Derrick Stafford. Generally, assertive officials are the best ones, but Stafford goes a step beyond assertive, bordering on pompous. Hanzlik, occasionally mentioned as a viable head coach someday, got a mouthful from Stafford.

"Oh, you got two head coaches tonight. That's the problem," Stafford told Hanzlik. "I can't wait for you to get a head coaching job, so I can give you a 'T' that means something."

Hanzlik knew that served as his final warning before he would receive the promised technical foul, possibly two. Considering the Hornets already trailed, 67-55, and had missed six straight shots, Hanzlik wisely grew quiet.

The Pistons' lead grew to 14 after Mourning was whistled for a technical foul. He argued with Stafford after throwing an elbow at Laimbeer while trying to get to the basket. Bristow kept up the debate with Stafford, saying the Hornets weren't getting the same treatment as the home Pistons.

Suddenly, the Hornets scored six straight points to climb back into the game. Detroit's Olden Polynice was whistled by Stafford for elbowing Mourning after losing the ball.

"See, Allan? Same call," Stafford said next trip downcourt.

The Hornets forced four straight turnovers from the Pistons to close within one late in the third quarter. Then, Mourning blocked three consecutive Detroit shots in the last four minutes. Remember what he said weeks earlier? — it isn't how many shots you block, it's *when* you block them. Mourning's timing on this night was superb.

RoboCop actually smiled after this one, Charlotte's fifth straight victory. Mourning not only grinned, he boasted when reminded that no previous Hornet team had won in eight trips to Auburn Hills.

"That's the has-beens," Mourning said of Charlotte teams that had lost to the Pistons. "We are the new nucleus!"

CHAPTER FIVE

"Guess Grandmama didn't wanna play no more."

A hotel room is a lousy place to spend Thanksgiving. A prison cell is far worse. So Alonzo Mourning spent part of Thanksgiving Day in Boston visiting former Georgetown teammate Charles Smith, who was serving time for vehicular homicide. The van Smith was driving hit a pedestrian, Smith panicked and sped away, and was eventually identified and convicted as the driver. At the time of the accident, Smith was playing point guard for the Celtics.

Smith had served as Mourning's surrogate big brother during Mourning's first year at Georgetown. Mourning never forgot that kindness.

"He carried me that year. He helped me out a great deal," Mourning told *The Gaston Gazette's* Mike Smith. "Smitty never said anything to anybody. He just got involved in a freak accident. It's a shame that happened, because it could have happened to anybody.

"Anytime I'm in a position to help out Smitty, I'm going to. I remember how he helped me out. All it takes for me is a little time. I've got plenty of that for Smitty."

This was an entirely different side of Mourning than most see. As opposed to Larry Johnson, who can't help but laugh and smile every 10 minutes, Mourning spends much of his life wearing an ominous scowl. Ask him for a minute of his time, and he often acts like you're asking for his eyes or his lungs.

But Mourning is also intensely loyal to those who have earned his friendship. "Smitty," doesn't get a lot of other visitors among his former teammates. Georgetown coach John Thompson said in the spring that Mourning sends Charles Smith money in prison every month.

Mourning hauled along another ex-Hoya to that visit to prison. David Wingate, who joined the Hornets November 20 after Johnny Newman broke his hand, also played at Georgetown and knew Smith. But Hornets president Spencer Stolpen suspects Mourning had reasons beyond school ties for talking Wingate into visiting Smith. Stolpen suspects Mourning was expressing a little tough love for Wingate, too.

You see, Wingate could easily be living life in a jail cell as well. Twice before, he had been charged with violence against women, though neither charge resulted in a conviction. Still, Wingate was considered damaged goods in the NBA because of his brushes with the law. After his contract ran out with the Washington Bullets, Wingate wouldn't re-sign for what the Bullets were offering. He thought he'd get other, richer offers.

None came, and Wingate sat until the middle of November when the Hornets called. Because the Hornets had already reached the salary cap of $14 million by signing Mourning, all Charlotte was allowed to offer Wingate was a league-minimum contract of $140,000 for one year. And even that contract was unguaranteed.

A month earlier, Wingate would have considered such an offer an insult. He had played six years in the NBA and was one of the league's better defenders; certainly his skills were worth more. But the bills were piling up — legal fees had been expensive — and Wingate needed a team to at least showcase his talent. So he was ready to come to work for the Hornets if they wanted him.

As purely a basketball decision, this made great sense. Bristow had been pleading for defensive help along the perimeter, and at 6-5, Wingate could guard a small forward, shooting guard, or point guard. He had played all three of those positions one time or another with Philadelphia, San Antonio, and Washington. Bristow had urged Tom Hammonds and Kevin Lynch to concentrate on defense if either expected more playing time, but neither could or would become the Hornets' designated stopper.

However, Wingate's past troubled everyone. The three coaches had a closed-door session with Wingate before the signing, warning him that a single incident — what Stolpen called a "whiff" of trouble — would be enough to get him waived.

Signing Wingate became a public relations problem, and rightly so. Shinn had talked continuously the first two seasons of how he wanted good people, not just good players, on the team's roster. Sure, the Hornets had a sense of charity — they hired former N.C. State great David Thompson as a youth programs coordinator after Thompson wasted his career and fortune on drugs — but this was different. Thompson was a danger only to himself. Bringing in a player with a reputation for violence against women made everything Shinn had said look hypocritical.

Observer columnist Ron Green, not normally quick to criticize, took the Hornets to task the day after the Wingate signing. It was among Green's better columns in recent years. Green wrote that the Hornets had now joined all those other major league franchises that placed winning above principles. To Green — and he certainly wasn't alone in this thought — the team that started each home game with a benediction had lost its innocence.

Actually, the Hornets' innocence started eroding several years earlier. Shinn's long-winded speeches about placing a priority on signing and keeping good people were little more than rhetoric. Kurt Rambis, the classiest, wisest person ever to wear a Charlotte uniform, was traded away the second season because then-coach Dick Harter thought Rambis was getting old. When Bristow first arrived in Charlotte, as team vice president, he said he never would have traded Rambis — that the leadership a Rambis provides would make him worthwhile on one leg.

There were other examples. Shinn once said Hornets cheerleaders would be inappropriate in a relatively conservative Southern town like Charlotte. But in the fourth season, the franchise introduced the Honey Bees, about 20 young knockouts whose various outfits grew tighter and shorter each month.

Actually, the Honey Bees were a big hit in Charlotte. Their bottom lines are monitored nearly as closely as the team's. According to one ex-Honey Bee, each woman's body fat is checked regularly. If it exceeds 17 percent, that lady can't perform without going on a diet.

Literally hundreds of women from around the Carolinas auditioned to be Honey Bees. As a result, the Hornets treat their cheerleaders as easily replaceable ornaments. According to one ex-Honey Bee, the women were paid just $35 a game, and were expected to practice six nights a week. The team promised to provide some personal appearances to make more money, but this cheerleader made only four such appearances over the course of a season.

There were other complaints. The team demanded the cheerleaders stay in top shape, but wouldn't provide a gym to work out. Also, the team made the Honey Bees pay for tickets for friends and family up-front, then often didn't distribute those tickets until just before game time.

The Honey Bees set up a meeting with Stolpen to discuss their problems. After a few minutes, Stolpen broke up the meeting, saying he had to take his family to dinner.

Wingate stayed clear of the Honey Bees and just about anything else that could get him in trouble the rest of the season. He answered any question about his old legal problems with the same cliche: "My past is behind me." (Isn't everyone's, and was that any guarantee he'd stay out of trouble?)

Wingate's only difficulty in Charlotte was money.

At mid-season, Wingate's agent approached the Hornets about some sort of advance or loan against Wingate's salary so that he could pay off some bills. Because Wingate's contract was unguaranteed, the Hornets couldn't advance him money under the NBA's salary-cap rules. The team couldn't even co-sign a loan for Wingate, because the strict morals clause in his contract could negate the deal before the loan was paid off. Finally, Stolpen helped Wingate secure a loan with a Charlotte bank on Wingate's own credit.

Wingate acquired a nice support system in Charlotte. He knew Mourning from Georgetown and had played with point guard Muggsy Bogues at Baltimore's Dunbar High School. He seemed popular among most of his teammates, though he never quite came out of his shell with the local media.

It really is the quiet ones you should watch out for. A neighbor of Wingate's at a south Charlotte apartment complex said he tests the power of his stereo speakers regularly at 2 a.m.

On the court, Wingate was a nice Band-Aid solution to the Hornets' defensive weaknesses. On most teams, the small forward or shooting guard is the most dangerous scorer. When a Dominique Wilkins or Michael Jordan was lighting up the Hornets, Bristow now had a specialist on the bench to address the problem. Wingate was no Dennis Rodman, but he knew how to get in a scorer's way, how to keep a hand in his face, and how to draw a charge. As a free agent pickup drawing a minimum salary, Wingate was the team's most cost-effective player as long as he stayed out of trouble.

Players learn to live with being on the road for Thanksgiving or Easter. It happens to everyone sooner or later. If a team is really good and draws high television ratings, like the Chicago Bulls, the league and NBC-TV will even schedule it to play Christmas Day.

Working on holidays is a touchy subject for the Hornets after Bristow made his team practice on New Year's Day in 1992. That was a violation of the league's collective-bargaining agreement with the players association. The team was fined, and Bristow had to provide the players with another day off as compensation.

The Hornets spent Thanksgiving at Boston's Long Wharf Marriott, near Quincy Market. Rather than make the players order room service, the team arranged for a banquet at The Chart House restaurant next door. There was the traditional Thanksgiving menu, plus enough shrimp, oysters, and even lobster to satisify the biggest appetites.

When the players weren't eating, most shut themselves off in their rooms to watch football. Players don't play tourist much on the road, particularly in Boston, where the autograph hounds are the most aggressive in the league. The season before, some kid had knocked on every door for several floors of a Boston hotel, looking for Larry Johnson. When J. R. Reid opened his door, he was surprised to find that the kid with the trading card and pen just wanted Johnson's room number.

Most players are good about signing autographs, but it's amazing how bad fans' timing can be, particularly at the Boston

Garden. Some have even walked onto the court during pregame or halftime warm-ups, demanding a signature.

When Rex Chapman was a Hornet, he had a simple policy when confronted with a slew of autograph seekers. He'd search out the youngest face in the crowd, and sign that card first. Chapman figured a little kid really wanted his signature as a keepsake. The adults were probably card dealers, looking to make a buck in what had become a lucrative collectibles market.

Bristow hates playing games the day after a holiday because he's convinced his players lose their edge with all the big meals and socializing. The season before, the Hornets were in Phoenix for Thanksgiving and lost by 20 the next day to the Suns.

The first half of the Boston game suggested otherwise. Still riding the momentum of a five-game winning streak, the Hornets were consistently beating the older Celtics downcourt for a series of dunks. They were mugging for television, talking trash to their elders, the Celtics, and leading by six at halftime.

Things changed quickly in the second half. The Hornets scored only 13 field goals and shot 10 of 17 from the foul line after halftime. Worse yet, Johnson got himself ejected with three minutes left in the third quarter for mouthing off twice at veteran official Mike Mathis.

Johnson got upset when Boston's Xavier McDaniel pushed him out of the way to grab a rebound. Johnson repeatedly berated Mathis for missing the call until Mathis charged him with a technical foul. The next time Charlotte had the ball, Johnson scored over McDaniel, then screamed again at Mathis.

Very bad move. Mathis immediately ejected Johnson, which essentially ended the Hornets' chances of recovering in a 111-102 loss to the Celtics. The winning streak was over.

Mathis is among the league's most capable and assertive officials. He is also a major league smart aleck. As he walked over to the scorer's table, he joked, "Guess Grandmama didn't want to play no more," referring to the character Johnson portrays in Converse's sneaker commercials.

"The first technical, he questioned my mother," Mathis said after the game. "The second one, he screamed at me. . . . He should have known he had one technical."

Everyone in the Hornets' locker room seemed a little disappointed that Johnson couldn't contain his anger better. Dell Curry, one of the more even-tempered Hornets, said, "Once you get one (technical), the referee is looking for you. You could hear (the Celtics) working the refs. They just know the refs and what they can do."

Added Bristow, "We're a young team and and we've got to learn the referees. That's part of winning. Mike Mathis is a good ref. How many times have Robert Parish and Kevin McHale had him? They know his personality. Larry's got to learn he can't do that."

Not that Bristow was anyone to talk. During the second half, he turned away from the game to tell off some hecklers at courtside. Apparently, coaches lose their tempers and focus, too.

Johnson was far from repentant afterward. Reporters looking to get some sort of comment out of him diplomatically suggested this was a learning experience he had to endure. Johnson, who said the previous season he was "never a rookie," thought otherwise.

"My learning experience was last year," Johnson said. "I didn't learn nothing from being ejected."

Johnson's sour mood suggested more was wrong than being tossed from a basketball game. It wouldn't take many days for Johnson to go public with what really troubled him.

The game was an all-around waste with a scary ending. The Boston Garden, opened in 1928, is dirty, smelly and dangerously cramped. As Mourning left the court following the game, a fan reached out and hit him on the top of the head with a fist. Assistant coach Bill Hanzlik had to intercede to keep Mourning from going after the fan, and potentially causing a riot.

"He better be glad I wasn't up in the stands," said Mourning, flashing that trademark scowl. "I guess he got excited by the win, or he had a little (beer). Alcohol does that."

Bristow provided some comic relief in the postgame interview. The Celtics had gotten off to a terrible start, going 4-8, yet were 2-0 against the Hornets.

"They clean our clocks. We're 40 percent of their wins," Bristow said.

Try 50 percent. Apparently, Bristow slept through his math requirement at Virginia Tech.

The Hornets and Indiana Pacers met in Charlotte the next night in another one of those important games between playoff contenders. Both teams figured to be chasing the last two of eight playoff spots in the Eastern Conference. Already, the Pacers had won once against the Hornets this season, when Johnson failed to score in Charlotte's last two possessions.

This game wouldn't be close like the last one. Pacers shooting guard Reggie Miller scored 57 points, most ever by a Hornets opponent, in a 134-122 blowout. At one time or another, Miller was guarded by Curry, Wingate, Kevin Lynch, and even Johnson. The Hornets' starter at shooting guard, Kendall Gill, was still on the sideline with a sprained left ankle.

Miller complains even more than he scores. First, he whined about how the Pacers should have a following like the Hornets'. Then Miller wondered aloud why he isn't more often mentioned as an elite shooting guard, alongside Chicago's Michael Jordan and Portland's Clyde Drexler.

Several preseason magazines had suggested Gill was on the verge of reaching that Jordan-Drexler level. Told of Miller's comments, Gill called himself the second-best shooting guard in the Eastern Conference "with a bullet." Bad ankle and all, Gill could still talk trash.

The real fireworks occurred long after the game's conclusion at Johnson's locker. Johnson often spends an hour or more in the trainer's room following home games, to calm his emotions before meeting with reporters. His dawdling is murderous on newspaper and television deadlines, but it's Johnson's way. On this night, no amount of waiting would keep him from expressing what needed to be said.

Johnson needed the ball more. He was the Hornets' go-to guy, a versatile and cunning scorer whose dribbling and passing opened up opportunities for others. But Mourning had gotten so carried away with this new offensive freedom that often he held the ball for too long. Regularly, Johnson would call for the ball and Mourning would simply ignore him before putting up something ill-timed or ill-conceived.

When the Hornets were in a five-game winning streak, Johnson could live with this. How could he rightfully complain when the team was on the longest winning streak in franchise history? But now the Hornets had lost two, and it was time for Johnson to reassert his status.

That wasn't easy for Johnson. He is genuinely selfless to a fault when it comes to accommodating his teammates. In fact, point guard Muggsy Bogues, primarily responsible for the team's shot distribution, has often told Johnson he hurts the team when he chooses not to shoot.

Think of it this way: When Larry Johnson takes charge of the offense, he joins a tiny group of dominant power forwards that includes Phoenix's Charles Barkley and Utah's Karl Malone. When Johnson defers to others offensively, he plays more like Portland's Buck Williams, a solid, tough power forward, but far short of what Johnson can be and needs to be for the Hornets to win consistently.

In the losses to Boston and Indiana, Johnson had averaged 10.5 shots, about six short of his average for the season. That was due in part to his ejection during the Celtics game, but it was primarily because Johnson wasn't demanding the ball. That had to end.

"I haven't had a decent game in the 13 we've played," Johnson said. "I try to get a lot of our guys involved, but maybe I'm passing up too many shots.

"Maybe it's my fault. Maybe I don't look to shoot enough. Maybe that's hurting the team. I don't know."

That's as close as Johnson has ever come to publicly criticizing his Charlotte teammates. It was clear something was about to change on the Hornets' four-game Western Conference road trip.

America West Arena is a tribute to the NBA's prosperity in the '80s and '90s. Relative labor peace (thank you, salary cap!) and lucrative contracts with NBC-TV and TNT cable meant everyone was making money in a well-run league where the talent was fairly distributed. The Suns had just moved out of dingy Veterans Coliseum and into the next century. America West, (named after an airline that paid handsomely for the advertising), had a separate, glass-enclosed practice court, banquet facilities, a gigantic bar with open-air access to the games, and a whirlpool in the home locker room the size of a master bedroom.

The Suns had just traded three players to Philadelphia to acquire perennial all-star Barkley. Along with being one of the league's great talents, Barkley is even more blunt and colorful

than Doug Moe. When Moe was hired as 76ers coach, management apparently decided two such strong personalities couldn't
coexist. Besides, the Sixers needed to rebuild, and at 29 Barkley
was more valuable to a team on the verge of title contention. The
Suns were just such a team.

It's a shame Barkley moved to the Western Conference
because that means he and Johnson now play each other only
twice a season. Barkley is the player Johnson most resembles in
size and style. Like Johnson, Barkley is a power forward who can
dribble, pass, and shoot from the outside, along with posting up
and rebounding. Also like Barkley, Johnson is short by the
standards of his position.

Johnson is only 6-5 1/2 in his stocking feet, while Barkley
is about 6-4 1/2. That's shooting guard or small forward height
on the NBA scale. But both make up for height with bulk,
strength, and the will to finish among league leaders in rebounding.

"You can have all the technique and height in the world,
but you've still got to go get the ball," Barkley once said of
Johnson's rebounding desire. "That's what it's all about, and
that's what he does. He's a hell of a player."

Former Hornet Armon Gilliam says Johnson's rebounding
dominance against taller players is all a matter of leverage.

"It's so hard to root him out of where he wants to stand,"
Gilliam once said. "Those are some shoulders, and he's got a
lower center of gravity than the rest of us."

Also, Johnson's height doesn't factor in his exceptionally
long arms. The Hornets measured Johnson's swing span at 7 feet,
1 1/2 inches, which is several inches longer than many players 6-
9 and taller.

But Johnson thinks his rebounding productivity basically
comes down to the simple strength to beat on his opponents all
night.

"I'm stronger than most of those other guys. I bring
something different," Johnson said. "Some 6-10 guy can jump
out of the gym, but he can't be used to 250 pounds pounding on
him like this. Most of my rebounds I get jumping this high,"
Johnson said, while holding his thumb and index finger about
four inches apart.

Johnson made good on his promise to take more shots —
27 in all against the Suns — and he outscored Barkley 27-13. But

the Hornets never figured out a way to contain Phoenix reserve forward Cedric Ceballos. Ceballos scored 20 on 15 shots, and the Suns won easily, 109-90.

Mourning tried some psychology on Ceballos that backfired badly. After watching Ceballos light the Hornets up from the outside, Mourning tried to bait Ceballos to drive with a taunt.

"When I got the ball, he told me to drive (saying), 'You can't hit that jump shot,'" Ceballos recalled Mourning's words.

Ceballos drove past Mourning, hooked in a shot and picked up a foul from Tom Hammonds for a three-point play.

"Is that what you wanted me to do?" Ceballos asked Mourning.

Not surprisingly, Mourning was incapable of laughing it off. Ceballos tried to shake Mourning's hand to calm the situation, but Mourning refused.

"I made him take a tough shot, what I wanted him to do," Mourning said afterward. "It just fell in."

Actually, this was typical of the bravado emerging as the Hornets' new persona. It wasn't enough that they were good, they wanted to remind everyone of it. The Hornets had taunted the Celtics a week earlier when they were ahead in the first half. After the Celtics won, Boston center Robert Parish made a point of commenting on the Hornets' new strut.

"I didn't know they talked so much," said Parish, so stone-faced during games that he's nicknamed The Chief, as in the grim expressions on totem poles. "It was nice to feed them some humble pie."

Charlotte's coaches set about toning down the players' sideshow immediately, though to limited success. Bristow didn't threaten punishments ("I'm not a big believer in saying, 'Hey, you act like that, you sit'") but the players said they'd adjust.

"I'm trying to keep my mouth closed," Mourning said, "but it's hard."

As the season went on, the Hornets would find less offensive ways to display emotion. Johnson, a former amateur boxer, took to shadowboxing along the baseline after a big dunk. Mourning started slapping hands with front-row spectators after big blocks.

And the Coliseu n crowd ate it up.

But the Hornets didn't totally give up trash talk. Late in the season, Portland guard Terry Porter had the final word on the team's brashness.

"Every team has one or two players who talk," Porter said. "They all talk."

The next night the Hornets had their rematch with the Golden State Warriors, this time at Oakland Coliseum. It looked as if Charlotte's losing streak would reach four when the Warriors pulled ahead by nine with 4:30 left. That's when Johnson took over. He scored nine of Charlotte's next 11 points for a one-point lead with a minute left. The last of those baskets was Johnson's best — an 18-footer that swished with no time left on the 24-second shot clock.

The Hornets would end up winning by one, off a boneheaded play by Warriors reserve Jud Buechler. The Warriors were trailing by three with about two seconds left, so their only realistic option was shooting a three-pointer. With the Hornets all on the perimeter, defending the three-point line, Buechler had a brain freeze and put up an uncontested layup with 1.5 seconds left, effectively ending Golden State's chance of winning the game.

Warriors coach Don Nelson was livid at Buechler, saying he would never again be put in that position. The Hornets' locker room was euphoric. Johnson had scored a career-high 36 points on just 18 shots from the field. He was 18 of 19 at the foul line; had Johnson made his last free throw, he would have tied an NBA record for most made without a miss in a game.

The go-to guy was again the go-to guy. But his teammates didn't want him to get a swelled head. So when Johnson returned from a postgame radio interview, he found the dress shoes he'd worn to the game on a table in the middle of the room, encircled with signs reading "Check *these* out!!!"

Johnson's shoes were blood red. They were only slightly less gaudy than Dorothy's ruby slippers.

Johnson's big night dominated ESPN's SportsCenter, but he had a more important forum coming up the next day. He had accepted an invitation to appear on the Arsenio Hall Show in Los Angeles, which meant catching an afternoon flight to L.A., then another flight right up to Sacramento following the taping.

NBA players love appearing with Hall, a close friend of Magic Johnson's. Hall gets appearances from athletes all the time for three reasons — he dresses like them, he talks like them, and he's a master of fluff. The toughest question a jock will ever hear

Hall ask is, "Now who made that tie, and where can I get one just like it?"

Players want to look their best when they appear on Arsenio, and Johnson discovered as he got to Los Angeles that he'd forgotten his stud earring. Now, how anyone would notice Johnson wasn't wearing his stud earring is a reasonable question, but Johnson was hell-bent on getting one before the taping. So the limo drove around Los Angeles until Johnson found what he needed at a jewelry store.

Johnson looked striking in a mustard-colored suit, black shirt, and multicolored polka-dot tie. The interview by Hall was predictably light. Hall asked Johnson about the gold tooth that has become almost a trademark. Johnson turned on all his teddy-bear charm to answer that one.

"One girl — and I hope she's watching — said it makes me look dangerous. And that's sexy," Johnson said.

Linda McCartney, wife of ex-Beatle Paul McCartney, was Hall's next guest. Paul McCartney was backstage, and as Johnson was leaving, he asked about all the security guards surrounding McCartney. In explaining the security, someone mentioned the shooting death of ex-Beatle John Lennon.

Who?

Johnson initially didn't know who John Lennon was. Actually, that wasn't all that much of a surprise — Johnson is 26 years younger than McCartney, and "Hey Jude" and "Yesterday" probably weren't played much in the Dallas ghetto where Johnson grew up. But it also says something about the way Johnson approaches life. He's much like the piano prodigy who has little time for anything but his craft. During his rookie year, Johnson was careful to minimize his business interests outside basketball. He bought a secluded home in a wooded area on Lake Wylie, a South Carolina suburb of Charlotte, and guards his privacy vigilantly.

It usually takes a while for Johnson to know people on a first-name basis, understandable since nearly everyone in Charlotte wants a piece of him. Johnson keeps everyone happy by grinning and saying, "Hey, big guy!" to anyone he thinks he's supposed to know.

But unlike Mourning, Johnson understands his goodwill ambassador responsibilities as a high-profile young star. Johnson now does interviews in the locker room before games, a customary courtesy in the NBA. The Hornets convinced Johnson to do so by showing him a videotape of Michael Jordan chatting with reporters before games. Johnson decided that if Jordan wasn't too busy to grant such interviews, then who was he to say no?

Mourning doesn't give those pregame interviews, and it's a fair guess he never will. Mourning just gets too hyped up an hour before a game to chat with beat writers like some baseball player hanging out during batting practice.

Johnson's hot streak continued against the Sacramento Kings — he shot 11 of 19 for 27 points. But more important, the Hornets got back shooting guard Kendall Gill, who had missed the previous seven games with that sprained left ankle. Gill had struggled even before the injury, shooting 43 percent from the field. He was no longer getting as many good shots now that Mourning had joined Johnson as a low-post scoring option. With those two finishers, the offense naturally gravitated closer to the basket.

But on this night, Gill was his dominant old self, hitting seven of 13 from the field and nine of 10 from the foul line for 24 points. Bristow wanted to blend him back into the lineup slowly, so as not to overwork the ankle. But Gill turned the game around on a three-pointer in the fourth quarter, then Johnson hit a free throw with eight-tenths of a second left for a 112-111 victory.

The victory assured that the Hornets would finish the cross-conference trip no worse than 2-2, a first for the franchise, and the Hornets were feeling rather smug afterward. An hour following the game, the coaches were leaning on a trainer's table in the visiting locker room, each drinking a beer. Hanzlik turned to a reporter and said, "You know what the secret to this game is?" No, Hanz, what is it?

"The secret is staying out of the fetal position."

The little room exploded in laughter. No one would let Bristow forget how he slept in the womb the previous season.

There was still a winnable game left against the Los Angeles Clippers. The Clippers had improved somewhat in recent years from their usual status as a lottery team, but the Hornets were 5-5 all-time against the team, 2-3 at the Los Angeles Sports Arena.

The Clippers buck the NBA trend of escaping to the suburbs. They resist the temptation to join the baseball Angels and football Rams in Orange County, instead remaining in the inner city, playing in an antiquated building next to the Los Angeles Coliseum. The Clippers don't do this out of great loyalty to the city game. Rather, owner Donald Sterling likes the ego trip of the big city after moving the team north from San Diego.

The Clippers were coached by ex-North Carolina player Larry Brown, who was in his seventh pro or college job in 20 years. Brown becomes disenchanted easily — he would leave the Clippers for the Indiana Pacers at the end of the season — but always manages to land on his feet because he is a wonderful rebuilder. One of Brown's assistants was former Duke point guard Quinn Snyder, the youngest assistant in the NBA at 25. Snyder just happened to be Brown's son-in-law, a total coincidence, of course.

Before the game, another ex-Blue Devil, Mike Gminski, went over to the Clippers' locker room to chat with Snyder and Brown. The door to the coaches office was closed, so Gminski diplomatically knocked, in case strategy was being discussed. Inside were Brown and Snyder, watching . . . the Duke-Carolina game on television.

Gminski had plenty of free time to socialize; Bristow had chosen not to play him in nine straight games. The presence of Mourning, Kenny Gattison, and J. R. Reid left Gminski as little more than a vastly overpriced insurance policy at center. After restructuring his contract to help the Hornets sign Mourning, Gminski would make $1.4 million this season, about $1.8 million next season, and at least a $1 million guarantee the following season.

Late in the season, Gminski would joke with *USA Today* columnist Peter Vecsey that he was like the MX missile — very expensive and never used.

Bristow sent Gminski in for his first playing time in nearly three weeks late in the first half against the Clippers. The look of surprise on his face said something glib was about to pop out. As he reached the scorer's table, Gminski broke up the beat writers by deadpanning, "Anybody got a map?"

Actually, it was rookie point guard Tony Bennett who could have used a blueprint of the court. With starter Muggsy Bogues taking a rest late in the third quarter, Bennett couldn't break the Clippers' trapping defense. Bennett looked like a petrified teenager in his first day behind the wheel at driver's education; the Hornets committed four turnovers in three minutes and never recovered in a 119-109 loss.

You see some wild outfits in an NBA locker room following games. Bogues once slipped on a full-length mink coat that had everyone calling him "Cousin It," the hairy little creature from the Addams Family. Seldom do you see a tuxedo, but that's what Gminski slipped on as his teammates boarded the bus to the airport for the charter flight back to Charlotte.

A friend of Gminski's was getting married that night in Los Angeles, so he hustled over following the game for the reception. He would fly home commercially the next morning, a day off for the Hornets.

Now that most NBA teams fly private charters to and from games, the general public seldom sees athletes on airplanes. Gminski's presence drew some attention a few rows back when a woman told her friend, "I think he's a ball player. . . but he read the whole newspaper in an hour!'

Typical fan assumption. If he's a jock, how could he have a mind, right? Wrong.

Gminski is a voracious reader and a man of considerable depth. Once, when asked at dinner who he would most like to meet, he said Jesus Christ, because he wants to know how Christ set out to convince the whole world who he was and why he was there. Gminski has Republican political aspirations (he once met with former President Richard Nixon to discuss his goals), and his wife, Stacy Anderson, belies every preconception about players' wives being vapid Barbie dolls.

A former New York investment banker, Anderson now advises inventors how to capitalize their projects. Anderson and Gminski have organized a charity event in Charlotte called a "top hats and high tops ball," which has been a huge success.

Gminski has occasionally been booed in Charlotte, and that is grossly unfair. Fans somehow blame him instead of management for the Gminski-Armon Gilliam deal not working out. Gminski didn't want to leave Philadelphia, but when the Hornets made the trade in January 1991, he set out to, as he put it, "run for mayor" in Charlotte. He bought a local home, got involved in local causes, and tried to be the Hornets' first successful center.

The incentives for the trade were questionable. Gilliam wasn't getting along well with his teammates, and Shinn, still preoccupied with marketing, even though the Coliseum was always sold out, liked that Gminski played up the road at Duke. It was predictable that Gminski's body would start breaking down after 11 NBA seasons in New Jersey and Philadelphia. And it wasn't his fault the Hornets were lucky enough in the draft lottery to get Mourning, making Gminski obsolete.

Still, fans booed or called local sports talk shows suggesting ridiculous ideas to rid the team of Gminski's salary. They would advocate cutting him (sorry, the guaranteed salary still counts against the salary cap). They'd advocate trading him (and which other team is going to take on a contract that size for a player who isn't playing?) Finally, they would advocate convincing Gminski to retire and take the money owed him as a television analyst or assistant coach.

That last suggestion, which came up often, was particularly silly. Did fans really think the NBA's salary-cap enforcers would look the other way while the Hornets paid Gminski $1.4 million to be an announcer or assistant coach?

Once it became obvious Gminski wouldn't play much, the Hornets tried to justify the trade by saying he'd be a tutor-mentor to Mourning. Originally, the Hornets had hoped Gminski might help fill the leadership void that existed after Kurt Rambis was traded to Phoenix. But Larry Johnson, Muggsy Bogues, and Kenny Gattison served as a troika in that leadership role.

Gminski couldn't very well lead if he wasn't playing. As for being Mourning's tutor, the Hornets didn't orchestrate that very well. As one insider described, the team sold Gminski on playing teacher, sold the public on Gminski-as-teacher, but never sold Mourning on Gminski-as-teacher. When Mourning finally signed four games into the regular season, he gravitated toward the advice of Gattison, just as Larry Johnson had. And why not, in the eyes of a rookie? Gattison was playing — he'd been the team's starting center the season before — and Gminski was sitting.

This might have worked out better had Mourning been in training camp, when there's more time to drill one-on-one. In that atmosphere, Gminski would have had more of a chance to offer some pointers. As it turned out, it would be months before Mourning felt comfortable enough around Gminski to exchange more than a passing thought on the game.

So Gminski stayed in shape, read thick books on the road, and did his best to lighten up practice with a joke or two. Really, it's not a bad job — extensive travel, no heavy lifting, and a seven-figure salary. But he still thought he could play, and no one seemed to believe him.

CHAPTER SIX

"I don't think anyone was turning back flips over Sidney Green."

Shootarounds are incredibly boring exercises, particularly if you are not among those shooting around.

But they're a tradition in the NBA. The coaches roust the players out of bed by scheduling these informal workouts at 10 or 11 a.m. wherever the team is playing that night. The theory is that by shooting in the arena — particularly on the road — players adjust to the baskets, lighting, and background before their shots count in a game. There's some truth to this. However, as much as anything, shootarounds are an excuse by the coaches to make sure the players aren't lounging around on game days, getting soft.

Because players and coaches are there, media show up, too, particularly the radio and television crews in need of pre-game sound bites. Newspaper reporters often show up as well, though morning newspapers have no deadline between shootaround and game time.

The shootaround on December 9 before the home game against the Phoenix Suns showed why reporters hang out at shootaround. Midway through the hour-long session, Hornets public relations director Harold Kaufman told coach Allan Bristow he needed to call San Antonio Spurs vice president Bob Bass.

That, by itself, was no big deal. Bass and Bristow had been friends for years from when Bristow played in San Antonio. They share a love of fishing and speak often during the season. But about 15 minutes later, Kaufman again walked over to Bristow to say Bass *really* needed to speak to him.

Something was clearly brewing. A reporter from *The Charlotte Observer* (this author) and WBT radio play-by-play announcer Matt Pinto nodded and winked, having both over-heard the conversation.

The Spurs were hurting for power forwards. Terry Cummings was out for the season with a knee injury and Antoine Carr would miss a few weeks with a foot injury. The Hornets were loaded with power forwards and would happily move J. R. Reid if they could get a first-round pick in return. It was clear Reid had grown miserable in Charlotte. Larry Johnson figured to be the team's starter at Reid's natural position for perhaps the next 10 years. Kenny Gattison got most of the playing time behind Johnson and center Alonzo Mourning. Reid played a total of 12 minutes in the Sacramento and Golden State games, and was quietly brooding about it. The two times Bristow sent him into those games, Reid casually sauntered up to the scorer's table, missing his first chance to enter the game each time.

The No. 5 overall selection in the 1989 draft, Reid was considered by many Charlotteans a wasted lottery pick. Hornets management at the time — General Manager Carl Scheer, Coach Dick Harter, and Director of Player Personnel Gene Littles — felt pressure to take Reid because owner George Shinn wanted a high-profile Tar Heel on the roster. The way Harter saw it, Shinn in essence told them that unless they could find a compelling reason to take someone else, Reid had to be the man chosen.

Shinn now says his instructions were more benign than that."My directions to my people were very simple. My *sugges-tion* to my people was very simple. If it comes down to the point where the better of two players was an absolute toss-up, and one's an ACC player, take the ACC player," Shinn said. "Ninety percent of the people who come to our games are ACC fans. So if everything else is equal, take the ACC player. If I had to make the same choice now, I'd do it that way."

It didn't help any when former all-star Julius Erving told Shinn that Reid would be an NBA star. (Erving is a Hall-of-Famer, but he's obviously no general manager). When word got out that Shinn was pressing his basketball people to take Reid, rather than let the decision be made in a vacuum, Shinn took considerable criticism from national media. Jan Hubbard, then the NBA columnist for *New York Newsday*, wrote that Shinn needed to learn to just write checks and cheer. Shinn shot back that if all he did was write checks, then he wouldn't have much to cheer about.

Just as the Hornets' pre-draft background checks predicted, Reid was terribly immature and irresponsible coming out of North Carolina. A few weeks into Reid's first pro season, Harter gave the team a Saturday off, but scheduled a practice for Sunday morning. Reid drove off to Chapel Hill in his new Porsche, and never made it back for practice. The next day he told reporters his car's fan belt had broken. The morning Reid's excuse appeared in print, a reader called *The Observer* newsroom to say he owned the same car as Reid, and there was no such part in that model.

The franchise showed great patience in trying to develop Reid. Part of the incentive for trading away Armon Gilliam was that Reid said he needed to play Gilliam's power forward spot, rather than center, to succeed. Much like Rex Chapman, Reid was a player who excited the general public more than professional scouts. He had some skills, including a feathery 10-foot jump shot, plus a wide, strong butt that made him hard to push out of the lane. But he had few offensive moves and was a slow learner when it came to picking up techniques. Within weeks of arriving in Charlotte, Larry Johnson was showing Reid where to stand in various defensive situations. Rookies aren't supposed to have to tell third-year players where to stand.

Reid tried the patience of every Hornets coach. Team president Spencer Stolpen claims Littles's exasperation with Reid — Littles once leveled Reid with public criticism after a loss to the Dallas Mavericks — was a factor in Littles losing the coaching job. Harter, Littles, and Bristow each came to roughly the same conclusion that Reid was not close to a player worthy of a No. 5 overall pick.

If Reid was just overrated, it wouldn't have been such a problem. But he was also a threat to team chemistry. First off, he was a trash-talker before the Hornets were close to good enough to brag. Reid's confrontation with Charles Barkley and Jayson Williams set off a bench-clearing brawl between the Hornets and Philadelphia 76ers the season before.

Also, while Reid wasn't a bad guy, his immaturity was infectious. Given a choice between going home to sleep or going out to party, Reid was often successful in convincing a few teammates to chase the night life. Pro basketball players don't have to be monks, but Reid was partying far too much. For a while he lost his driving privileges after the speeding tickets piled up.

In a nutshell, J. R. Reid just liked the status and lifestyle of being a pro basketball player more than he liked playing basketball.

The fans' reactions to Reid's performance and personality says plenty about Charlotte's love/hate relationship with North Carolina basketball. At first, Charlotteans, many raised on the propaganda that a Tar Heel can do no wrong, felt the local media were unfairly criticizing Reid and harping on his liabilities and habits. Then, after Littles started ripping Reid midway through Reid's second season, public opinion shifted dramatically. It was as if the problems had hit some saturation point, and suddenly everyone was a Reid-basher.

Tar Heels fans felt he was discrediting the program's reputation for developing good people and great NBA players. Tar Heel-haters (they're nicknamed ABCs for "Anybody But Carolina") took great joy in seeing one of Dean Smith's players failing just down the road from UNC's campus.

If Reid deserved more criticism early in his Charlotte career, then he surely didn't deserve to be crucified later on. He was often booed at home for no reason other than being J. R. Reid. One fellow with a seat in the third row of Charlotte Coliseum would scream out, "No, Allan. . . Not J. R.!" in a singsong voice every time Reid approached the scorer's table.

Reid did his best to ignore the mocking for several weeks. Finally, Reid turned his head until he made eye contact with the heckler from about 20 feet away. In that voice of Reid's that is several steps below bass, he yelled out, "Shut up, Motherfucker!" loud enough to be heard clearly 10 rows up.

Message received. The fan never again screamed out "Not J. R.!"

Reid's ties to the Carolinas provided him with some financial advantages, including a local Gatorade commercial. But he held no special affection for Charlotte, particularly after the fans turned against him. There was a rumor in the preseason that the Dallas Mavericks had some interest in Reid, a deal that would have solved the Hornets' cap problem in signing Mourning. Reid said he'd welcome a move to Dallas if it meant more playing time. But Dallas didn't want Reid unless it amounted to a "giveaway," in the words of one Mavericks official.

Though the Los Angeles Lakers and Minnesota Timberwolves both expressed interest in Reid before the 1992 draft, nothing happened. By the start of the 1992-93 season, the beat writers in Charlotte all knew that sooner or later, Reid had to be dealt. One day Hornets director of player personnel Dave Twardzik mentioned to John Delong of the *Winston-Salem Journal* that Delong should lose a few pounds. Delong laughed, mentioned Reid, and told Twardzik, "You unload your excess baggage and I'll unload mine."

San Antonio made sense as Reid's new destination. Back when he was Hornets vice president, Bristow had nearly pulled off a deal that would have sent Reid and Chapman to the Spurs for guard-forward Willie Anderson. The deal was done, then undone when league lawyers reminded the Hornets of a clause in Reid's contract that paid him a six-figure bonus for being traded. Shinn wouldn't pay the ransom to make the deal, and neither would Spurs owner Red McCombs, so the trade fell through.

With so many power forwards hurt and the Spurs in danger of missing the playoffs, McCombs was now more agreeable to Reid's new contract. Reid would make an average of about $1.7 million over four seasons, a fair salary to a team prepared to play him 25 to 30 minutes per game. The Spurs were offering the Hornets a first- and second-round pick. But to make the deal work under the salary cap, the Hornets also had to take veteran forward Sidney Green.

A holdover from Larry Brown's days in San Antonio, Green was playing little with the Spurs, even though his college coach, Jerry Tarkanian, was now San Antonio's coach.

Green and Reid each made just over $1.2 million in 1992-93, so their salaries were an easy swap under the salary cap. The difference was that Reid was owed a ton of money over the next three seasons, while Green's contract expired after one more season at about the same salary.

This was the Rex Chapman deal all over again — trade a disappointing player with a big contract for a bench warmer making less over the long haul. Only Reid's height and bulk allowed the Hornets to also get two draft picks out of the deal.

If there was any question Green was a throw-in, Shinn settled it during the trade's announcement, telling reporters, "I don't think anyone was turning back flips over Sidney Green."

Nice welcome to your new home, huh, Sid?

Players learned of the deal as they showed up around 6 p.m. for the 7:30 tip-off against the Suns. Dell Curry, one of Reid's closest friends on the team, learned of the trade as he asked team vice president Tom Ward for extra tickets to that night's game.

Curry's reaction that night illustrates how quickly players adapt to losing teammates. Curry went to call Reid at home, but first made a quick stop by Reid's locker to confiscate his ex-teammate's tickets for the game. Hey, sentiment can wait when your wife needs two more seats for the relatives.

"I don't know that J was happy here," said Gattison, expressing the consensus.

And certainly the Hornets weren't happy with his contribution or his contract. As Shinn said, "There've been a lot of questions about his maturity." But Bristow wouldn't use that as an excuse.

"That can irritate people sometimes. But you can't be that narrow-minded to think that's why he didn't make it," Bristow said. "His personality at times can be construed as sometimes not caring, but he added something to the locker room. He was happy-go-lucky.

"J was going to be the fourth big man on this team. We (drafted) Larry last year and Zo this year (with Gattison already on board). I would have been happy with him as our third big man, if he was our third-best big man. I tried to play both (Reid and Gattison) at the same time and it didn't work out."

Reid told San Antonio reporters that night that playing time was the issue, but he also mentioned that he'd been unfairly billed as a savior in Charlotte. If that's true, then failure was everyone's fault — Reid's for not trying hard enough, Shinn's for his obsession with marketing, and the fans for viciously turning on Reid once he didn't fulfill their fantasies.

The separation was best for everyone concerned.

The only one disappointed by the trade might have been Charles Barkley in the visitors' locker room. After the Suns beat the Hornets, 110-101, Barkley was reminded he'd once offered several hundred dollars to any Sixers teammate who would take loudmouth Reid out of the game. That had led to Jayson Williams's sucker punch and the ensuing brawl.

"Does this mean I can't put another bounty on him?" Barkley asked.

Quite the contrary. Now, Barkley and Reid had both moved to the Western Conference. They would see plenty of each other from now on.

While Barkley provided his usual postgame one-liners, to the delight of Charlotte media, Ailene Voisin, a veteran NBA writer with the *Atlanta Journal-Constitution*, was interviewing Johnson in the Hornets' locker room for a feature story.

Women reporters have been a common sight around NBA locker rooms for years. Six of the 27 teams were covered regularly by female reporters during the 1992-93 season, and Jackie MacMullan of the *Boston Globe* is among the elite writers covering the league. The NBA makes a point of informing rookies during their orientation session that women reporters have the same locker room access as men reporters, and should be treated with the same courtesy.

Either Mourning slept through that part of his orientation, or he simply ignored it. Wearing a towel around his waist after taking a shower, Mourning walked up to Voisin and asked her to leave while he put on his pants. At the time, Voisin had her back to Mourning while interviewing Johnson.

Another reporter, *The Observer's* Charles Chandler, was taping the interview with Johnson so he had a record of the confrontation that ensued.

Mourning: "Could you leave the locker room while I get dressed, if you don't mind?"

Voisin: "No, I'm standing here talking to Larry. It's in the NBA rules. I can be here."

Mourning: "If you was playing ball, I wouldn't walk in the locker room on you."

Voisin: "I'm just standing here talking. I've been doing this 12 years. If you have a problem with that, that's tough."

Mourning: "Don't give me that shit. I don't care how many years you've been doing it. This is our locker room."

Voisin: "It's your job to play, not to give me a hard time."

Mourning: "Fuck you!"

At that point, Johnson interceded. Like Johnson, Voisin graduated from Nevada-Las Vegas, and the way things were headed, Johnson just might have saved a fellow Runnin' Rebel from a black eye or worse. But the argument was not over.

Mourning: "Don't tell me what my job is. Don't tell me what my fucking job is."

Voisin: "This doesn't have anything to do with your job. Act like a pro, rookie."

Mourning: "What's that got to do with it?"

Mourning finally went into another room to dress.

"I asked her politely to leave the room while I got dressed. That's when she got rude and that's when I got rude," said Mourning. "I mean, hey, if the shoe was on the other foot, and this was a women's locker room, I wouldn't walk in here at all. It's just out of respect. I don't care how long she's been doing this, 12 years or 50. It's the principle I'm talking about. All I wanted to do was get my pants on."

Of course, Mourning conveniently ignored the fact that often locker rooms are the only places where athletes make themselves available for interviews. He also failed to mention that he interrupted Voisin, who wasn't even talking to him.

Voisin was perplexed. She knew the right thing to do was complain strongly to the league. But she worried about becoming the new Lisa Olsen. A reporter for the *Boston Herald*, Olsen had been harassed by several New England Patriots in a locker room while covering that team. When Olsen filed a complaint with the NFL, she became the story rather than the players who harassed her. To the general public, the question wasn't whether those football players reacted like neanderthals, but rather whether Olsen was really some sort of voyeur.

Women sportswriters do their best to respect players' dignity while getting their quotes on tight deadlines. In general, they are far more professional about this touchy arrangement than the athletes they interview.

You can debate all day whether any sportswriters — male or female — belong in locker rooms before or after games. But it's been that way for decades. The alternative, massive post-game press conferences, would be a far greater inconvenience for players, so the leagues open the locker rooms.

Mourning certainly wasn't the first male athlete uncomfortable with women in the locker room. For instance, Bobby Jones, who played for Denver and Philadelphia, had problems with it as a moral issue. But unlike Mourning, Jones understood he didn't have the right to tell others how to do their jobs. Jones changed his postgame routine, rather than expecting other professionals to change theirs.

Mourning's reaction to Voisin was typical of the inflexible way he often deals with outsiders. Early in the season, he often started sentences with, "This is our locker room, and. . .," and then throw a tantrum. Mourning had no trouble adjusting to NBA basketball, but the little inconveniences that go along with being a professional tied him up in emotional knots.

Certainly, Mourning didn't learn good press relations at Georgetown. CBS-TV reporter Lesley Visser was physically removed from the Hoyas' locker room about a decade ago when she worked for the *Boston Globe*, covering Big East rival Boston College.

Georgetown coach John Thompson had a rule that his locker room was open to the press no longer than 15 minutes following games. The 15-minute window opened when Thompson started his news conference in another room, so reporters had to choose whether to talk to the coach, the players, or frantically run between the two rooms with the clock ticking. One day during the NCAA tournament in 1985, Thompson was in a particularly chatty mood, so a reporter from Washington tried to lobby Thompson for more latitude.

"Coach, you just don't understand our deadlines," the reporter said.

"No," Thompson replied, grinning widely, "I *do* understand your deadlines."

Thompson has mellowed somewhat since then. Georgetown publicist Bill Shapland makes a point of saying the Hoyas now grant equal access to all reporters.

As news of the Mourning-Voisin incident spread, reaction from Hornets management was varied. Stolpen was sufficiently

concerned that he called the league to report it. Meanwhile
Bristow felt *The Observer* made too much out of it. He thought it
would have been no big deal had Mourning had this hassle with
a male reporter.

Quite the opposite was true. Mourning avoided a possible
suspension because Voisin didn't want to become the focus of a
national story. A male reporter would have raised hell if Mourning told him to leave the locker room. Quietly, the NBA raised
hell with Mourning, telling him he'd just used up his one indul-
gence for his career. Mourning agreed to apologize to Voisin.

Of course, peer pressure was the best punishment. For the
next month or so, whenever a female reporter entered the Hornets' locker room, some teammate would immediately start
spoofing Mourning, telling him to cover up. Mourning even
learned to laugh about it.

Mourning had plenty to take his mind off the Voisin
controversy. Over the next two games, he would face each of his
Georgetown buddies, in New York against Patrick Ewing and
then at home against Denver's Dikembe Mutombo.

It had to be eerie for Mourning to finally face Ewing in a
game that counted. Since watching Ewing block all those shots in
the national championship game against the Tar Heels, Mourning had virtually patterned his life after Ewing. His hair style was
the same, down to the little razor-stroke hash marks at the
temples. And Mourning's wristbands — double-wide — were
just as Ewing wears them.

But Mourning denied this first meeting with Ewing
amounted to some sort of test of status.

"I'm anxious to go to New York to win that ball game, not
to show Patrick what I can do," Mourning said. "He knows what
I can do. And I know what I can do."

Despite that disclaimer, there was clearly a game within a
game. As they met at midcourt, the two bumped chests in a
gesture that looked half aggression, half friendship. Then they
tore into each other, with Mourning ending up with the slightest
of edges. Mourning had 22 points and a professional-high 17
rebounds and six blocks in a shocking 110-103 Hornets overtime
victory at Madison Square Garden. Ewing had 28 points, nine
rebounds and three blocks. It was a crazy, wonderful game in the
biggest media market in the country. People would take notice
of the Hornets off this game.

The Knicks had previously been 10-0 at home, and New York coach Pat Riley had warned reporters that his team was "ripe" for a loss there.

He was right. The Hornets stayed in it through regulation, then held the Knicks scoreless for 2 1/2 minutes of the extra period. Mourning did a great job in holding Ewing scoreless in the overtime.

"He forced me not to get the ball. I got impatient and stepped out (of the lane) to get it," Ewing said.

Meanwhile, the Hornets allowed shooting guard John Starks to self-destruct. Starks is the Knicks' only consistent offensive threat after Ewing, but he has a terrible temper and sometimes gets so excited he loses all sense out there. In overtime, Starks committed two turnovers, two fouls (one flagrant), and allowed Mourning to twice block his shot.

"We beat them at their own game — bump and grind," said Bristow, no fan of the Knicks' roughhouse tactics. "Since I've been in Charlotte, it's always been the Patrick Ewing show against us — 40 points and umpteen rebounds. Now we at least have a guy who can neutralize that."

The Hornets hustled to get across the river to New Jersey and their charter flight home. A "Nor-easter," half-hurricane, half-blizzard, was heading up the coast, and the Hornets just beat the storm's approach before airports all around New York closed for two days. Much of Metropolitan New York was flooded with inches of freezing rain and sleet. To the north, in New England, snow closed down entire towns for nearly a week.

The Hornets' jet climbed quickly after takeoff, then banked a little too sharply for Bristow. His ex-boss, Doug Moe, was so scared of flying that Moe sometimes drove between games and met his team at the next city. Apparently, all those years around Moe made Bristow jumpy during air travel. Two days later, team equipment manager Dave Jovanovic asked a reporter if Bristow's knuckles were still white with fear from the rough flight.

Charter air travel has become virtually universal among NBA teams. Bristow lobbied for charter travel as team vice president, then got it when he took over as coach before the 1991-92 season. Flying charter is one of the few ways an NBA franchise can improve the players' chances of winning that isn't regulated by the salary cap.

Charter flights sound like a silly and costly luxury. They're not, when you consider that two or three extra wins over an 82-game schedule can make the difference of home-court advantage in the playoffs or even making the playoffs at all.

Every time some newspaper takes a poll of NBA players, the No. 1 complaint about the league is the schedule. A team's schedule is determined by arena availability, not an even spacing of games.

The Hornets played 22 sets of games on back-to-back nights in different cities in the 1992-93 season. If they had flown commercially, their daily schedule would have looked like this: Play the game in one city, return to the hotel and order room service, get to sleep around midnight. Get up the next morning around 6 a.m. to catch the first flight available (required by league rules), get to the next city late morning, nap, be at the arena at 6 p.m. for the game.

Flying charter, the Hornets schedule looked like this: Play the game, bus to the charter flight, eat and sleep on a plane that is entirely first-class seating with maximum leg room. Get home around 1 a.m., get up late-morning for a midday shootaround. Or just sleep in, play with the kids, then show up for the game at 6 p.m.

Now think about it — in a league where you can't spend a dollar on talent without it counting against a salary cap, isn't an extra couple of hundred thousand for charter travel a worthwhile way to stay rested and competitive? That's about what the Hornets paid Kevin Lynch, their 12th man.

Chartering also allows team management a certain subtle monitoring of the players' diet and lifestyle. The catering on the plane is nutritionally balanced, not fast food. And as Bristow often says, charters maximize the time the players get to sleep in their own beds.

What Bristow didn't say was that charter travel minimizes the time players might sleep in other people's beds. By traveling charter, the Hornets probably spent 20 fewer nights on the road last season. Those were 20 fewer nights for boys to be boys.

There are plenty of devoted husbands and fathers among NBA players. It's neither fair nor accurate to assume, as many fans do, that most NBA players spend their spare time chasing women on the road. But it's undeniable that the temptations are out there in every city. Young, attractive women make themselves available to players all the time. And as Magic Johnson's HIV-positive status demonstrates, the risks of promiscuity in the '90s are great.

The NBA and its players association have cooperated on a program of AIDS and safe sex awareness since Johnson's tragic announcement.

"I think the guys hear the talk and it goes through their minds," Los Angeles Lakers forward A. C. Green told the *Portland Oregonian*'s Kerry Eggers. "But I don't think what happened to Magic has drastically changed anyone's behavior. I don't see that."

The Hornets' all-time night owl had to be Robert Reid, who played for the team in two different stints over the first two seasons. Good-looking and exceptionally charming, Reid seemed to have women chasing him at every stop. A few years later, Reid ended up coach of the CBA's Yakima (Washington) Sun Kings. The idea of Reid being an authority figure over 12 young players in the CBA struck his former Hornets teammates as hilarious.

But Reid, always ready with a line, had one waiting when a Charlotte reporter chuckled at the notion of him doing bed-checks. "They say the class clowns end up as the best teachers," Reid said, flashing that wide grin.

Groupies aren't always particularly subtle, as one incident in Atlanta demonstrated a few years ago. The Hornets had hired a sideline reporter to glitz up local telecasts of away games. Hornets fans from South Carolina often drive to Atlanta for games against Charlotte because the Hawks draw so poorly that tickets are always available at the Omni. So the sideline reporter was assigned to find some devoted Hornets fans in the crowd to interview during a timeout.

Instead of finding a middle-aged couple dressed in teal and shaking pom-poms, the sideline reporter started interviewing some woman wearing a tight black dress. Before the interview was abruptly concluded, viewers could easily deduce this woman wanted to do more for the Hornets than just cheer. Several players' wives called the team offices over the next few days, to inquire about this apparent bimbo who so obviously wanted their husbands.

As the team returned to Charlotte for the game against the Nuggets, they were met by new teammate Sidney Green. Green is the NBA's definitive nomad — this was his sixth team in 10 pro seasons. Green played for Chicago, Detroit, New York, Orlando, San Antonio and now Charlotte, but his family parked the moving van for good in Orlando. Green and his wife decided the city Mickey Mouse built was a great place to raise their two children. So when Green was traded to San Antonio, the kids and wife stayed behind in Orlando.

Other than phone calls or the occasional road game in Orlando, Green's only link to his two children during the season was videotapes of his daughter's dance recitals and his son's basketball games. Late in the season, Green's Charlotte apartment was burglarized. In the act of swiping Green's video camera, the burglar also grabbed those prized tapes. Green put out the word through the local media to please send back the tapes, no questions asked. The lost jewelry, the lost camera meant nothing. The memories stored on those videotapes were invaluable.

It's understandable why Green would want to move his family to the Magic Kingdom. He grew up in a rough Brooklyn neighborhood. Green decided to get out of New York as a high school junior after an older brother, Joe, was gunned down for a disability check. Green moved 2,000 miles away to play for Nevada-Las Vegas, then was taken No. 5 overall in the 1983 draft by the Chicago Bulls. Green moved his mother out of Brooklyn, to Pennsylvania, when he turned pro.

Green's presence relieved the Hornets of Reid's long-term contract, but didn't balance the roster. At 6-9 and 240 pounds, Green was just like Reid — a backup power forward who could play a little center. Only Green was older and obviously not as good as Reid, since the Spurs gave up two draft picks to make this swap. Bristow essentially gave Green the same message he'd once given Tom Hammonds — there isn't much playing time available, but if you can play defense, I'll find you some.

Unlike Reid, Green was old and wise enough not to openly brood about circumstances. He wasn't playing much before in San Antonio, so this wasn't going to be any worse, right? He took a seat at the end of the bench and struck up a friendship with Gminski, his only contemporary on an otherwise young team.

Green found little ways to help that Reid never would have accepted as a calling. Like cheerleading from the bench. Green and rookie Tony Bennett were always the ones slapping starters' backs during timeouts trying to keep the mood positive. Green often pumped up Mourning, coining the term "Zo-lentless" to describe Mourning's intensity. One day Green said in print that he'd love to be "fan of the game," the promotion fans vote on during a timeout at home games. Sure enough, Green's face was up on the overhead scoreboard the next game, along with the faces of two unsuspecting fans.

But this was more than just benign towel-waving. Green spent a lot of time on the bench during games working the referees. Most of the time, he reminded officials how opponents would ward off Johnson or Mourning in the lane with two hands, technically a foul.

"He's hand-checking! Please, Mr. Official, call two hands!" Green would shout about a dozen times a game from the bench.

Bristow won't tolerate attitude problems at the end of the Hornets' bench. It's unavoidable that three of the 12 players won't play much. It's also unavoidable that they won't be happy about it. Unhappy is one thing, disruptive is another. The Hornets had a big problem a few years ago with a player they acquired from Portland, Richard Anderson. When the Hornets traded for him, it looked like Anderson would play a lot, but his defense was awful, so Anderson sat. He moped and occasionally ignored team rules. He flew his girlfriend (now wife) to Los Angeles to accompany him on the road during a Western Conference trip, which infuriated his teammates.

Muggsy Bogues once got so mad at Anderson that he grabbed Anderson's necktie and yanked it apart while it was still tied around Anderson's neck. Bogues had called Anderson "whopper," apparently referring to Anderson's out-of-shape appearance, and an argument escalated into Bogues destroying Anderson's tie.

The last three players on the Hornets' bench the 1992-93 season — Green, Mike Gminski, and Kevin Lynch — were pros about their situations. They didn't like not playing, and they were occasionally sarcastic about it, as in Gminski's "MX missile" joke. But they practiced hard and stayed in the games mentally. That's all Bristow had the right to ask of them.

The Hornets swept Georgetown week, beating the Denver Nuggets and Mutombo, 109-100, to improve to 11-9. Mourning upped his team record for blocked shots in a game to seven, including rejections of LaPhonso Ellis and Todd Lichti in the fourth quarter to settle things.

"Coach Thompson always reminded me, 'Time and score.' It's not how many blocks you get, it's when you get them," Mourning said.

By now, Mourning was among league leaders in rejections. He would finish fourth in the league at 3.47 per game, behind Houston's Hakeem Olajuwon (4.17), Orlando's Shaquille O'Neal (3.53), and Mutombo (3.50).

"He was just going after another high-jump record, going after every shot," Bristow gushed after the Denver game. "You know you'll see another game with him in there — Zo makes the game different for the other team."

Mourning's presence on the team was telling in the Hornets' defensive statistics. The season before, the Hornets had the second worst field-goal percentage defense in the league, allowing opponents to shoot .496. Milwaukee had been slightly worse at .498.

But over the first 20 games of this season, the Hornets held opponents to .458 shooting. Had they done that the entire previous season, they would have finished tied for the fifth-best defense in the league, rather than second worst.

Fans were starting to come around to Bristow's reasoning that field-goal percentage was a better indicator of defense than points allowed. A team holding the ball all the time — the first two seasons of the Minnesota Timberwolves for instance — could keep opponents below 100 points just by being deliberate on offense. But was this really defense? Field-goal percentage defense, the kind Mourning contributed by making opponents hesitant to drive the lane, meant the Hornets were really stopping teams when it mattered.

There was clearly a connection between the Hornets' improved defense and their success on the road. The Hornets won six of their first 11 road games, and everyone on the team attributed the initial road success to the defense. A foreign arena — strange rims, bad lighting, a nasty crowd — can throw off a shooter's rhythm. But defense is a constant whether played on your home floor or in pitch dark on the playground. The Hornets were starting to learn that.

The next game illustrated how important Mourning was to that newfound defense. Mourning suffered a scratched left eye early in a road game against the Chicago Bulls. He missed 5 1/2 minutes with the injury and played the rest of the game with blurred vision. The two-time champions saw their opening and shot 59 percent from the field in a 125-110 spanking.

Early in the game, Gill reinjured his left ankle in a pileup with Michael Jordan. But he played on it that way for another 25 minutes, and ended up missing the next four games.

Was Gill toughing it out, not realizing how badly he was hurt? Or was this just foolish bravado for the hometown crowd? Gill grew up in suburban Chicago idolizing Jordan almost as much as Mourning idolized Ewing.

Sometimes it's hard to tell where the natural similarities end between the two, and where Gill has simply appropriated Jordan's style. They're built similarly and have the same long stride. They are both "power" shooting guards who outmuscle most people guarding them. Gill's jump shot is just fair — he shoots it with little arc, so there's not much room for error. That means he has to score inside with power and quickness.

The cosmetic similarities are obvious. Gill wears his wristband up high, near the elbow, as every school kid knows Jordan does.

The day Gill lounged around the Hornets' locker room in a pair of University of Illinois practice shorts was a bit much. It's part of the Jordan legend that he wears North Carolina practice shorts under his Bulls uniform every game.

"Every guard in the league — every player in the league — measures himself against Michael," Gill once said.

But Gill does so more than most. He says Jordan is great, but adds, "there's a new one on the horizon."

They hang out together in the summer when both are in Chicago, sometimes practicing at a local health club. One day the previous summer, Jordan flashed past Gill so quickly that Gill never got to move his feet before Jordan dunked.

"You forgot about that first step, huh?" Jordan asked Gill.

"Nah, you're almost 30 years old. I thought you lost your first step," Gill needled back at Jordan.

Jordan clearly had his first step... and his second and third step, in scoring 16 of his 25 points in the first quarter.

Gill often talks of attaining something approaching Jordan's greatness. He knows he has exceptional ability, and unlike many blessed with such gifts, he's an exceptional worker. When Gill had trouble reading defenses his rookie season, he spent hours watching videotape on his own to correct his mistakes. When he realized at the end of his first season that he had to get stronger, Gill pumped so much iron the following summer that he became muscle-bound.

Syracuse coach Jim Boeheim once called Kendall Gill the toughest player in college basketball. Gill played the second half of an NCAA tournament game against Syracuse with a split lip caused when Orangeman Derrick Coleman elbowed him in the mouth. The cut was so hard to close that the front of Gill's uniform was drenched with blood, yet Gill played on.

There's no doubt Gill is tough and bright. But he's not always wise. He talks of needing to be on a winner, and yet he has a hard time sharing the spotlight. Until Gill becomes a Jordan (and that itself might be impossible), Gill can't be the best player on a big winner in the NBA. Most shooting guards simply don't have that kind of impact on a game. There are too many good shooting guards and too few good centers for Gill's position to have that much impact.

Gill was growing frustrated, and no wonder. Due to the chronic ankle sprain, he would miss 11 of Charlotte's first 25 games and shoot just 41 percent from the field in the other 14. Gill had a clause in his contract that gave him the option to become a restricted free agent at the end of the season. Gill and agent Arn Tellem thought that escape clause could be worth perhaps double the $1.9 million Gill made this season. But NBA general managers usually don't open their vaults that wide for 41 percent shooters. Not if they expect to keep their jobs.

The Hornets' 93-91 loss to the Utah Jazz was a prime example of Charlotte's inability to hold leads, particularly at home. The Hornets held the Jazz, a preseason contender for the NBA finals, to 35 percent shooting in the first half for a 10-point Charlotte lead. But the Hornets ended up losing by two when Larry Johnson's three-pointer fell short with about a second left.

Of course all of that was secondary to the night's sideshow, probably the most embarrassing moment Allan Bristow will ever experience as a coach. He was ejected with about 7 1/2 minutes left in the game, after going so berserk that he punted his suit coat at NBA official Hue Hollins.

Now, there are officials in this league who could expect Bristow to kick coats at them. Bernie Fryer comes to mind immediately. Fryer has thrown Bristow out twice since Bristow took over as coach of the Hornets. A former player for the Portland Trail Blazers, Fryer played against Bristow, and the two just don't get along. Bristow jokes that he shut Fryer down defensively once. For whatever reason, there's a strong possibility that Bristow will spend part of any game Fryer officiates in the locker room, watching via television.

But Hollins isn't a hothead; he's one of those soothing officials. He and another referee, Tommy Nunez, probably missed their calling in psychotherapy the way they finesse coaches. But on this night, Hollins tossed Bristow, and with cause.

Johnson had been called for an offensive foul that negated a basket. Rather than see Johnson get tossed (he was livid), Bristow marched onto the court to draw an automatic technical. That wasn't good enough. First, he yanked off his coat and threw it to the floor. A second passed, two seconds passed. . . Oh what the heck. . . Bristow kicked the coat at Hollins like some baseball manager tossing dirt at an umpire's shoes. What theater! What drama! What a way to get a new suit of clothes.

"Probably the most depressing thing is that my jacket is torn," said Bristow, who will never match a Pat Riley or Chuck Daly in the wardrobe department. "Now my wife has got to buy me a new suit for Christmas."

If Etoila Bristow was going to have to shell out all that money for a new suit (she replaced it with an olive double-breasted that is nicer than anything he previously owned), then she was going to have a little fun first. She made sure both daughters were up the next morning to see replays of their father's antics on ESPN's SportsCenter. Imagine the breakfast conversation: "Come on, girls, put down your Cheerios. Daddy's on TV making a fool of himself again."

ESPN and CNN each ran Bristow's madman act about 10 times over two days. And no doubt, local sportscasters around the country used it, too, like that tape of the minor leaguer running through a fence to catch a home run.

By the way, his players loved Bristow's blowup, and not just for its comedy value. The Hornets came back from eight down to nearly win. "It fired us up, it brought us together," said Johnson, who outscored Utah superstar Karl Malone, 29-21.

It gave the local sports talk shows plenty to chatter about for days, and inspired a halftime promotion. For several home games, the Hornets sponsored coat-kicking contests, judging both distance of the punt and dramatic appeal of the acting.

Bristow accepted all the kidding in good humor, but he also acknowledged that he needs to control his temper better. This wasn't the first time Bristow had been reminded of that. The previous season, Bristow led the league's head coaches in technical fouls with 15, and Hanzlik topped all league assistants with six.

Fiery is one thing, crazed is quite another.

The Hornets went back out on the road to win two straight in Washington (126-117) and Atlanta (130-114) to improve to 13-11. The Bullets game was significant only because Gminski sprained his left knee when ex-Hornet Rex Chapman ran into it. Gminski going on the injured list would avoid cutting someone to reactivate Johnny Newman, who had recovered from a broken left hand. If the Hornets had made a cut, it wouldn't have been David Wingate, who was signed when Newman went out. Bristow called Wingate's defense "a lifesaver."

The road victory over the Hawks was particularly important because Atlanta figured to be one of the teams the Hornets would fight all season for playoff position.

Hawks management started out the season trying to decide whether to keep this group intact or break it up and rebuild. They had talent, but no chemistry. Dominique Wilkins and Kevin Willis were always fighting over the ball and Rumeal Robinson was a point guard who didn't understand his job was to pass first, shoot second. The Hawks dealt with one problem by trading Robinson to the New Jersey Nets for Mookie Blaylock.

It was another of those trades that had more to do with subtraction than addition. Blaylock was keeping second-year point guard Kenny Anderson from playing, and the Nets had to develop Anderson to justify using the second pick of the entire 1991 draft to acquire him. Robinson was generally hated by his Hawks teammates, particularly Wilkins and defensive specialist Stacey Augmon, a college teammate of Larry Johnson's.

The Hornets would have loved to acquire Blaylock as a complement to Muggsy Bogues at the point. But they thought he wasn't available. In other words, the Hornets had nothing expendable that New Jersey wanted. Robinson, who could play some at point and shooting guard but excelled at neither, would back up both spots for the Nets.

Wilkins was out for the Hornets game with a broken finger and surely his scoring would have been helpful in keeping up with Charlotte. Atlanta's defense was virtually nonexistent in a 130-114 loss. Charlotte shot 56 percent from the field, and Johnson topped the night off with a dunk that nearly brought down a rim.

Johnson flashed between Travis Mays and Adam Keefe to steal a pass, then attacked the basket without a defender in sight. Johnson had lost in the finals of the NBA slam-dunk contest the previous February. The slam he made in Atlanta would have won that contest on pure force.

"I put a little extra mustard on that hot dog," Johnson said afterward.

Wilkins, nicknamed the Human Highlight Film for his own showmanship, didn't enjoy the view from the sidelines.

"You don't let teams toy with you, showboat on you, in your own gym," Wilkins said afterward.

The Hawks would remember this night and reply in Charlotte later in the season.

CHAPTER SEVEN

"He won't admit it because he's Napoleon."

Thinking back to the night of December 23, Bill Laimbeer would probably now decide his mistake wasn't what he did, but rather when he did it. Alonzo Mourning had already scored 27 points and grabbed 18 rebounds before Laimbeer baited him into a fight with four minutes left in the fourth quarter.

Laimbeer, Detroit's center and master of the sucker-punch, waited until the game was all but over before getting himself and Mourning ejected during a timeout. What Laimbeer did belonged in the back of a school bus, like Laimbeer was trying to extort lunch money from the new kid in the neighborhood.

Laimbeer and Mourning crossed each other's path at mid-court, headed toward their respective benches. Mourning looked the other way — never a wise move when Laimbeer is nearby — so Laimbeer chucked Mourning in the face with his shoulder. Mourning immediately retaliated by throwing a punch at Laimbeer, automatic cause for ejection in the NBA. Since Laimbeer had instigated the incident, he was also ejected.

What followed belonged in a Charlie Chaplin film, except Mourning was dead serious. He left the Hornets' locker room, looking for Laimbeer. The funny part was Charlotte strength coach Chip Sigmon's honest effort at holding back Mourning. As one would expect of a strength coach, Sigmon is rock-solid. But he's slightly under six feet, so he's a foot shorter and probably 50 pounds lighter than Mourning, whose rage was growing by the minute.

Accordingly, Sigmon used a greater dose of coaxing than brute force to try to avert a Mourning-Laimbeer rematch in the Pistons' locker room. Sigmon laced his arms around Mourning's waist from behind, trying to slow him down, while Charlotte Coliseum security helped block Mourning's path. "No, Zo... No, Zo." Sigmon called out, until Mourning cooled off enough to return to his own locker room.

The sight had eyewitnesses chuckling afterward. Mourning and Sigmon looked like they were doing a little line dance. Perhaps conga lines were coming back in style. Anyway, it was not a common sight at an NBA game.

Sigmon's efforts probably kept Mourning from being suspended, though this wouldn't have been the first time a fight started on the court and ended in a locker room. A few years earlier, Armon Gilliam, then playing for the Phoenix Suns, got into a hassle with Dwayne Washington, then with the Miami Heat. After both were ejected, Gilliam went to the Heat locker room and decked Washington. Whatever Washington did to upset Gilliam must have been considerable, because Gilliam is no thug. In fact, when Gilliam played for the Hornets, some of his teammates thought he was soft as Jell-O on defense.

In the locker room after the Hornets won, 107-95, Pistons forward Dennis Rodman said Laimbeer was "the best in the league at that" — "that" being agitating an opponent out of the game one way or another. But the Pistons were still 0-2 against the Hornets this season, an important turnaround from the 14-2 dominance Detroit had over Charlotte previous to this season.

Not incidental to that reversal was that the Hornets weren't letting teams push them around anymore. In the past, physical teams like the Pistons would give the Hornets a few elbows, then watch them settle for outside jump shots the rest of the game.

NBA games are more like gang warfare than the league's marketers would like to admit. If a team like the Hornets got rattled by being pushed around, then word would spread and they'd be pushed around even more. The Hornets used to get bullied all the time this way.

The Hornets rallied around Mourning's ejection, just like they rallied around Bristow's ejection three games earlier, to say they wouldn't be pushed around anymore.

"Before, there were maybe one or two players" with such attitudes among the Hornets, said Kenny Gattison. "Now we have a whole team with a mean streak." Mourning seemed to be the source of this new fierceness. "If it's helping us win, I hope it is getting around," Mourning said following the Detroit game.

Which is just about all Mourning had to say. He declined comment on the fight, and not in a particularly polite manner. First, he told one group of media he didn't want to discuss it. Then, when another group happened by and unknowingly asked about the fight, Mourning yelled out that if he heard one more question about the fight, he was cutting off all interviews.

Ah, well, this was still an improvement. The last time Mourning blew up at a journalist, it was over her mere presence in the locker room. Now, at least, you had to ask him a particular question for him to lose his temper.

Christmas Eve cost Mourning $5,000, but made Gattison a whole lot more. Before leaving for the holiday, NBA vice president Rod Thorn levied a $5,000 fine on Mourning and a $6,500 fine on Laimbeer. Mourning was fortunate to be getting off that easy, considering he headed for the Pistons' locker room following the ejection. Bristow said it was "a little bit misconstrued how determined" Mourning was in stalking Laimbeer. Maybe so, maybe not. Those who witnessed Mourning's rage sure didn't think he was on his way to invite Laimbeer to dinner.

Gattison got the nicest Christmas present of his life when he signed a four-year, $5.5 million contract extension. At an average of just more than $1.37 million, Gattison more than doubled his salary from the $598,000 he was making this season. Gattison signed the deal just before leaving with several teammates to deliver Christmas baskets to the needy.

As much as anything, the contract extension demonstrated management above Bristow finally recognized Gattison's importance to the locker room. That "You trade Gatt, you trade me," line from Johnson must have opened some eyes. "He's a big stabilizing force for our team — our player representative, our senior spokesman," Bristow said. "People really respond to him, particularly off the court."

The deal also illustrated how the fax machine has changed how the NBA does business in the '90s. Stolpen finalized the package from a tropical island where he was vacationing.

Small forward Johnny Newman also got a Christmas present when he was reactivated for the December 28 game at New Jersey. Newman missed 18 games with the injury. This was the second straight season he broke a hand bone.

Newman was devastated by the injury because he had started the season so well. With Johnson, Mourning, and Gill around, Newman's status seemed diminished with each draft. But over the first seven games of the season, Newman was shooting 52 percent from the field and averaging 18.9 points. He was even rebounding, normally his big flaw, averaging 3.8 boards per game. The injury, against the Dallas Mavericks November 17, had come at a terrible time.

"I've never seen an athlete as disappointed," Hornets team physician, Dr. Glenn Perry, had said after setting Newman's hand. "He really wants to play."

David Wingate and Dell Curry had both played well at small forward in Newman's absence, so Newman's well-known paranoia had to be brewing. Wingate's strength — defense — was what Bristow wanted most from his starting small forward. Normally, small forwards are primarily scorers (Newman is typical in that regard), while the power forward is more the complementary player.

Power forward Johnson's presence as the Hornets' top offensive option reverses all that. With Johnson taking so many shots, the logical player at small forward would be a Dennis Rodman or Stacey Augmon — a good defender who looks for offensive rebounds rather than demanding the ball. Karl Malone's presence in Utah prompted the Jazz to use Thurl Bailey and Tyrone Corbin as just that type of complementary small forward.

Newman's game was scoring, and he led the team in that category his first season in Charlotte, averaging 16.9 points in 1990-91. Newman even set the Hornets' single-game scoring record with 41 against the Indiana Pacers.

As team vice president, Bristow brought Newman to Charlotte, signing the then-restricted free agent to an offer sheet the summer of 1990. Newman's previous team, the New York Knicks, could have matched the Hornets' offer and retained him, but decided to let him leave. Bristow had coached Newman in a pre-draft camp in 1986, and liked his athleticism. Newman was a great driver, what basketball junkies call a "slasher," and had three-point range as a jump-shooter.

As Johnson's and Gill's stars rose, Newman felt he was being left behind. That put an even greater strain on the always touchy Bristow-Newman relationship. Newman often acts like Bristow has a special responsibility to foster Newman's career because Bristow signed him. Bristow regularly reminds Newman that all he was promised was four years of employment and a chance to show what he could do.

"I'm the one who signed him," Bristow said. "We didn't promise Johnny he'd be a starter or score 20 points a game. He'd had some problems up there (in New York). We gave him a fresh start."

Two seasons ago, Newman publicly accused Bristow of turning him into a "decoy." In Newman's mind, the team was getting Gill all the good shots from the outside. Bristow thought this was pretty funny, since the passing game the team ran almost exclusively at the time had no refined structure to showcase or not showcase Newman's skills. It was up to each player to find the open shots, and Gill just did a better job of finding those shots than Newman did at the time.

Bristow, Stolpen, and director of player personnel Dave Twardzik have to spend too much time finessing Newman's thin-skinned personality. It's funny that Newman complains about how Bristow coaches him, because Newman used to complain to Bristow about how Gene Littles used him. Stolpen has told Newman that his biggest problem — his only real problem — is how his insecurity skews his judgment.

If Newman's only problem was a lack of confidence, then it wouldn't be a big deal. The coaches would just pat him on the back a lot. But Newman also has an ego that can run out of control. There's a tiny window between giving him too much and too little praise.

An example: Newman agreed to push $75,000 of his 1992-93 salary to the next season to help the Hornets sign Alonzo Mourning. The Hornets weren't yet ready to give Newman a contract extension, so they asked Newman to move the money within his current deal as a sign of good faith.

Newman agreed, but then Stolpen didn't see the signed contract changes for days. When he called Newman about the papers, Newman asked Stolpen, "Why don't you like me?"

They do like you, Johnny. That's why the Hornets paid you $1.175 million for the season. As Bristow has said time and again, probably the Hornets value Newman's skills more than any other team in the league. And there's evidence to support that statement — two different summers, the Hornets looked to deal Newman for any draft pick because they were so in need of room under the salary cap. No one made a deal with the Hornets, not even at this fire-sale price.

Perhaps all this insecurity began when colleges started recruiting Newman out of George Washington High School in Danville, Virginia. A rawboned player from a relatively small town, Newman wasn't heavily recruited initially. Richmond's Dick Tarrant, always known as a sharp judge of talent, saw Newman's potential early and recruited him hard. But ACC schools like Virginia showed serious interest only after Newman had big games in the state tournament his senior year.

Newman rewarded Tarrant for his loyalty by signing with Richmond and leading the Spiders to the NCAA tournament. But he's played basketball with a chip on his shoulder throughout his pro career. He got himself released in Cleveland because he wasn't playing, left New York because the Knicks had traded for Kiki Vandeweghe, and now frets over his status in Charlotte. You get the impression from Newman's moods that he believes no coach since Tarrant has appreciated his contributions.

It's too bad, because Newman is in many ways a great guy. He's giving of his time with all kinds of charity work in Charlotte and has tried hard to become more than a basketball mercenary in the community. He just always finds a way to be unhappy about his career.

Newman struck up a friendship with Larry Johnson that seems to have loosened him up some. Johnson can needle Newman in ways others can't. One day in practice late in the season, Newman was playing good defense on Johnson, cutting off a drive to the basket. It was obvious Newman felt pretty good about himself, so Johnson explained to everyone within shouting distance what Newman had done and how proud he was of it.

"I like that, Johnny. I like the way you did that. That was

good what you did, Johnny, bodying me up and everything like that," Johnson needled. "It didn't work, but I liked it."

Johnson's sarcasm broke up the assembled reporters, who were laughing a little too loud. Newman lost his cool, yelling, "Hey, that's not funny!" at the media.

Sorry, Johnny, but it was hilarious. Learn to laugh at yourself like us clutzes. You'll live a happier, longer life.

Newman's return to the active roster would have forced the Hornets to cut someone — probably Hammonds — had Gminski not sprained his left knee against the Bullets. This was Gminski's first knee injury and it was semi-serious. He would end up missing 14 games.

The Hornets demonstrate more integrity than most NBA teams in not exaggerating injuries to avoid cutting players. The Chicago Bulls, for instance, are infamous for discovering their 12th man has a pulled hamstring at the most convenient times when a Scottie Pippen or Horace Grant is ready to come back from the injured list. Chicago beat writers think the Bulls maintain a one- or two-player taxi squad at all times by trumping up injuries, yet the league looks the other way. When Charlotte orthopedist Glenn Perry signed on as the Hornets' team physician, he was stern in two demands — he would never let a player go on the injured list unless he really couldn't play, and he would have absolute authority to keep a player off the court if there was any health risk. Perry loves sports. He says he'd love to be a sportswriter, and sportswriters tell him they'd love to make his salary. But Perry is also a skilled, highly principled surgeon who once served a similar role with baseball's Philadelphia Phillies. The Hornets were lucky he was in town when they were looking for a team physician.

The first game after Christmas was in New Jersey against the Nets, another of those important games against a team in the middle of the muddle of playoff contenders. After years of being a league-wide joke with an arena in the middle of a reclaimed swamp (the Exit 16W Nets, they were tagged), New Jersey had improved around a core of Derrick Coleman, Kenny Anderson, and a Yugoslavian shooting guard named Drazen Petrovic.

"Petro," as he was called, grew up in Eastern Europe but adapted quickly to the American basketball custom of trashtalking. He loved to get under Gill's skin after hitting a 20-footer.

Petrovic proved that trash talk was a truly international language by giving Gill grief in several dialects, none of them English. Gill didn't know what Petrovic was saying, but he could tell from the tone, the hand motions, and the timing of the comments that Petro wasn't wishing him a safe trip home to Charlotte.

Petrovic, who tragically died the summer of 1993 in a car crash, was an exquisite outside shooter; he would eventually be voted third-team all-NBA. But the young Croatian was about as good a defender on the basketball court as a placekicker is on the football field. So when Gill, Muggsy Bogues, and Kenny Gattison charged downcourt, with only Petrovic to stop them with five seconds left, the Hornets looked in great shape to win one at Brendan Byrne Arena.

"I thought I was in big trouble," Petrovic said.

He should have been. But Gill, the best finisher of the three, inexplicably gave up the ball. It ended up in the hands of Gattison, and Petrovic slapped down to knock it free. In the scramble for the loose ball, the clock ticked out, giving the Nets a 104-103 victory.

Gill grabbed the rebound that set up the Hornets' last possession and never should have given up his dribble. At least, he probably would have drawn a foul from Petrovic for two free throws that could have won the game.

"I thought they made a mistake by going to Gattison instead of Gill," said Petrovic. "I thought it was a very good defensive play."

Petrovic might have lacked for modesty, but his point on Gattison versus Gill was well taken. Gill knew he'd screwed up, saying, "We should have won this game."

The Bulls made their first trip to Charlotte this season, and that is always an occasion. Michael Jordan is considered some sort of natural resource of the state, so Bulls games always sell out first on Charlotte's home schedule. Usually the 2,000 or so tickets available on a single-game basis are gobbled up within hours of going on sale for any Bulls-Hornets games.

Jordan grew up in Wilmington and played his college ball in Chapel Hill, but his mother now lives in the Charlotte area, so it's sort of a second home. Jordan's friends from around the state always pressure him for tickets, so his life is even more chaotic here than elsewhere in the league. Also, Jordan's last public appearance in Charlotte hadn't been a pleasant one. He testified in federal court in Charlotte to having lost tens of thousands of dollars in gambling debts to one James "Slim" Bouler.

Bouler is a convicted cocaine dealer who lives in the Charlotte suburb of Monroe. Bouler admits he makes money as a professional gambler. There was nothing illegal about Jordan losing all that money to Bouler on the golf course in South Carolina. But hanging out with the Slim Boulers of the world didn't exactly fit the "Be like Mike" image in the Gatorade advertisements. Jordan's fame means he lives in a fishbowl, but he and agent David Falk have to take some of the blame for creating an image no one could live up to.

When *The Observer* broke the story of Jordan's connection to Bouler, reader reaction was interesting. Some saw the extensive coverage as a cheap shot at a positive black role model. Some others were glad that, in their minds, a Tar Heel was finally getting some bad press after all the negative coverage of Jim Valvano's ouster at N.C. State.

Neither assessment was accurate; *The Observer* had no agenda. Two *Observer* reporters learned of the federal investigation into the Bouler-Jordan connection somewhat by chance. The newspaper treated Jordan as it would any other prominent Carolinian in such a mess. Of course, it's hard to imagine a Carolinian more prominent than Michael Jordan.

The Hornets lost their 17th straight to the Bulls, this time 114-103. Jordan, who is quite a gamesman along with being the greatest basketball talent on the planet, added some weight to the Hornets' burden following the game.

"We are aware of those 17 straight wins," Jordan said after assembling a triple-double of 28 points, 12 rebounds, and 11 assists. "It keeps you awake — when are they going to come at you?"

The Hornets' only victory over the Bulls was in their first meeting back in 1988 on national television. *The Observer* treated that first game against the Bulls like a visit from the royal family. The front page of the sports section was filled by a line drawing of Jordan, prompting then-Hornet Kelly Tripucka to ask if Jordan had been traded to Charlotte without anyone's knowledge.

Kurt Rambis tipped in a shot at the buzzer to win that game. Rambis, now a Los Angeles Laker, says five years later he still gets letters with North Carolina postmarks thanking him for that shot.   Gill didn't like it when told that Jordan was keeping track of the 17 straight victories since Rambis's tip-in.

"That's good, but M. J. will have his day," said Gill. "There will be a day when we do that against the Bulls."

Newman, back in the starting lineup, scored 28 points on the Bulls while hitting 10 of 12 shots from the field. But Mourning was awful, shooting two of nine and grabbing only four rebounds in 29 minutes. Perhaps Mourning was finally hitting the wall, that hypothetical point in a rookie's season when the demands of the pro game wear him down. The Hornets had played 27 games already — nearly the length of a college season — but the NBA schedule was not quite a third over.

Gill made up for giving up the ball in New Jersey, hitting a 15-footer with four seconds left to beat the Nets in Charlotte, 118-117. Gill was bouncing between hero and goat almost daily. In the Hornets' next game, Gill missed an easy layup with 12 seconds left in a 107-103 loss to the Boston Celtics. Gill was hard on himself afterward. Asked what went wrong, Gill just said, "Me," in a virtual whisper following the game.

Gill's confidence was taking a terrible bruising. He was shooting just 40 percent from the field and occasionally hearing boos from Charlotte fans when he entered games. It didn't help any that *The Observer* ran a giant picture the next day of Gill sitting on the floor following the missed layup, looking like a beaten man. The picture accurately described what happened, but it heaped even more pressure on a player in a terrible slump. Gill shot just five of 17 and might have been better off on the bench.

Newman probably thought so. He had left the game with 4:47 left in the third quarter, never to return. The famous paranoia was showing through.

"I just go out and work hard, do what I'm asked to do. That's not working," said Newman. "Nothing surprises me."

Newman wasn't just sharing time with Dell Curry and David Wingate anymore. Now, Kenny Gattison was getting extra playing time in a big lineup that moved Johnson to small forward. If Newman wasn't having a big scoring night, then Bristow had to go big against the Celtics to counter Boston's height.

The biggest problem of the night was not the loss, but the cracked bone Mourning suffered in his left thumb. Celtics center

Robert Parish, a martial arts student in his spare time, chopped down on Mourning's hand trying to knock loose the ball and instead broke Mourning's thumb just above the joint.

Perry and trainer Terry Kofler decided Mourning could play with the injury, but how effective would he be? In order to protect the fracture, Mourning played with the thumb encased in a soft plastic and foam rubber splint wrapped in an Ace bandage. Play-by-play announcer Matt Pinto described the wrap as a "corn dog," which was most accurate and a cute turn of phrase. Question was, could Mourning play with the corn dog and the throbbing pain? Much of what makes Mourning so good offensively is that he can shoot jump shots and dribble far better than the average center. Would the corn dog rob him of those skills?

Apparently not, on the basis of the next game against the Los Angeles Clippers. Mourning scored 20 points and grabbed 13 rebounds, and he hit eight of 19 shots in a 115-101 victory.

The game marked referee Bernie Fryer's first appearance at a Hornets game since the preseason. It had taken 30 games for the Hornets to be assigned Fryer, so it was apparent the league was aware Bristow and Fryer had problems. Remember, Fryer threw Bristow out of games twice, the most recent in that preseason exhibition in Las Vegas against the Portland Trail Blazers.

What made Fryer's long absence from Hornets games all the more interesting was that Darell Garretson was the lead official on the game. Garretson is both a working referee and the NBA's chief of officials. Yes, Garretson holding both jobs is the absurd conflict of interest it appears to be. Many referees hate the system where they are on the floor working with Garretson one day, then having him evaluate them the next. Worst of all, Garretson is essentially an arrogant curmudgeon on a power trip. He manages through intimidation, as he demonstrated that night at Charlotte Coliseum.

The Hornets are proud of their music selection during games. The mix of music and sound effects has always been part of the building's successful atmosphere. Sometimes the timing of the music or sound effects goes too far in helping the home team in Charlotte. Garretson couldn't be diplomatic in explaining that to the scorer's table. Instead, during a timeout five minutes into the game, he marched over to the game operations staff and growled, "You better play it at both ends, or I'll put someone else on the record player!"

A real sweetheart, that Garretson.

USA Today's Peter Vecsey had just written a column, suggesting Garretson shouldn't be kept on as an official, much less a supervisor. That gave a Hornets fan some material to heckle.

"Hey Garretson, Vecsey's right!" the fan screamed out.

"At least you can read," Garretson responded.

"At least I can see!" the fan yelled back.

Garretson's presence in Charlotte sure made it look as though the league wanted a watchdog around when Fryer and Bristow were on the same court. It looked even more suspicious that Garretson was also there the next time Fryer officiated a Hornets game.

Bristow says he honestly doesn't know what the friction is between him and Fryer, and he wishes he could smooth things over.

"You know me, I could have a beer with him right now. What do you do?" Bristow said after Fryer ejected him in the preseason.

Actually, that's exactly how Bristow looks at life. For someone with such a wild temper, he cools off quickly, then forgets whatever he was mad about.

After the Clippers game, some of the Hornets got together to celebrate point guard Muggsy Bogues's 28th birthday. Apparently, Bogues celebrated a bit too much because he showed up at practice the next day complaining of a mysterious stomach ache. His teammates knew a hangover when they saw one — Johnson needled Bogues by urging a reporter to get the real scoop on Bogues's ailment.

Bogues showed up in a sweat suit, figuring to sit out practice. Bristow is pretty lenient about letting players sit out practice to rest soreness, but this was different. Bristow told Bogues to go on home if he wasn't up to practicing. Bogues got the message, changed into his practice gear, and participated. Like most players at one time or another, Bogues wanted to be coddled.

Boston's Kevin McHale once called Bogues the toughest player in the league, concluding he'd have to be just to compete at 5-3. Despite that tough outer shell, Bogues's height makes him somewhat insecure and paranoid.

Who woudn't be, considering what it took for Bogues to get this far? Bogues has been told all his life he can't play basketball. Even in high school, players from opposing teams would sometimes laugh at him before the opening tip-off of games. Then Bogues would strip those jokers three or four times for layups and everyone would stop laughing.

There's a strut about Bogues that compensates for his lack of height. Knicks point guard Doc Rivers, known for a biting wit, described Bogues's pride well: "Obviously, he'd love to be six foot. But he won't admit it because he's Napoleon."

Leon Howard, formerly a director of a Baltimore recreation center where Bogues played, recalls Bogues always wanted to be the center of attention, the leader. Howard says Bogues always wanted to hold the flag for the pledge of allegiance.

"Even then he was the smallest kid around," Howard told *The Observer's* Charles Chandler.

Bogues has had an all-around challenging life — when Bogues was 12, his father was sentenced to 20 years for armed robbery. He's risen above that neighborhood back in Baltimore. He's charming, charismatic, and has turned his lack of height into a marketable distinction. His agent thinks there is money to be made in a book and/or movie on Bogues's life.

But don't be deceived; Bogues is not as cuddly as he appears. There's a testy agenda about Bogues that apparently evolved from coaches constantly questioning whether he could compete.

Dick Harter was probably hardest on Bogues. When reporters would ask why Harter questioned Bogues's ability, Harter would drop to his knees and wave helplessly to illustrate why Bogues can't deny the entry pass. Then Harter would jump up on a chair and hover to illustrate how easily NBA guards can contest Bogues's jump shot.

Harter demanding that the Hornets trade away Bogues was a primary factor in Shinn deciding to fire Harter.

But Bristow has no such problem with Bogues. In fact, he prefers short, quick point guards who can pressure the ball because those players excel in the passing game. Bristow knew that before he ever got to Charlotte, having coached Michael Adams back in Denver.

Bristow's only complaint with Bogues's game is that he passes up open shots. That sounds like a pleasant problem, considering how many unabashed gunners there are in the NBA. But in fact, passing up an open shot in an NBA game is an unpardonable sin. With the 24-second shot clock ticking down, there might not *be* another open shot. Bogues becomes so absorbed in being a playmaker that he appears to forget about shots. Or perhaps he doesn't always have the faith in his shooting to take them.

Bogues's reluctance to shoot allows opposing teams to double-team off him constantly. That creates problems for Johnson and Mourning, who draw those double-teams.

Bogues presents one other problem — he almost never wants to leave a game to take a rest. This seems admirable, except he often gets downright contemptuous when Bristow substitutes for him with the game still in doubt. Watch Bogues's body language. As he walks back to the bench ever so slowly, Bogues places hands on hips and subtly shakes his head. Then, once past Bristow, he looks back and squints as if to say, "This guy is crazy for ever taking me out!"

The coaches are amused by Bogues's annoyance with leaving games, but somewhere down the road the Hornets will draft a point guard who challenges Bogues for the starting spot. Bristow has often said Bogues would be more effective in shorter doses, though it's hard to believe Bogues will buy into that theory.

No matter how bad the Mavericks get, the trip to Dallas is a big one for the Hornets because Larry Johnson comes home. Johnson's friends and family sell out an entire section of seats at Reunion Arena. He put on a show against the pitiful Mavericks, scoring 24 points in a 132-113 victory.

Kenny Gattison's candor got him in a bit of trouble after the game. Gattison just said what every other NBA player thought — that the Mavericks were putrid.

"They're bad on paper and bad on the floor," Gattison said. "They need everything from top to bottom. Three more players are not going to make this a good team. They've got to build a starting five and a solid bench. They're at least four years away.

"Any team they beat this year is an upset."

There was nothing inaccurate about Gattison's statements, and he didn't intend to sound cruel. But a baseball writer filling in for the *Dallas Morning News'* regular beat writer made it sound like Gattison was taunting the Mavericks. Gattison was just being his normal, honest self, but he made headlines the next day.

The Hornets had two nights off before their game at Houston, so they stayed an extra night in Dallas. That allowed Johnson to throw a massive dinner party for his teammates. It was classic Johnson — generous, social, considerate.

Johnson's mother cooked half the food and the rest was catered. Strangely enough, entertainment was provided in part by the Hornets' quiet man, David Wingate, who piped up with some impromptu rap music.

Whenever Johnson is in Dallas, his agents, Steve Endicott and Sherwood Blount, aren't far behind. Endicott, a former college football coach, is the agent of record when reporters call. Endicott is low-key and doesn't take himself too seriously, which distinguishes him from almost every other agent in the country. Blount stays in the shadows, but it's clear Endicott works for Blount. A Dallas real estate developer, Blount has reason to keep a low profile — he was knee deep in the recruiting scandal at Southern Methodist.

The NCAA forced SMU to disassociate itself from Blount, one of the school's big boosters, as part of the so-called "death sentence" that caused the school to shut down its football program for a year.

Johnson originally signed to play for SMU, but left the school when its administration demanded that Johnson sit out competition his freshman year for academic reasons. Johnson eventually ended up at Nevada-Las Vegas.

Blount never wanted to be quoted during negotiation of Johnson's first contract with the Hornets, which was fine with reporters since Endicott is so pleasant. The funny thing was that while Blount didn't want to be quoted, he constantly injected himself into interviews. One day he took over a phone interview for about 15 minutes. The only thing Blount revealed in that conversation is that he knew next to nothing about the NBA salary cap. Blount said it didn't matter whether a veteran was signed before a rookie, as far as those contracts' effect on a team's cap room was concerned. Just the opposite is true, as the reporter illustrated to Blount with two different examples. Finally, after this little class in remedial cap-ology, Blount backed off his claim and acknowledged he was wrong.

Johnson's mother cooked at a Dallas-area country club where Blount and Endicott play golf. They befriended her, which obviously didn't hurt their chances of signing Johnson, despite their limited experience representing NBA players. Blount and Endicott's agency is more football oriented. Dallas Cowboys wide receiver Michael Irvin is probably their highest-profile client other than Johnson.

It became clear quickly to the Hornets that Johnson's agents didn't know much about negotiating an NBA contract. After learning of Blount's background, various members of the Hornets' management team have quietly expressed concern that Johnson's money isn't being handled by the best of managers.

Then again, with a $20 million initial contract that the Hornets already want to extend, it's hard to imagine Larry Johnson ever worrying about his next meal or his next Mercedes.

CHAPTER EIGHT

"Everybody wants to be shooting stars, superstars."

After mowing down the Mavericks, the Hornets thought they had everything figured out. They were full of themselves, having won three of four. Budding confidence had bloomed to arrogant cockiness. That made Bristow fret even more than usual. His players still weren't as good as they thought they were.

"There's still a seven-game losing streak in these guys," Bristow had said at the start of the Texas swing.

Bristow also mentioned that less than a year ago some guy was living on a billboard along Independence Boulevard, Charlotte's busiest street, promising to stay up there until the Hornets won two games in a row. The coaches and players resented that guy to no end. He was chasing publicity for a foam-rubber "stinger" novelty he was marketing. They thought he was mocking the team's difficulties rather than showing his loyalty.

Bristow would remind the players and the media of that billboard-sitter whenever he thought the team was losing perspective. He didn't have to use that trick after the Houston game. The Rockets did everything necessary to show the Hornets they still had plenty to learn.

Hakeem Olajuwon treated Mourning like. . . well, like the rookie he was, in grabbing 19 rebounds and scoring 14 points. The surprising part was how badly Houston rookie Robert Horry showed up Johnny Newman. Horry dunked continuously on Newman to score 18 points in the first half and a career-high 26 overall.

"The Dallas game gives you fool's gold," said Bristow. "For us to be a good team, we have to be mature just as much mentally as physically."

It was clear Bristow thought about shaking up the lineup and nearly as clear that shakeup would send Newman to the bench. Newman, the team's most temperamental player, would see this as a demotion, though that wasn't Bristow's purpose. It was just more logical to have Newman, a scorer, playing with the second unit, which needed his scoring. Wingate, who didn't need to score to contribute, was a more logical complement to Johnson, Mourning, and Gill.

But Bristow knew that if he made the change now, Newman would perceive it as punishment for his poor defense against Horry. "I hate to do it off of one game," Bristow said.

The Hornets completed their Texas swing with a trip to San Antonio, where ex-teammate J. R. Reid was thriving. Shortly after Reid was traded to the Spurs, the team fired Jerry Tarkanian and hired former NBA point guard John Lucas as coach.

It was a bold move. Lucas was a recovering drug addict who ran a dependency rehabilitation program in Houston when he was hired by Spurs owner Red McCombs. Lucas was exceptionally bright and motivated, but his only previous coaching experience was running a summer-league team in Miami to give recovering ball players somewhere to play.

And yet, Lucas was an excellent choice. The Spurs needed someone with his training to restore the team's confidence. Tarkanian hadn't worked out, and there was a strange mix of personalities on this club, including Lloyd Daniels, a New York playground legend who never made it to college ball. Daniels had been shot in a drug deal gone bad.

Lucas, who grew up in Durham, North Carolina before playing for Maryland, saw immediately that Reid would never have grown up if he'd stayed in Charlotte.

"Living in North Carolina, going to North Carolina, there was an undue pressure on him to succeed," Lucas said. "He hasn't had a chance to develop as a person."

It was clear that the move had helped Reid already. Now, he was just one of the guys, not someone constantly showing off to justify his status. And he admitted relief at being out of the spotlight.

"Nobody likes to be booed, and I wasn't enjoying (Charlotte) as much as I should have been," Reid said. "I was happy that I was the one to leave. I was hoping someone (in the frontcourt) would go. Someone *had* to go. I was just happy I wasn't going to Detroit. I don't like anybody there.

"I knew something would happen eventually. That's why I never bought a house in Charlotte."

Then Reid asked about the Charlotte crowd booing Kendall Gill. He was upset for his ex-teammate, but not surprised. Reid had heard plenty of boos in Charlotte Coliseum.

"The people in Charlotte have got to relax. They have a very talented team," Reid said.

But the fans hadn't relaxed; they got all over Gill for his shooting. Perhaps they resented the way Gill marketed himself. He had allowed a company to plaster his face on billboards around town, organizing a Kendall Gill fan club. People don't normally pay to join fan clubs for players shooting 40 percent and missing game-winning layups. A 40 percent shooter should pay fans to join his club. The billboards looked increasingly silly with each bad game.

Bristow took Gill aside several times to remind him the team had confidence he'd bounce back from what had become a two-month shooting slump. Gill eventually decided that he needed to simplify his life, to pull back from some of his marketing and business diversions.

That pleased the Hornets, but another decision Gill would make within weeks would have just the opposite effect.

David Wingate continued his quiet-man routine, which was wise considering his past in San Antonio. Surrounded by military bases, San Antonio is quite the party town, and Wingate had been quite a partier as a Spur. There's a story San Antonio writers tell of a strip joint that put out a "Welcome Home David Wingate" sign when he showed up in San Antonio with the Bullets.

The fall at Houston started the week-long losing streak Bristow feared. San Antonio center David Robinson scored a career-high 52 points to beat the Hornets, 124-111, completing the road trip.

The Houston-San Antonio weekend would have been a total loss, except Mourning did prove he wasn't always RoboCop.

During shootaround the morning of the Spurs game, John Delong of *The Winston-Salem Journal* tripped on the edge of the court and did a pratfall á la Chevy Chase. Mourning nearly fell over, too, with laughter. Either he was a fan of slapstick comedy, or Mourning just enjoyed watching sports writers hurt themselves.

It was obvious Bristow was about to move Wingate into the starting lineup and Newman out. The Hornets had allowed the Rockets and Spurs to shoot 51 percent in the two losses. Newman wasn't a bad defender, but it was obvious Wingate was better. Also, even Newman agreed that Johnson and Mourning would get into their offensive rhythms faster with him coming off the bench.

Bristow tried his best to finesse the situation, but it was obvious what was coming. The day before the next game, at home against the Atlanta Hawks, Newman practiced with the reserves while Wingate practiced with the starters. But no one would officially confirm the obvious when asked by the media.

The Hornets stayed close this time, but lost on a fluke — a 7-foot-tall fluke. Hawks center Jon Koncak reached over Gill and tipped in the winning shot off the glass from six feet away for a 102-100 victory.

Koncak proves that if you are a 7-footer and have any control over your four limbs, you can make a ton of money in the NBA. Koncak was drawing a $2.45 million salary for the season, though even he basically admitted he wasn't worth it. Koncak was booed by Hawks fans far more than Reid or Gill ever were in Charlotte. In fact, after Koncak hit the winning shot, he joked, "You better stop putting my name in a headline. Somebody might start liking me."

Dominique Wilkins scored 34, so Newman probably thought he belonged back in the starting lineup. Newman did a good job of keeping mum with his unhappiness. That is, except for a moment of weakness January 20 when Newman told *The Gaston Gazette*, "If I'm not going to play, then trade me. They know how I feel about that."

The Hornets had bigger problems than Newman. Much bigger problems. Apparently tired of being booed, Gill decided he wanted out. The Hornets received a brief letter from agent Arn Tellem January 20, confirming Gill's "desire to be traded."

It was disappointing, but not much of a surprise. Hornets owner George Shinn, a great believer in instinctual management, always had a bad feeling about Gill's loyalty to Charlotte. Gill was a big-city kid from Chicago and never seemed excited about settling into a middle-sized market. He wanted to be a star, and often talked of the off-court opportunities in Chicago, New York, or Los Angeles.

"I've just always had a feeling that Kendall was more of an individual player than a team player," Shinn would say in June. "He just didn't fit in."

Gill showed occasional signs of warming to Charlotte. He once talked of selling his uptown condominium to build a big house on Lake Wylie near Johnson's place. In September, over a deli sandwich at the Charlotte Hyatt, Gill had even talked of signing a long-term deal with the Hornets, getting married, and raising kids here.

The best reason Gill would want to stay is to play with Mourning and Johnson. Their presence in Charlotte assured the chance to contend for NBA championships. But Gill wanted it both ways. He wanted to win a title *and* be the center of attention. And that just wasn't going to happen. Gill is one of the 100 best players in the NBA and has potential to be one of the 50 best. But if he's the best player on a team, that team will win 40 games, tops. Gill is not Jordan, and Jordan still needs Scottie Pippen and Horace Grant to win championships.

Just about the time Gill dropped his bomb on the Hornets, they were losing at New York, 114-91. The game illustrated how fragile the Hornets could still be. They still weren't so overpowering with talent that they could ride out the rough spots.

"If we're not on the same channel, then we're a mess. That's what we're doing — making a mess," Gattison admitted. "Guys see us going South, and so they break out, try to do too much."

The Hornets assembled for a team meeting the next day in Chicago to clean up their mess — to discuss how they had lost their focus, how some players were trying to do things they had no business attempting. The word "selfish" came up often in this meeting. Players were reminded who were the kings, who were the knights, and who were the pawns. They needed that reminder.

"They're cocky," one team official said that night. "Everybody wants to be shooting stars, superstars."

The coaches went off to a Chicago dog track that night, to blow off steam. Predictably, Bristow couldn't pick a winner. What else could he expect in a week like this?

Worse yet, the Hornets were about to take their regular dose of bitter medicine from the Bulls. Remember what Jordan said? Seventeen straight and counting. When would the Hornets beat the Bulls? *Could* they beat the Bulls?

Gill's request to be traded hadn't become public yet, but Tellem was laying the groundwork to pressure the Hornets into a trade. Charles Chandler, a feature writer for *The Observer*, was researching a long story on Gill for the following Sunday. In the course of an interview with Chandler, Tellem said he recommended Gill not only exercise an escape clause to become a restricted free agent, but that he sign only the one-year qualifying offer the Hornets are required to provide. That would allow Gill to become an unrestricted free agent in two years and dramatically increase his options.

Tellem, who also represents baseball millionaires Bo Jackson and Mark Langston, predicted he could get a young, talented player like Gill a staggering contract on the open market.

"Never has there been a player of Kendall's status as an unrestricted free agent in the NBA. Having represented baseball free agents, it would be very interesting to see what the contract would bring if Kendall was a basketball free agent," Tellem said. "It is my opinion that I can bring a taste of baseball to the NBA with Kendall Gill."

Shinn and Stolpen know all about baseball economics. They investigated the possibility the summer before of Shinn buying the San Francisco Giants. Shinn adores baseball, it was his sport growing up, but a world of $7 million annual salaries is the last thing Shinn wanted for his basketball team.

"The thing I find a little scary is the suggestion of using Kendall to bring baseball salaries to basketball," Stolpen said. "This league has always prided itself on avoiding that silliness, and I will not respond to rhetoric."

Funny, Spencer, but it sounds like you just did.

The odd thing in all this was Gill's reaction. Remember, Gill's request to be traded — sent through Tellem — had not yet become public. When asked about Tellem's thoughts on free agency, Gill gave no indication he wanted out of Charlotte. In fact, he emphasized just the opposite.

"I'm just looking for what is best for me financially. I want to stay a Charlotte Hornet," Gill said of Tellem's statements. "I think we have a chance to win a championship here."

This is where it gets strange, and stayed that way for months. Obviously, Tellem didn't ask for the trade on his own. And yet, Gill wouldn't flat-out tell the Hornets face-to-face what he wanted. Maybe he didn't know, maybe he kept changing his mind, or perhaps he just didn't have the guts to say flat-out, without an intermediary, that he didn't like it in Charlotte.

At one point, Twardzik approached Gill before a practice because he wanted to hear it from Gill's lips whether Gill really wanted to be traded. Gill was noncommittal, like some 17-year-old recruit hesitant to tell a college coach he was going elsewhere. Shortly after that conversation, the Hornets got a call from Tellem reminding the team Gill wanted to be traded. Obviously, Gill had called Tellem to tell him to do the dirty work.

In fact, it took a June meeting in Chicago among Gill, Tellem, Twardzik, and Stolpen for Gill to finally say straight out that he preferred to leave Charlotte.

It's odd that Gill was like that. One of the more impressive things early in Gill's first three years with the Hornets was his directness. As a rookie in Portland, after his older teammates dogged their way through a loss to the Trail Blazers, Gill openly questioned whether his team had mentally given up for the season. That took great courage on Gill's part, and impressed management right away that Gill had the heart and mind of a leader.

Unfortunately, Gill shrank into a shell. Perhaps it was his shooting slump, or the boos, or the pressure of impending restricted free agency. Maybe Gill didn't like Charlotte's size, or perhaps he felt Johnson's and Mourning's growing stardom robbed him of his status. There was clearly friction between Gill and Bogues, the emotional hub of the Hornets' locker room. It's tough to pal around with Johnson or Curry or Wingate if you don't like socializing with Bogues. Gill didn't spend much time on the road with his teammates. Gill's absence from Johnson's party in Dallas was clearly resented by his teammates. Gill had another engagement that night, but some players wondered why Gill wouldn't break those plans considering how much fuss Johnson went to to entertain his teammates in his hometown.

Gill occasionally complained of not having many close friends among his teammates. If that's so, it's because he didn't make much effort to develop those friendships. Gill was always talking about greatness — he often said he had a goal of being one of the five best players in the league. Finally, someone from the Hornets' organization reminded him that one definition of greatness is making the people around him better — that giving up some of his game to merge it with others' is what great players do. That never seemed to register with Gill.

Gill is a good guy. In fact, he is quite considerate to people like reporters, who often are treated as pests by some other players. Other than Gminski, Gill would be the Hornet quickest to congratulate a beat writer or broadcaster on a new baby or promotion. But Gill's preoccupation with money and status annoyed many of his teammates. Gill had three cars in Charlotte — a Ferrari Testarossa, a red Mercedes convertible, and a Toyota 4-runner. He bragged to Chandler of having 100 outfits in his closets. He was trying to live the life of Michael Jordan before he was Michael Jordan.

Gill started living big quickly after signing with the Hornets. So quickly that early in his career in Charlotte, he had to ask the Hornets for an advance on his salary.

Every Hornet has a luxury car, usually more than one. But several teammates thought Gill's conspicuous consumption and Tellem's talk of using Gill to break new ground in player salaries was self-indulgent and totally unrealistic. The Hornets were already willing to sign Gill to a contract worth well more than $3 million a season. That would put Gill in a slot between Jordan and Reggie Miller, the highest-paid guards in the league.

Gill's parents moved to Matteson, Illinois, a mostly white suburb of Chicago, in the mid-1970s. Gill told Chandler he felt the sting of prejudice there. When he and a white friend jumped into the swimming pool at a country club, some other boys jumped out. After he made the game-winning hit in a district-championship baseball game, Gill was the only player not to receive a medal.

Those experiences hurt Gill, but the Hornets felt he was now preoccupied with status. As one team official said, no one on the team was kicking Gill out of the pool, so why would he want to leave? All they wanted was to pay him well and let him play his entire career, if he wanted to, in Charlotte.

This business of Gill's aspiring to be one of the league's top five players concerned Bristow.

"To a point, it's good to think like that. Confidence in yourself is a quality any great athlete has," Bristow told Chandler in January. "But you also have to realize where. . . I don't want to say where to draw the line because that's limitations. . . but you have to accept your potential.

"I think it will come naturally. He'll find his niche. Maybe he'll be one of the top five, maybe he won't. But, eventually, you have to accept it. If you fight it too much, you're never happy."

That, of course, became the question of the month: Could anything make Gill happy long term in Charlotte?

At one point, Hornets management flat-out asked Gill and Tellem what it would take to get him to sign a long-term contract. The Gill camp came back asking for an average of $4.5 million per season. No guard other than Jordan was worth that kind of money. To have made such a request meant Gill had to want out of Charlotte.

If anything was going to convince Gill how good life could be as a Hornet, the victory over the Bulls in Chicago January 23 should have been it. After losing four straight, the Hornets astoundingly beat the Bulls, 105-97. The victory, in front of his family and his hometown, had Gill gushing afterward.

"Just think, if we can beat the Chicago Bulls in Chicago Stadium, we can beat anybody anywhere," Gill said. "This is a turning point for the Charlotte Hornets."

The meeting, in which players talked openly of teammates trying to do things they weren't capable of, had obviously helped. As Mourning said, "a couple of team meetings cleared things up — like people's roles."

And strangely enough, the losses, particularly the thumping by the Knicks, helped. The Hornets had played so badly against the Knicks that they knew they had hit bottom. There was a certain serenity in knowing they could only improve the next game.

"We were playing so bad, we had nothing to lose," said Dell Curry. "We were playing the Bulls, we were not expected to win, so we just played."

The so-called "Big Three" of Johnson, Mourning, and Gill were all great. Johnson had a season-high 19 rebounds, plus 18 points. Mourning had 19 points, 14 rebounds, and a career-high nine blocks (one more rejection would have been the franchise's first regular-season triple-double). Gill had 19 points and five rebounds.

Best of all, Jordan finally had to break down his mental toteboard on which he kept track of the Bulls' successive victories over little Charlotte.

"We can sit here and make excuses all day, but they played well," Jordan said afterward. "How many games have we won against them? We figured one of these days they were going to sneak up on us."

Actually, there was nothing "sneaky" about the Hornets' approach. In fact, Mourning got pretty full of himself at the end, trash-talking to Jordan late in the game. Mourning might have been wise to discuss this with Gill before giving Jordan lip. It was one thing to give Jordan grief in a summer scrimmage. But as Gill once said, "You never talk to Michael in a game. He might score 50 on you."

Jordan and the rest of the Bulls would remember the Hornets' brashness following this victory. As Dominique Wilkins had the previous week, Jordan would remind the Hornets down the road about winning gracefully.

If the game in Chicago showed how fun it is to be young and brash and talented, then the home game two nights later against the Indiana Pacers showed how misleading such a victory can be. Once again the Hornets were the Pacers' chumps, losing by seven.

The weekend illustrated all the Hornets' traits for the season. How they could play shockingly well on the road or lose all concentration at home. How they would win at the exact moment fans were ready to write them off, but also how they didn't understand how to protect a lead.

One thing was certain after this loss — the Pacers brought out the worst in the Hornets for no easily explained reason.

"To beat them we need to have a 25-point lead with three minutes left to go," Gill said.

The Hornets didn't blow quite that much of a lead in this one, but there was a 21-point turnaround over the last eight minutes. Charlotte led, 98-84, on Curry's 19-foot jump shot with

8:04 left, only to lose, 112-105. It was gruesome to watch, as Pacers center Rik Smits, hardly a Dutch version of Hakeem Olajuwon, nearly outscored the Hornets in the fourth quarter. Smits had 11 points, the Hornets 15.

Observer columnist Tom Sorensen, who writes with more of an edge than colleague Ron Green, called the Hornets "mediocre" and "gutless" in the next day's newspaper for the way they played in the fourth quarter. Sorensen admonished the Hornets for their 8-9 home record, and Pacers guard Reggie Miller chimed in as if on cue.

"Charlotte always seems to let us back into games down here," Miller said. "They seem to get an early lead, and then get away from what got them the lead."

The Pacers were peeved at Mourning for grandstanding after nearly every basket in the first three quarters. Apparently, Mourning was still on a high from his performance in Chicago. After the game, Bristow said he needed to talk to Mourning about his demeanor. Told of Bristow's plan, Mourning threw another tantrum.

"You know what? I have always, since the first time I played the game of basketball, demonstrated my excitement about playing the game," said Mourning. "I will stop, if they give me a good reason why it's a detriment to the team . . . If they've got a problem, release me. Release me!"

Obviously, Mourning knew the Hornets wouldn't release him. Bristow already thought Mourning was among the top six or seven centers in the league. Mourning overreacted, just like he did on the court. The Hornets love his enthusiasm, his will, his desire — those are the qualities that set him apart from lesser centers of equivalent ability. They just wanted him to fine-tune his emotions — to learn the difference between celebrating and foolish, energy-sapping taunting. And Mourning would get better about this as the season progressed.

As Sorensen so aptly explained: "To wage war on every play, to invest that kind of energy and emotion, is to risk burning out early. Unfortunately, Mourning's war ended 12 minutes before the game did."

Someone should have taped Sorensen's column to Mourning's locker and highlighted those words in red ink.

CHAPTER NINE

"There's no place like road."

Mike Gminski's knee was healing, he would soon be ready to come off the injured list, and the Hornets would have to make a roster move. Most teams drag their feet in these situations, hoping that if another player is about to get hurt, it will happen before a cut is made.

Instead, Murphy's Law often applies. A day after one player is cut, another goes out for the season with an injury. Sometimes when that happens the team actually goes out and re-signs the player it just waived, which means it has to pay him twice. Sending two paychecks to a marginal player must be an agitating experience no matter how much money NBA teams make.

Hornets coach Allan Bristow doesn't like bending the rules on the injured list. If he has to cut someone, he'd just as soon have it behind him. So Bristow was ready to make a quick decision.

"Besides," Bristow joked, "the extra per diem (on the road) is killing us."

It is rather funny that a league paying the average player about $900,000 a year must also provide him with about $60 a day on the road in "meal" money. Hornets director of player personnel Dave Twardzik was astounded earlier in the season when Sidney Green wanted to be reimbursed for a $20 cab ride from the airport when he reported to Charlotte. First off, the Hornets had sent someone out to the airport to meet Green's plane but couldn't find him. Second, the Hornets were about to pay Green more than $1.2 million per season to sit on the bench. It's reasonable to assume Green could afford the cab.

Former Hornets coach Dick Harter always marveled at how he'd regularly buy players post-game beers, but the players, earning two, three, sometimes five times what he was, never returned the gesture. Some of his ex-players in Charlotte would respond that they're not cheap, they just didn't like Harter enough to buy him a beer.

For the Hornets, the per diem is often redistributed in card games on the charter flight. J. R. Reid was quite the card shark on these flights before being traded to San Antonio. Former Ohio State point guard Mark Baker once lost all his meal money on a cross-country flight in the preseason. Worse yet, the preseason game was in Las Vegas, and Baker was no luckier at the craps table. He lost a bundle in the casino and was waived a few weeks later.

Tom Hammonds was happy to give up his Hornets meal money for his freedom. Most extraneous players want to hide when it's time for the team to make a cut. Hammonds openly lobbied to be waived, and got his wish January 27.

Public opinion was mixed about who the cut should have been. The players getting the least playing time were Hammonds, Green, Gminski, and Kevin Lynch. Gminski was owed too much money over too many years. The same could be said about Green. Besides, Gminski and Green could fill in at center, and coaches worry they never have enough insurance against injury at center.

Lynch, a shooting guard, was the other extreme — highly expendable. He played little and the mechanics on his jump shot were all messed up (he looked like a shot-putter, launching the ball from around his chin). But Lynch made only $250,000 and was happy just to be in the NBA trying to improve. At that price, he was cost-effective and low-maintenance.

Hammonds complained more — he thought he should be playing — and so he was the logical departure. The Hornets ate what was left of his $850,000 guaranteed salary and sent him on his way.

Many fans called the radio talk shows, complaining that Hammonds hadn't been given a fair chance. Most of those callers also thought Lynch should have been cut rather than Hammonds. That was typical of the parochial way Carolinians looked at their pro team. Hammonds played his college ball at Georgia Tech, and there's incredible loyalty and pride shown toward the Atlantic Coast Conference around the Carolinas. People would always second-guess the Hornets for not drafting North Carolina's Scott Williams or wonder aloud why the team didn't give N.C. State's Chris Corchiani a free-agent contract.

The ACC has provided the NBA with plenty of talent. But as Mourning, Johnson, and Gill illustrate, so have the Big East, Big West and Big Ten. Hornets fans, many schooled along Tobacco Road, didn't always keep that in mind when they assessed who did and didn't belong on the Hornets' roster.

After the Hornets lost to the Los Angeles Lakers at home and beat the Washington Bullets on the road, they were 20-20, right on target for a playoff spot. But how they reached that record was quite amazing. The Hornets were 11-10 on the road and 9-10 at Charlotte Coliseum.

It made no sense to anyone who followed basketball. Teams were always supposed to be better at home than on the road. In fact, really good NBA teams often win just a third of their games on the road and three-quarters of their games at home.

It was particularly hard to explain why the Hornets were suddenly road warriors. The only advantage they had in their early years was a raucous home court. A poll of players by a Houston newspaper the Hornets' first season listed Charlotte as having the third-greatest home-court advantage in the league. The two arenas providing a greater advantage were the Boston Garden and Chicago Stadium, idiosyncratic old barns that baked in the noise like a pressure cooker.

Charlotte Coliseum was new and state of the art, so visiting teams had no problems with lighting or the court. It was the ravenous fans who made Charlotte such a tough road trip in that first season. Rick Pitino, then Knicks coach, now Kentucky coach, once said Charlotte Coliseum is louder than Duke's Cameron Indoor Stadium. That statement placed the noise level at roughly the volume in the front row of a heavy-metal concert.

But as the newness of the team wore off, the volume dropped. The Hornets still sold out every home game, but the enthusiasm was less resilient. In fact, several thousand in the crowd this season seemed more interested in beating the traffic by leaving early than they were in seeing the end of tight games. It's one thing to leave with five minutes to go when your team is up or down by 20. But why would fans run to the exits with time left in a two-point game?

"This arena is not a difficult place to play (as far as) floor or lighting, like the Boston Garden or Madison Square Garden," Bristow said after a home game. "Our crowd — that's where we've got to get our home-court advantage. We've got to turn that crowd on by our play."

The crowd was simply more critical. It was no longer sacrilege to boo a Hornet, or the entire team for that matter. The crowd's treatment of Reid and Gill showed Charlotte was no longer so forgiving of its players.

Carl Scheer, the team's general manager the first two years, saw this coming.

"That's the way it is, what fans are all about," said Scheer. "They start to expect more. It's not a cheap night out, it's $100 a night. If you buy a ticket to see Neil Diamond, you expect him at his best. When you don't, you get a backlash.

"I believe Charlotte is a terrific town, but it's no different than any other — you still have to win sooner or later."

The Hornets weren't winning often enough at home, but they were redeeming themselves on the road. The overtime victory over the Bullets was quite an escape. Dell Curry hit an astounding 28-foot three-pointer to throw the game into overtime. Curry scored a career-high 33 points, Johnson grabbed 19 rebounds, and the Hornets won, 127-121.

Gminski did his Dorothy-in-Oz imitation after the game, joking "there's no place like away." As others picked up on the wisecrack, it was changed for rhyme to "there's no place like road."

After the game, Bullets forward Buck Johnson touched on what makes Curry such a dangerous outside shooter.

"He must have strong wrists. He almost shoots before he touches it," said Johnson. "It throws you off because he doesn't jump when he shoots."

Curry might have the strongest wrists in the NBA. He is a former baseball pitcher whose fastball was hard enough to get him drafted by the Baltimore Orioles. Curry's wrists are so strong that he doesn't have to change his shot from outside the NBA three-point arc, as most players do. He also doesn't need as much time to gather himself to shoot off a screen because he doesn't use his legs like other players do. Curry doesn't exactly have a jump shot. It's more a stretch shot — often his tiptoes are still touching the court when the ball leaves his hands.

Curry's shooting range was a constant source of amusement to his teammates. Larry Johnson was feeling pretty cocky after practice one day, so he challenged Curry to a long-range shooting contest. Johnson set his feet on the edge of the center circle, 40 feet from the basket. He lofted a shot high in the air, and it fell in off the back of the rim. "Got him!" Johnson must have thought, considering the smile on his face. Curry walked to the spot Johnson shot from and put up a 40-footer like he was shooting a free throw.

Swish. Curry just smiled and shrugged as Johnson and a reporter or two fell over laughing at the ease with which Curry performed the feat.

Nonchalance is Curry's way. If Johnson's or Mourning's game is hard rock, then Curry's resembles jazz — all keyboards, flutes, and saxophone; no heavy percussion. He floats to open spots on the floor with an instinctual grace. And he understands how to run defenders through screens where, as Mourning describes, Curry's teammates love to "headhunt" for him.

It's defense where Curry gets in trouble. The same sleek grace that serves him so well offensively makes him look "soft" defensively. Curry hesitates to step in front of people, to rough it up on defense, and that costs him. It particularly hurt him in the eyes of Harter, whose Oregon teams were known as the "Kamikaze Kids" for their willingness to take charges. Curry and Johnson were playing one-on-one one day following a shootaround and Mourning found Curry's attempts at defense pretty funny.

"Dell can't guard his own shadow," Mourning said, shaking his head and laughing heartily.

Defense will never be Curry's forte, but Bristow maximizes what he does well — break up the passing lanes with anticipation

— by relying heavily on traps. Strangely enough, Curry appears to be more effective defensively against small forwards than shooting guards. Perhaps since he isn't particularly physical against either one, guarding a small forward allows him to rely on superior quickness. Also, Curry can wear the opposing player out at the other end by playing hide-and-seek behind those "headhunter" screens. After running through 10 or 12 screens set by Mourning or Johnson, the other team's small forward doesn't have much energy or will left to play offense.

Regardless of his liabilities, Curry is in high demand around the league. It seems whenever teams call looking to make a trade, Curry's name comes up. That's primarily because of his shooting range, but also because Curry is one of a handful of highly skilled NBA players totally comfortable with playing off the bench.

The Hornets campaigned for Curry to get the NBA's Sixth Man award, and until a cold streak late in the season, he was a viable candidate. Surely, he fits the mold. Curry doesn't need much time to get into his shooting rhythm, so he can quickly jump-start an offense. His hot streaks are so extreme that players and coaches often talk of "milking" his jump shot when they see he's on the upswing.

Unlike, say, Rex Chapman, Curry worked at making the adjustment to reserve, which is more difficult than it sounds. First off, almost every player good enough to stick on any NBA roster was a starter all through college. Few of those players can readjust their egos to happily play off the bench. Second, moving to the bench means changing your approach to conditioning, Curry says. As a starter, you pace yourself. As a reserve, playing perhaps 12 minutes per half, you have to exhaust whatever energy you have in that short burst to exploit any advantage over a tired starter from the other team.

Curry's baseball experience helped in this transition — he sometimes compares his role to that of a relief pitcher, another prized specialist who must wait his turn. That specialty makes Curry more marketable than a starter of his ability because teams love skilled players who have shown a willingness to blend in. There are so few players like this in the NBA — a Cliff Robinson in Portland, an Anthony Mason in New York, a Danny Ainge in Phoenix. Each one can play more than one position, each one is comfortable playing off the bench. And each one is in demand.

Owner GEORGE SHINN rose from a modest background to become one of the most powerful men in Charlotte. His optimism and energy helped drive the Hornets' success.

CARL SCHEER shepherded the Hornets through their first two seasons as General Manager and then left under strained terms.

A born pessimist, DICK HARTER's personality conflicted with George Shinn's and led to his dismissal as the Hornets' coach after only a year and a half.

GENE LITTLES' conflicts with J. R. Reid contributed to his departure from the Hornets.

Coach ALLAN BRISTOW with NBA Commissioner DAVID STERN at the draft lottery. The number one pick was superstar Larry Johnson.

ALLAN BRISTOW celebrates one of the team's many victories on the way to the Hornets' first playoff berth in 1993.

ROBERT REID (left), and KELLY TRIPUCKA (right), two of the expansion Charlotte Hornets' early stars.

J. R. REID was one of the first "big-name" players selected by the Hornets. George Shinn pushed for the drafting of Reid because of his ties to North Carolina, but later regretted the pick and eventually traded him to San Antonio.

Courtesy of Charlotte Hornets.

DAVID FALK (above) and SPENCER STOLPEN (below) played a game of chicken with top draft pick Alonzo Mourning that kept the rookie center out of the Hornets' lineup until after the fourth game of the season.

Courtesy of Charlotte Hornets.

Georgetown phenom ALONZO MOURNING became a superstar in his first year and gained the respect of his team and the rest of the NBA.

Backcourt mates KENDALL GILL (above) and TYRONE "MUGGSY" BOUGES (left) comprised one of the most talented young backcourts in the NBA. While Muggsy emerged as a team leader, the talented but disgruntled Gill became such a problem that the budding star was traded to the Seattle SuperSonics in the same deal that brought Hersey Hawkins in from Philadelphia.

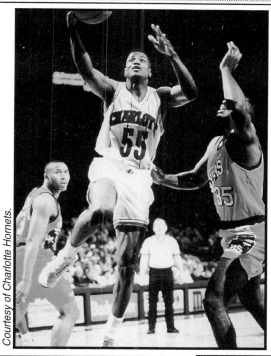

DAVID WINGATE, another Georgetown standout, was brought in to add hard-nosed defense to the young Hornets.

ENNY GATTISON'S skills and work ethic made m one of the most popular Hornets—so pular, in fact, that when the team tried to ade him, the players threatened to revolt.

JOHNNY NEWMAN, acquired from the Knicks, added instant offensive power to the Hornets.

From day one, LARRY JOHNSON established himself as "The Man" on the Hornets team and a force to be reckoned with.

LARRY JOHNSON sizes up the competition.

For that reason, it would be a tough sell to convince the Hornets to give up Curry in trade. But there was a time several years ago when the Hornets constantly dangled him as trade bait. The Hornets were loaded with shooting guards (first Chapman, then Kendall Gill), and Curry seemed extraneous. He was all but traded to the Indiana Pacers the Hornets' first season in a deal that would have acquired Stuart Gray and John Long. The deal was nixed only because Long wouldn't restructure his contract to make the salary cap work. That was a major break for the Hornets; Gray and Long are now long out of the league, while Curry has a bright future.

Curry spent his first few years in the league being shipped around like a foster child. He was drafted by the Utah Jazz in 1986, then traded to Cleveland the next season. Cleveland exposed him to the expansion draft after one season, primarily because Craig Ehlo was by far the superior defender.

Utah was an awful experience. Curry liked the stark countryside of Utah — he grew up hunting and fishing with his father in Virginia — but there isn't much for a black man to do in Mormon-dominated Salt Lake City. As Curry once joked, Utah drove him to marriage.

Actually, Curry is among the Hornets' most devoted fathers. He and his wife, Sonya, have two sons, Stefen and Seth, who are often at Hornets practices or shootarounds. Stefen might not take after his father — he's more a ball handler than a shooter. But that's not bad — point guards are harder to find than shooting guards.

Scheer thought Curry was far better than any other player available in the 1988 expansion draft, and time has proven Scheer correct. Curry, Bogues, and Orlando point guard Scott Skiles are the only three players chosen in the two expansion drafts who actually hung on long term as contributors to their new teams.

There was an obvious joy to the way Curry played the 1992-93 season. Perhaps it was finally having a stable role with a winning team. Or perhaps Curry just walks through life happy and content in a way Mourning hasn't yet discovered. Curry helps keep Charlotte's locker room loose, as he did in the playoff drive late in the season. The Hornets and a local supermarket chain had sponsored some silly contest for best legs on the team, and Curry discovered he won. So he paraded around the locker room before a game, hitching up his shorts to show off his thighs.

Everyone broke up at a time when the team needed a good laugh to loosen them up.

It's Curry's way. He's a streak shooter, remember? His job is to change momentum. In Las Vegas in the preseason, he walked up to an ice-cold craps table late one night and rolled nine straight passes, to the delight of the assembled crowd. Those who'd played with him knew enough to respect a Dell Curry streak, and bet heavily on his ability to keep rolling sevens.

The Hornets came home to face a tough Seattle SuperSonics team that would go on to reach the Western Conference finals. The Sonics had been on an incredible roll to build up a 28-13 record. And of course, the Hornets weren't playing well at home, so this looked like a sure loss.

Surprise. In a performance nearly as impressive as winning in Chicago, the Hornets beat the Sonics at home, 112-100. The only problem in the game was Mourning reinjured his cracked left thumb. He tripped over some Sonic and broke his fall with his left hand.

Considering the so-called "corn dog" wrapped around his thumb, Mourning had played astoundingly well since originally suffering the injury January 5. The coaches wondered if Mourning would lose all the touch in his shot and much of his ball handling skill due to the heavy bandaging. Yet in the 13 games following the injury, he averaged 20.7 points and 9.8 rebounds and shot 53 percent from the field. If his play was in any way affected by the bandage, then every center in the NBA should have his thumb wrapped similarly.

But Hornets team physician Glenn Perry was worried more about the long term. He feared that if Mourning kept refracturing the thumb, he'd eventually do some permanent damage. So Perry told the Hornets that if the injury didn't start healing by the end of the all-star break, then Perry would order Mourning to sit out of games.

"Dr. Perry said if it comes to that, it's his call because it doesn't look like it's healing," Mourning said after learning the thumb had re-cracked. "He's looking at the big picture. He's worried about the next 10 years. I'm worried about 30 or 40 games."

Of course, Perry had everyone's best interests in mind. Mourning didn't want to chance hurting a promising career over a 10- or 15-game absence. The Hornets had to be more interested in the health of a franchise center than whether he'd miss a few games his rookie season. And Perry wasn't about to do something shortsighted just to keep Mourning on the court.

Perry has the highest-profile job in the Charlotte medical community, as he discovered the previous summer. Larry Johnson needed some torn knee cartilage removed, a relatively minor procedure. But no procedure involving a Hornet of Johnson's status was minor to the local media. Perry held one news conference the day before the procedure and another following the operation because there were so many interview requests. Perry had done far more complicated operations, but never one quite so scrutinized.

The first week of February, the Hornets found out what it's like to be a real grown-up major league franchise — one young star was named a starter in the all-star game while another postured to be traded.

Johnson found out the fans from around the country had voted him to the Eastern Conference's starting unit by a wide margin. It was gratifying and also a little humbling. Johnson talked immediately of concentrating on rebounding and getting out of Michael Jordan's way whenever Jordan wanted to shoot in the all-star game. Johnson sounded so deferential to Jordan weeks before the game that Jordan probably could have asked Johnson to caddy for him when Jordan ran off to Arizona the Friday before the all-star game in Utah for a quickie golf round.

But the week's real news was a story planted with *USA Today* columnist Peter Vecsey. Vecsey speculated that Gill wanted out of Charlotte in the worst way, in part because he didn't see eye-to-eye with Bristow and in part because of Hornets point guard Muggsy Bogues's alleged "reluctance" to get Gill the ball, as compared to Johnson, Mourning, or Dell Curry.

Vecsey made no effort to attribute any of these allegations to even an unnamed source. But Hornets management immediately concluded it came from Gill or his agent, Arn Tellem, whom Bristow had roughed up when Bristow was team vice president.

Tellem denied being the source of the story. Gill said he didn't know who was saying these things to Vecsey, then apologized to Bogues. (Which raised an interesting question: If Gill didn't know who had said these things, then what did Gill have to apologize for?)

Amazingly, Gill continued to claim he didn't want to be traded, though it was evident he did. Hornets president Spencer Stolpen grudgingly admitted that, yes, trading Gill might be a possibility if there was some friction there. But Stolpen didn't reveal to reporters that day that he'd received a letter from Tellem two weeks earlier asking for a trade.

Bogues was perplexed, and rightfully so. There are some things about Bogues that could rub a teammate the wrong way — he's thin-skinned and paranoid about the Hornets bringing in other point guards — but Bogues is a fighter focused on winning. If Gill thought Bogues was choosing not to pass him the ball enough over some personality conflict, then Gill was way off base. As columnist Tom Sorensen wrote in *The Observer*, Bogues would pass to Saddam Hussein on the break if Hussein was in position to finish the play.

If Bogues *was* looking more to Johnson or Mourning or Curry, it indicated good judgment, not bad blood. At the time, Johnson was shooting 51 percent, Mourning 49 percent, and Curry 47 percent. Gill shot 42 percent, and had thrown away one chance for a game-winning shot by passing off in New Jersey and missed another by blowing a layup against Boston. Gill hadn't suddenly become a bad player, he just wasn't playing well. Who's to blame Bogues if he had more confidence in others at the time?

Stolpen knows dollars, not basketball, so he asked Dave Twardzik, the team's director of player personnel, for advice. Twardzik had been the point guard on the Portland Trail Blazers' NBA championship team, and had his jersey retired in Portland. Surely, Twardzik would sense if Bogues was to blame for this.

Twardzik said it's natural for a point guard to look for who's hot rather than someone who had failed to complete plays lately. Essentially, Twardzik was saying this was Gill's problem, not Bogues', which was the organization consensus anyway.

This wasn't the first time a personality conflict played out on the court for the Hornets. In the first season, Rex Chapman and

Kelly Tripucka didn't get along well at all. But back then, it was a minor annoyance on a bad team. This was something quite different — a potential barrier to the Hornets' reaching the playoffs.

Gill wasn't getting any sympathy from his teammates. As he would say within days, "I'm not the most popular guy in this locker room right now." Most Hornets, particularly Johnson, are protective of Bogues, partially because of his size. That Friday, Johnson would knock Milwaukee Bucks guard Eric Murdock to the floor with a vicious forearm because Johnson thought Murdock was roughing up Bogues.

If Team Gill thought criticizing Bogues would improve Gill's situation in Charlotte, then Gill's handlers were badly mistaken. And there probably couldn't have been a more offensive vehicle for that criticism than Peter Vecsey's column, as far as the Hornets were concerned. Vecsey runs on the wild side of sport journalism. Stolpen compared him to Hedda Hopper, the infamous Hollywood gossip columnist of the '40s and '50s.

"I don't comment on gossip columns," Stolpen sniffed the day Vecsey's little bomb appeared.

Vecsey made a name for himself covering the NBA for the *New York Post,* a lowbrow tabloid. He has great sources but is not known for being particularly cautious or precise with his reporting. Vecsey once reported that the Denver Nuggets were set to trade Todd Lichti to Atlanta for Hawks swingman Paul Graham, but that Lichti's serious knee injury killed the deal. What Vecsey either missed or ignored was that Lichti's injury occurred after the trade deadline. Oops!

Beat writers hate to see the teams they cover mentioned in Vecsey's column. It either means Vecsey is way out ahead on a story on your beat, or he's written something erroneous and you have to clean up the mess. The odds are about 50-50 either way. Two years ago, during the NBA Finals, one beat writer joked that Vecsey was in charge of delivering a *USA Today* to each reporter's door at the media hotel. Another writer said that explained why only half the papers were getting to the right rooms.

Vecsey seems to have it in for about a dozen coaches and general managers around the league (Utah Jazz president Frank Layden being the most prominent), and Bristow falls into that group. Since Vecsey never seems to have anything nice to say about Bristow, Bristow regularly turns down phone interview requests from Vecsey.

"Peter and I go way back. . . I don't know where it went wrong," Bristow once said.

Vecsey's NBC-TV connection (he appears with Bill Walton on the "Insiders" segment of the pregame show) gives him a certain clout to get videotape interviews. One day late in the season, Vecsey held up the departure of a team bus for nearly an hour while taping an interview with Mourning for NBC. Asked if Vecsey was the one delaying the bus, Bristow replied, "You mean dick-head?. . . Peter-head?. . . Asshole? Take your pick."

Yeah, Allan, that's the guy.

If the incentive in leaking such venomous stuff to Vecsey was simply to ignite trade talk, then the column served its purpose. Within days, GMs from around the league were calling the Hornets, asking if Gill really did want out. Of course, the other teams hoped that meant a fire sale, but the Hornets weren't giving Gill away.

Hornets owner George Shinn, who never particularly trusted Gill's loyalty, was ready to listen to all offers. Shinn wanted to make sure the team got something in return for Gill, and took it for granted Gill would bolt out of Charlotte once he reached unrestricted free agency.

Shinn would have jumped at a midseason trade of Gill for Atlanta Hawks guard Stacey Augmon (Augmon and Dominique Wilkins don't get along), but the Hawks had a bargain in Augmon's contract, compared to Gill's.

Bristow loved Gill's game and thought Gill could be coaxed back into the fold if the team just demonstrated some patience. Bristow was peeved that Gill's handlers blamed Bogues for Gill's slump, but thought time would solve that problem, too.

"Kendall Gill is perfect for this team. He's what we want," Bristow said. "He solidifies our backcourt, he's a defender and he's a player who can grow in our system."

Quoting Shinn, Bristow has more control over the roster than "any other person in the organization" — even the owner, who had finally learned to defer these decisions to a basketball guy he trusts.

More than anything, Bristow didn't want the Hornets making a rash deal that would fall well short of fair market value.

And right then, that's all the Hornets were hearing in return for Gill.

The problem was that Gill had de facto veto power over every viable trade. The escape clause in his contract meant he could become an unrestricted free agent in two years. What general manager with any sense would trade anything of value for Gill without a long-term contract extension that would supersede that escape clause? Twardzik looked into a deal that would have exchanged Gill for Portland guard Terry Porter, but Gill wouldn't sign long term with the Trail Blazers. The Knicks wouldn't give up anything the Hornets wanted, and the same was true of the Lakers. So the logical team to talk with was the Clippers.

Clippers coach Larry Brown liked Gill's game as much as Bristow did. There would be many discussions between the two teams before the trade deadline February 25.

Despite the Gill distraction and the possibility of Mourning sitting out with his bad thumb, the Hornets were cruising along quite nicely. They beat Washington, Seattle, Philadelphia, and Milwaukee for a four-game winning streak. Only Bristow refused to call it a streak.

"We're still in the incubator stage," Bristow would say.

Not surprisingly, Gill looked tense throughout this span, particularly in a home victory over Milwaukee. He shot six of 19 against the Bucks and was whistled for two charges. "I just try and block it out," Gill said of the distraction. "I just try to play ball. I'm not sending any messages."

Meanwhile, Johnny Newman was actually growing to like playing off the bench. For all the private fussing Newman did over the move, he was actually coming around to Bristow's reasoning that there were more shots available playing with the reserves. And he was getting more compliments from Bristow than he ever did as a starter.

"I understand what my role is. It's more defined," Newman said. "I can do a little bit of everything now. Before, when I started off the games so early, it would slow the other guys down."

Funny, hadn't Bristow said the same thing about two months ago?

Johnson finished the week by leveling Milwaukee's Murdock with that infamous forearm. Replays showed that he belted

Murdock in the side of the head, going far beyond what is allowed in the lane. Murdock is a mouthy, annoying pest, but Johnson's forearm was out of line.

"He just hauled off and hit him in the side of the head," said NBA vice president Rod Thorn, who fined Johnson $8,000. Thorn added that Murdock "didn't know what hit him."

Bucks coach Mike Dunleavy was furious that Johnson wasn't also suspended.

"He's lucky, he should have been suspended," Dunleavy said. "Hopefully, he learned a lesson."

What Johnson actually learned is that you can't get fined by the league without taking some ribbing from your teammates later. About an hour before game time in Milwaukee the next week, Johnson was handed a note by a ballboy. The note said Johnson was about to get his "ass kicked," and was signed Murdock. But the handwriting looked suspiciously like Newman's, and half the locker room muffled laughter as Johnson read the note.

CHAPTER TEN

"It ain't Godzilla versus the X-monster."

The Cleveland Cavaliers own the Charlotte Hornets whenever the two teams play. Maybe it looked like the Indiana Pacers owned the Hornets, but that was more like a one-season lease. What the Pacers did to the Hornets the 1992-93 season, the Cavaliers do to the Hornets nearly every season.

The Cavaliers are among the NBA's best teams, but they are limited. They're soft, and they are too system oriented. When a team like the Chicago Bulls bullies the Cavaliers out of their finely tuned patterns (as the Bulls eventually did to sweep Cleveland in the playoffs), the Cavaliers panic like cattle in an earthquake.

The Hornets never seem to get Cleveland out of those patterns. Center Brad Daugherty chases a triple-double, point guard Mark Price hits all the big shots, and the Cavaliers beat the Hornets. It's written on a stone tablet and buried in a tomb somewhere — the Cavaliers beat the Hornets.

The Hornets knew the Bulls were a better team and knew the Knicks were a better team, but they also knew the Cavaliers had an easier time beating them. It's all about matchups. The Cavaliers were the biggest of the top three teams in the East with 7-0 Brad Daugherty, 6-11 John "Hot Rod" Williams, and 6-10 Larry Nance. The Hornets are among the smallest teams in the East, even with 6-10 Alonzo Mourning. The Hornets know

Cleveland's big weakness — the Cavaliers are so preoccupied with blocking shots that when they don't, they're always out of position under the boards. So teams with offensive rebounders like New Jersey have success against the Cavaliers. The Hornets don't have great offensive rebounders, so they consistently lose to the Cavaliers.

It was predictable, then, that the Hornets' four-game winning streak would end against the Cavaliers. At least this time it was close — 107-103, after Larry Johnson intentionally missed a free throw trying to get back the ball at the end for a desperation field-goal try. Johnson tried so hard to miss that foul shot that he put up an air ball, giving Cleveland automatic possession and the game.

"Cleveland knew we were there," Bogues said afterward. "They were in a game."

True, but such moral victories mean little or nothing in a playoff race, and the Hornets seemed destined to play Cleveland in the first round. Cleveland had little chance of overtaking New York or Chicago, so the Cavaliers were a lock to be third seed in the East. With New Jersey and Boston playing strong at midseason, the Hornets figured to be sixth seed at best. That meant a first-round pairing with the Cavaliers in an eight-team Eastern Conference playoff. The way the Hornets played against the Cavaliers, that could mean being swept.

Two nights later, the Hornets had a far more winnable, and memorable, meeting with the Orlando Magic. Memorable because it was the first time Mourning would play against Orlando rookie Shaquille O'Neal.

It's amazing that it took these two 20 years to meet. Their fortunes seemed so intertwined. O'Neal turning pro early after three seasons at Louisiana State had cost Mourning the status of being the No. 1 overall pick. But it also did Mourning the favor of sending him to Charlotte, where he could play with Johnson. O'Neal had to hold together the Magic his first season with little help, except for an occasional drive to the basket by Nick Anderson.

O'Neal was as grand as the $40 million contract he signed. He had the dimensions of a young Wilt Chamberlain, and he happily described himself as a childhood superstar "like the Jackson Five." And he was often handy for a one-liner. Asked the previous summer if he could settle in Orlando, O'Neal deadpanned and played the big ol' kid routine: "I like Mickey . . . I like Goofy."

Madison Avenue devoured this guy's marketing potential. Pepsi had the cutest commercial, a spoof of Coke's decades-old ad where a kid hands Pittsburgh defensive lineman "Mean" Joe Greene a bottle of soda pop after a tough game. Riding the antihero culture of the '90s, Pepsi instead had a kid blow off O'Neal when O'Neal asked for the child's soft drink. The ad concluded with the towering O'Neal pleading with the kid for a taste.

Almost instantly, O'Neal was among league leaders in nearly every statistical category. But it drove the average Hornets fan nuts that it was a foregone conclusion O'Neal would be voted rookie of the year over Mourning.

To Charlotteans mad enough to call the radio shows, this was some sort of plot by those nasty reporters who vote on the award. Wasn't our Zo good enough to win rookie of the year?

Of course, he was, but O'Neal was consistently just a little better. O'Neal topped Mourning in every major statistical category for a center — scoring, rebounds, field-goal percentage, and blocks. Sure, there was a wider gap between Mourning and the rest of the rookies than between O'Neal and Mourning, but that wasn't the point — reporters could only vote for one rookie of the year, and it was obviously O'Neal.

Finally, Charlotte fans started dreaming up their own criteria to rationalize their anger. They called in to the talk shows saying Mourning has a more versatile game (he does) and that all O'Neal ever does to score is dunk (close to true).

Of course, the implication that Mourning should be rookie of the year because O'Neal only dunks is roughly like saying Larry Csonka wasn't a great football player because all he did was run over linebackers for touchdowns. O'Neal dunked all the time because he was so strong and so quick that no one could keep him from dunking all the time.

The other paranoid argument Charlotte fans made was that O'Neal would win rookie of the year only because the league and Reebok, the sneaker company O'Neal represents, were his unofficial campaign managers. If anything, the hype hurt O'Neal. By their very natures, reporters are contrarians — they distrust and generally dismiss any campaigning for awards. If anything, O'Neal won despite the hype, not because of it.

The ridiculous part was not that fans thought with their hearts rather than their brains. It was how some of the Charlotte media humored this silliness, even fostered it. Paul Cameron, the sportscaster for WBTV, might as well have been Mourning's campaign manager. And the two radio sports talk shows did little more than verbally nod when fans would whine about O'Neal's impending award.

Consciously or not, the Hornets have managed to place team employees in charge of both radio call-in shows in the Charlotte market. Matt Pinto, who moderates WBT-AM's "Sports Huddle" most nights, does radio play-by-play for the Hornets during road games and is paid by the team. Gerry Vaillancourt, the host of "Sports Talk" on WAQS, does analysis on all the Hornets' radio broadcasts and is a full-time employee of the team. Clearly, there is a conflict of interest there. How much would either Pinto or Vaillancourt criticize a team which employs them? To their credit, Vaillancourt and particularly Pinto acknowledge that conflict of interest and try their best to walk what must sometimes be a thin line between their conflicting responsibilities.

It's strange how such arrangements are common in sports broadcasting and unthinkable in other forms of journalism. Can you imagine a newspaper or television station allowing its city hall reporter to work part time for the mayor?

Sadly, the Hornets no longer have their general manager field calls every Monday night on WBT-AM. Carl Scheer started the show, then Allan Bristow, and finally Dave Twardzik showed up for the weekly grilling. Fans would call in with tough questions on topics ranging from ticket prices to the team's lack of depth at point guard. And since these were season-ticket holders calling, not nosy reporters, the GM couldn't blow them off on the air. It was must listening, because fans asked so many blunt and often insightful questions.

When the Hornets renewed their contract with WBT-AM, the team replaced the GM show with the comparatively tame "Hornets Sports Line." Vaillancourt and in-house play-by-play man Steve Martin host the show, and don't always have a guest. Vaillancourt and Martin are nice guys who travel with the team, but they aren't the Hornets' decision makers. That's who fans grew accustomed to calling, and grilling, on Monday night.

While Charlotte fans raged on about O'Neal's front-runner status for rookie of the year, Mourning reacted with a shrug. Individual awards are of little consequence to Mourning. In fact, whenever Mourning would win rookie of the month or player of the week, he'd treat it as a nuisance rather than an honor. Mourning had his reward — a $24 million contract — and his team was winning. Winning is all that mattered to him, and should matter more to other players caught up in their own statistics.

Bristow must have loved Mourning's disinterest in those awards. He wanted his players focused more on team achievements than they were in the past, and set the agenda early in the season by coaxing the players to ban statistics sheets from the locker room. The ban was a little thing, but it was a positive symbol. In the old days when the Hornets lost two out of every three games, some players couldn't wait to see what they had contributed in points or rebounds or assists, as if to say, "Hey, I did my part, don't blame me."

This preoccupation with individual statistics was petty but could be highly amusing. Bogues once called a team statistician into the locker room after a home game to grill him on why Bogues wasn't credited with more assists. Assists are assessed somewhat subjectively. If in the statistician's view, a pass led directly to a basket, then the passer gets an assist. In Bogues's mind, statisticians in other NBA cities — particularly Salt Lake City, where assist leader John Stockton plays — were more generous in crediting assists than the Charlotte statisticians were.

Reporters had to muffle their laughter watching Bogues chew out some innocent statistician getting paid a few dollars a game. Basketball isn't the only sport where such silliness occurs. Traditionally, reporters used to score baseball games for the home team, but most baseball writers no longer agree to score because it causes so many unnecessary conflicts. If a close play is scored an error, then the fielder is mad at the reporter scoring the game. If it's scored a hit, then the pitcher is mad. Reporters don't deserve this grief and neither did the statistician called into the locker room by Bogues.

Mourning and O'Neal played to a magnificent draw in their first meeting. O'Neal had 29 points, 15 rebounds, and four blocks. Mourning had 27 points, 14 rebounds and two blocks.

"(Mourning) is going to be a superstar," O'Neal said, sounding like he was inviting Mourning to his private little club.

With O'Neal and Mourning neutralizing each other, the game came down to the Hornets' trapping defense. The Hornets went on a 19-3 run in the third quarter, when Orlando committed four turnovers and shot one of seven.

"When we're pressing, Shaquille O'Neal doesn't even have a chance to score," said Hornets guard Kendall Gill. "(Magic point guard) Scott Skiles, he really doesn't bring the ball up well against Muggsy. We were trapping all over the place tonight."

Gill and Skiles, former Big Ten rivals, don't like each other. Gill thinks Skiles gives out cheap shots. Gill got so mad at Skiles late in the season that he threw gum at him following a game. No, Gill didn't threaten to pull Skiles's hair or scratch his eyes out. The girlie fight was limited to gum-throwing.

Gill's agent, Arn Tellem, didn't expect his client to be traded by the February 25 deadline, and that just made sense. Major trades in the NBA almost never happen around the deadline. Summer is the time to make such deals because contracts are expiring, so teams have more flexibility in their salary caps. To deal Gill, the Hornets would have to find a team with the right player and contract to exchange. The player Charlotte would receive would have to be of equivalent value to the Hornets and make within 15 percent of Gill's $1.9 million salary.

On top of that, Gill would have to be traded to somewhere he wanted to play, so that the other team could sign him to a long-term extension. No general manager in his right mind would give up something of value for Gill without an assurance Gill would stay for more than one year.

In many ways, a Gill-Danny Manning swap looked like a great idea. First off, their salaries were close enough to matching that something could be worked out that the league would approve. Also, Manning, a 6-10 forward, grew up in Greensboro, about 90 miles from Charlotte. He liked the Carolinas so much he wanted to buy a franchise with Krispy Kreme, the region's semifamous hot donut maker.

Manning would be a good fit with the Hornets because he wouldn't mind being third banana behind Mourning and Johnson. In fact, Manning doesn't seem comfortable with being the top player on his team, though he was drafted No. 1 overall and led Kansas to a national championship.

The problem was that Manning was no quicker to sign a long-term contract extension than Gill was. Manning would become a restricted free agent over the summer, and his agent, Ron Grinker, saw a gold mine ahead if Manning reached unrestricted status in the summer of 1994.

"Frankly, I can get $5.5 million per season," Grinker once claimed.

Grinker said all the right things about how Manning liked Charlotte and would love to play with Johnson and Mourning. But Manning wouldn't sign long term to facilitate a trade. It sounded fishy to the Hornets. Why trade one problem for another?

Stolpen thought there might be a point in the future, if it became obvious that Gill would never re-sign long term with the Hornets, when a Gill-Manning swap would make sense. But this was not that time.

The Hornets kept their eyes open for a veteran point guard to complement Bogues. Tony Bennett was all right as a third point guard — a practice player with a chance to improve — but clearly the Hornets could use experienced help at the position. When Gill wouldn't sign long term with Portland, Terry Porter stopped being an option. Dallas's Derek Harper was also a possibility. But Gill would never sign with pitiful Dallas, so to acquire Harper, the Hornets would have to arrange a three-way deal that would send Gill to the Clippers and something of value from the Clippers to the Mavericks.

All the tension around Gill was clearly distracting him. While playing against Cleveland, Gill yelled at Bristow along the sidelines. This wouldn't be the last time this season that Gill would scream at a coach during a game.

"I was waking up every morning saying, what's in the paper this morning?" Gill said. "That got rough, so I haven't been reading the paper the past four or five days.

"Lately, I've just tried to forget all the stuff going on around me. I was thinking about it, and it was affecting me."

Gill scored 20 in Miami as the Hornets beat the Heat, 116-107, in a game closer than the final score suggested. Mourning blocked Grant Long's hook shot with 35 seconds left, then Bogues hit two free throws to settle what had been a tight game.

Hornets-Heat games are always tense because of the two teams' shared origin. The crowd got on Johnson during a trip to the foul line, so each time he hit a free throw, Johnson pointed to the fans behind the basket, as if to say, "You keep screaming, cause I'll keep making them." Both Miami coach Kevin Loughery and Bristow were assessed technical fouls by game's end.

Bristow was even louder and more animated than usual along the sideline, running from one end of the bench to the other to ride the officials. Once Bristow finally sat down, NBA referee Joe Forte turned and said, "Hey, Allan . . . you know you coach a lot better when you're sitting?"

Bristow broke up at that one. Good referees — and Forte is definitely one — can make their point and keep control without being confrontational.

The Hornets playing the Detroit Pistons on Valentine's Day seemed nearly as inappropriate as the Bulls and those thug Knicks tangling on Christmas Day. The Hornets have no affection for the Pistons, and things got worse, rather than better, between Mourning and Pistons chief goon Bill Laimbeer.

The last time Laimbeer and Mourning had faced each other, Laimbeer sucker-punched Mourning into a fight that got both ejected. This time, Laimbeer was playing as a reserve, so Bristow took Mourning out in the first half whenever Laimbeer entered the game. Mourning was still too volatile and Laimbeer too cunning a cheap-shot artist to take a chance on Mourning being ejected.

Bristow's decision to keep Mourning and Laimbeer separated as much as possible looked justified in the second half, when the two finally faced each other. At his first opportunity, Laimbeer chopped down on Mourning's broken left thumb as Mourning held the ball. Technically, it was a legal play — no foul was called, and you could clearly hear that Laimbeer hit the ball, too — but Laimbeer knew exactly what he was doing.

Mourning hit the floor in massive pain. Fortunately, an examination showed Laimbeer had done no serious damage to the injury.

"I knew something like that was going to happen, particularly with him on the court," Mourning said later. "I just think he's a dirty player. Hands down, he's the dirtiest player I've ever played against. I never played in college against someone like Laimbeer, not that temperament. He's in a class by himself."

That "temperament" didn't serve Laimbeer well the rest of the game. The surly center was assessed two technical fouls in the fourth quarter, an automatic ejection, for arguing a call with referee Luis Grillo. The Pistons had come most of the way back from a 23-point deficit before Laimbeer's technicals. They fell apart in his absence and lost, 117-107.

"It was unfortunate what happened and I feel bad," Laimbeer said of the technicals. "Like I said, I'm tired of getting the short end of the stick. Four or five years ago, we could have played over things like this."

Four or five years ago, the Pistons were contending for NBA championships. Now they sounded like nasty, bitter old men.

The Hornets had won seven of eight to rise to 26-21. The team had never before been five games above .500. Better yet, they headed to Milwaukee for a game with the Bucks, a sure lottery team. Bristow always said consistently beating the league's bad teams was the best way for the Hornets to make the playoffs. So far, the Hornets were 10-0 against Washington, Dallas, Golden State, Sacramento, Milwaukee, and Philadelphia, all destined to miss the playoffs.

Then, the Bucks served the Hornets another slice of that "humble pie" Boston center Robert Parish referred to earlier in the season. The Hornets lost at Milwaukee, 128-122, in what might have been their worst defensive performance of the year. Rookie Jon Barry, who missed much of the season in a contract dispute with Boston before being traded to the Bucks, scored 18 points. Milwaukee shot 54 percent as a team.

"If we'd won this game, we would have stolen it," Bristow said afterward. "The offense was good, but the defense let them score at will."

Afterward, Mourning was in one of his frequent sour moods, so a radio reporter from Milwaukee picked the wrong moment to ask Mourning about an upcoming game against Knicks center Patrick Ewing.

Mourning hates talking about individual matchups. He thinks that when reporters compare him to Ewing or O'Neal, it sounds more like a heavyweight title fight than a team sport. So that Milwaukee radio reporter got more than he bargained for when he flipped on his tape recorder.

"It ain't Godzilla versus the X-monster!" Mourning popped off, providing probably his best quote of the season.

Most of the Milwaukee media were circled around Bennett, the Hornets' rookie point guard who played up the road at

Wisconsin-Green Bay. Bennett's father, Dick, is the coach at Wisconsin-Green Bay and previously coached Portland Trail Blazer Terry Porter at Wisconsin-Stevens Point.

Homegrown basketball players aren't exactly commonplace in Wisconsin. Midwesterners joke that Wisconsin is famous for dairy products and short, white people, and not necessarily in that order. Bennett was a coach's son with just enough ball handling and shooting skills to be drafted in the second round.

Bennett doesn't look like an NBA player and doesn't act like one. He is 6-foot, and looks more like he is 17 than 23. One day a guest in a New York hotel asked why one kid was giving autographs to the other kids.

Why that's no kid! That's Tony Bennett!

Bennett has this blockish head that makes him look a little like Bart Simpson when he smiles. Except unlike Bart, Bennett is an overachiever. He knows he's fortunate to be in the NBA, and as professional athletes go, Bennett is refreshingly modest. He understood during his rookie season how to stay confident without becoming cocky. Sadly, such an outlook is seldom present in the NBA.

"Just seeing a Ewing, an Olajuwon, a Robinson. . . just watching the game itself is exciting," Bennett said at mid-season. "If I'm still playing in this league eight years from now, maybe it will be different. But right now, I enjoy being a rookie."

Miami Heat managing partner Lewis Schaffel says most rookies show up at training camp already having acquired a strut and talking trash. Even mediocre players get told they are so wonderful so early, first by recruiters and then by agents, that they all think they're the next Michael Jordan. And when they don't become stars, or even starters, many tend to blame coaches, general managers, or the media . . . anyone except themselves.

Bennett was more patient, perhaps because he had to be, and more mature than some 10-year NBA veterans. Gill and Newman could learn much from Bennett about patience and teamwork.

"I try to stay upbeat and positive. I want to play, but I have to look at this season as an apprenticeship," Bennett said. "At times I've said I have to improve, I have to get better. But I never thought this was above me. My Dad says there's only one queen bee, but there are a whole lot of worker bees. I know I'm helping, even if it's just in practice. You need worker bees.''

If the NBA hadn't changed Bennett's personality, it at least reworked his wardrobe. Larry Johnson had purchased designer leather jackets, each worth $2,700, for his teammates, plus the coaches, trainer, and equipment manager. It was a classy move — the jackets were created by Jeff Hamilton, who styles many of Arsenio Hall's outfits. They were bold, with purple, teal and silver patches on a black jacket, and personalized with each player's name printed in script on the back.

This jacket had to be flashier than anything Bennett previously owned, and he got a big kick out of wearing it out of the arena following home games.

"I was wearing my shades and this jacket, and I looked baaaaad!" Bennett said one day. "They won't recognize me in Green Bay."

Young Tony Bennett — the baddest dude from Green Bay, Wisconsin.

CHAPTER ELEVEN

"I'll have 80 on 'em next time. Eighty!"

Larry Johnson finished second in the NBA's slam-dunk contest as a rookie. He decided to skip the contest his second year in the league to save himself for the all-star game the following day. As things turned out, Johnson could have competed in the slam-dunk contest, the three-point contest, partied all Saturday night, and still retain all the energy he needed for the all-star game.

As things turned out, Johnson should just as well have skipped the all-star game.

Johnson played only 16 minutes as a starter in his first all-star appearance. Maybe the Knicks' Pat Riley, who coached the Eastern Conference all-stars, forgot about Johnson. Maybe Riley wanted to get bigger, so he played New York center Patrick Ewing some at power forward. Maybe he wanted to add experience, so he played Cleveland forward Larry Nance. Or maybe, as many Hornets fans assumed, Riley had some secret agenda that kept Johnson on the bench.

"I got 12 guys," Riley said afterward. "How many (minutes) did Johnson play? I would say (Joe) Dumars, (Brad) Daugherty, Detlef Schrempf all played about that. It works out that way. It's not a conscious decision."

Johnson saw it differently. To him, Riley's substitution pattern amounted to an insult, and Johnson would promise to punish the Knicks for Riley's decision.

"I'll have 80 on 'em next time," Johnson said. "Eighty!"

What started out as a dream weekend in the Rockies proved to be a total embarrassment for Johnson. For three days, he had been the toast of Salt Lake City, charming every reporter in sight, chatting constantly with kids. Johnson was the official spokesman for the league's licensed apparel, and took this goodwill ambassador's role seriously in Utah.

Johnson didn't get paid much money for the endorsement, but the exposure and prestige involved with the relationship was a marketing coup. Hornets president Spencer Stolpen had played matchmaker between the league and Johnson on the deal, and the NBA was smart enough to jump on Johnson's bandwagon.

Unlike the Clippers' Danny Manning, Johnson has the outgoing persona to match his formidable talent. Johnson is a showman, a performer. The Grandmama series of commercials Converse designed were perfect for him, because Johnson can be simultaneously tough and cuddly and get away with it.

Originally, Converse wanted to market Larry Johnson in a series of commercials with Magic Johnson and Larry Bird. The idea was that Bird and Magic would conjure up the perfect basketball player, then naturally name him "Larry," for Bird, and "Johnson" for Magic.

That was cute, but this was cuter. Johnson agreed to pull on a house dress like his granny, then run over everything in sight, spreading the word that Converse's shoes could make even a geriatric into a basketball nightmare.

Converse's image had grown a little stuffy, so the sneaker company had lost much of its target audience — teenagers and young adults — to the more hip companies like Nike and Reebok.

Converse saw Johnson as their bridge to the younger generation. He was a bit of a rebel, and yet he was also funny and approachable. And Johnson is wonderful with kids — probably only Muggsy Bogues has more magnetism with the younger crowd among Hornets. As Johnson once said in Las Vegas: "Hey, I've never had trouble with kids. It's the adults I have a problem with."

Like Tom Hanks or Chevy Chase, Johnson has never lost touch with the child inside. He can tweek anyone and anyone is allowed to tweek him. For instance, Hornets director of player personnel Dave Twardzik was out scouting college talent for several weeks over the winter, then suddenly showed up at a shootaround.

"Where you been?" Johnson asked Twardzik.

"Out looking for a new power forward," Twardzik jabbed.

"Ohhhhh, well maybe I'm looking for a new general manager," Johnson needled back.

Johnson can laugh at himself as well as he can laugh at others. He loves telling the story of what a baby he was during his minor knee operation in the summer of 1992.

"The guy over here was moaning, the guy over there was moaning, so I started moaning. Ooooooh! Ooooooh!" Johnson would recall.

Here's another surprise. Big, tough Larry Johnson is afraid of dogs. Johnson and Stolpen were at a car show once, and Johnson wouldn't walk within yards of a dog he thought looked a little nasty.

It's these frailties, and his admitting to them, that make Johnson so . . . yes . . . lovable. The Grandmama commercials work because Johnson is secure enough to put on a dress, read dialogue about leg wax, then laugh off the inevitable jabs by his teammates.

Grandmama was everywhere at all-star weekend. Converse is the NBA's official shoe company, so it got prominent floor space in the trade shows that accompany all-star weekend. TNT announcer Craig Sager even dressed up as Grandmama to surprise Johnson at an appearance.

There was quite a battle for air time among the various sneaker makers. Reebok was rolling out a line of commercials comparing Shaquille O'Neal to all-time greats like Wilt Chamberlain and Bill Russell. In fact, Reebok stuck a cutout of O'Neal's gigantic footprint under every hotel door in Salt Lake City during all-star weekend.

Nike paired Michael Jordan with Bugs Bunny in a commercial that sent the two to outer space and poked fun at the millions Nike pays Jordan.

The competitor that he is, Johnson even talked trash about the opposing companies' commercials.

"Mine is more funny, more catchy, and kids like it," Johnson said. "Shaq says one line (in the Reebok commercial) . . . The Bugs Bunny commercial can't hold a candle to Grandmama."

Johnson always talks of his Grandmama persona in third

person, like she's a separate being. "She is," Johnson joked during the playoffs.

His fellow all-stars didn't care much about the commercials, but they were impressed with Johnson's game. Utah forward Karl Malone sees himself in Johnson's toughness.

"Some people think he's a horse's ass, but Larry's a great guy," said Malone. "I don't like soft players. They whine and moan. They can dish it out at one end and not take it at the other. I'm not like that, and neither is Larry."

Amid all this goodwill, Johnson put out the word that he wants to sign a long contract extension and spend the rest of his career playing in Charlotte. He quickly grew attached to the small-town friendliness of Charlotte, so why not let the Hornets be the team to pay him his tens of millions over the next decade?

"Charlotte — that's where I want to spend my whole career," said Johnson, who originally planned to finish his career in hometown Dallas.

Stolpen was sold. At mid-season he said he'd happily extend Johnson's contract a dozen years.

While Johnson was pledging his allegiance to Charlotte at one end of Salt Lake City, Twardzik was shopping around Kendall Gill at a hotel on the other side of town. Most of the league's general managers show up at all-star weekend to attend rules meetings and to talk about trades that never happen. Twardzik didn't hear anything particularly appealing, so he left to scout college games late in the weekend.

In doing so, he managed to miss what Johnson would regard as Riley's great snub.

The fans had voted Johnson and O'Neal onto the all-star team as starters. Johnson replaced perennial Eastern starter Charles Barkley, who had moved West to play for the Phoenix Suns. O'Neal overtook Knicks center Ewing on the fan ballots, which annoyed Riley. To Riley, Ewing was not only a deserving all-star starter, but also a viable candidate for most valuable player.

Riley would rip the media later in the season for giving Ewing only a handful of votes for MVP. In the all-star game, Riley played Ewing 25 minutes, starter Johnson 16. Only six of a possible 120 starters in the previous 12 all-star games played 16 or fewer minutes. And remember this game went into overtime.

Perhaps it was a coincidence, but Ewing clearly got most of

the minutes Johnson logically would have played in the second half as a starter.

In fairness, Johnson didn't give Riley much reason to keep Johnson in there. Johnson said several times he wanted to set screens, grab rebounds, and stay out of Jordan's way. Johnson was perhaps too deferential to his veteran teammates. Ewing and Nance were more assertive, so they played more. As Riley said after the game, Johnson never complained to him, only to the press.

Hornets fans back in Charlotte reacted, as always, with paranoia. They searched for a conspiracy, and many decided Dick Harter was somehow to blame. Harter had been fired as coach of the Hornets and was suing the team for lost income from various benefits. He was now Riley's top assistant in New York and sat right next to Riley during the all-star game. Fans in Charlotte figured this was somehow Harter's revenge on Charlotte.

Harter was incredulous when the theory was passed on to him: "We weren't trying to screw Larry," Harter said afterward. "He's a great kid."

If Harter was incredulous, Riley was indignant. He had coached a half dozen NBA All-Star teams, and Johnson was the first player to publicly complain about playing time. He thought the whole situation was absurd, particularly considering he would have preferred to have the weekend off and let some other coach work. He originally made plans to spend the weekend in Malibu before the Knicks' record obligated him to coach in Salt Lake City.

Whether the slight was real or imagined, Johnson was deeply hurt by the experience. He still seethed over it two days later, after scoring 17 points and grabbing 14 rebounds in a victory over the New Jersey Nets.

"I would rather play 35 minutes with the Hornets than 35 minutes with Pat Riley," Johnson said. "It's justified that I was, excuse the expression, pissed. I was voted to play in the all-star game and I should have gotten more than 15, 16 minutes, since the game was 53 minutes.

"I felt bad for the fans. . . Fans wanted to see me, Hornets fans. I thought I could have made a bigger impact and given them something to be proud of.

"If I go next year, I bet you I play more than 16 minutes, if I have to check myself in."

CHAPTER TWELVE

"Hope I see you guys Thursday."

The all-star break hadn't helped Kendall Gill's shooting any. He was four of 16 against New Jersey in the Hornets' first game after the break. Coach Allan Bristow made much of Gill's defense on Drazen Petrovic — Gill was excellent in that regard — but Gill appeared to be having an out-of-body experience. That is, his feet were in Charlotte, but his head was off in Los Angeles. Gill wanted to be a Clipper.

Gill had told the Clippers he would sign a long-term contract if they could acquire him from the Hornets. That, by itself, should have confirmed Gill was badly confused. The Clippers have been an awful franchise, playing in an awful arena ever since moving to L.A. from San Diego. They will forever be second to the Lakers in the hearts of Los Angeles basketball fans.

A reporter who regularly covered the Clippers once went to his editor and suggested a detailed story on all the mistakes that the team has made. The editor said that would be one heck of a story, except for one important issue — nobody cared enough about the Clippers in L.A. to wonder why they were so bad.

Gill's agent, Arn Tellem, knew all this. He once worked for the Clippers and their eccentric owner, Donald Sterling. According-ing to someone who would know, Tellem tried to convince Gill he wouldn't like playing there. The Clippers go through a new coach just about every season or two (Larry Brown would leave at the end of this season), and their best players were always trying to leave. Charles Smith used impending free-agency to force a trade to the Knicks, and Danny Manning contemplated a similar move. One solid player who wanted to stay, Ken Norman, lost patience with the team's slowness in extending his contract and signed the summer of 1993 with Milwaukee.

If so many others wanted to ditch the Clippers, then why would Gill want to embrace them?

Perhaps the exodus of potential stars from Clipperland was the reason. Perhaps Gill wanted to regain what he once had in Charlotte — to again be what Tony Bennett's father describes as the "queen bee." What Gill doesn't understand is that any NBA team with him as its best player is not going to win a title. Unless his name is Michael Jordan, no shooting guard is likely to lead the Clippers to an NBA championship. Clyde Drexler couldn't do it in Portland, and the Trail Blazers had a far better, deeper team than the Clippers.

Gill wanted to live in a big city. He was dating a dancer and liked living large in New York or L.A. Not that he admitted much of this. Though it was obvious he was leveraging the Hornets toward a trade, Gill still would not flat-out admit he wanted one.

The closest he came to saying he might be gone was as he left the locker room following the Nets game. He turned to the beat writers and said, "Hope I see you guys Thursday," referring to the impending trade deadline.

The Hornets played the Spurs at home the night of the trade deadline. The game represented the return of former Hornet J. R. Reid, but Reid's presence was only a minor subplot. First, the weather was threatening. Snow and freezing rain were forecast, and any hint of a winter storm sends Charlotteans scrambling to the supermarkets to stock up on milk and bread. Southerners freak out over the possibility of snow, not because they aren't hearty but because their towns are not equipped to move the snow or ice off the roads. Essentially, Southern towns all but shut down over flurries.

That the weather didn't scare off many from attending that night's game is a tribute to how important the Hornets are to Charlotte. Or perhaps fans just couldn't contain their curiosity over whether Gill would still be a Hornet by the end of the night.

Gill was there for the player introductions, but team president Spencer Stolpen and director of player personnel Dave

Twardzik were nowhere in sight. They were still up Hive Drive (yes, Hive Drive — it's silly but catchy) at the Hornets' offices, fielding calls about a possible deal. Owner George Shinn had told Stolpen and Twardzik he didn't want to see them in the Coliseum before the 9 p.m. trade deadline. Most of the talk still centered on a three-way swap with Dallas and the Clippers. The Clippers were willing to send forward Loy Vaught and point guard Gary Grant to the Mavericks. The Hornets would get Derek Harper and the Clippers would get Gill.

Dallas general manager Norm Sonju, whose team still hadn't signed No. 4 overall pick Jim Jackson, was lukewarm on the deal. Harper wanted to leave for a contender, but he was one of Dallas' few assets. If Harper left, the team would be a lock to end up with the worst record in NBA history.

Sonju had tentatively decided to hire NBC-TV analyst Quinn Buckner as the team's new coach, so Sonju consulted Buckner on the proposed deal. Buckner said he didn't want Gary Grant, which wasn't much of a surprise. Grant had been a disappointment as a pro after a fine college career at Michigan. Also, Grant has a sour attitude, hardly the kind of player who would fit into a rebuilding effort.

So Dallas passed, killing the Hornets' best chance at a viable deal. About a minute before nine, Stolpen and Twardzik slipped into the back entrance to the Coliseum. Gill would be a Hornet the rest of the season.

Not surprisingly, Gill played the most self-conscious game of his life. He shot three of 15 from the field. Every time either team called a timeout, Gill turned sharply as if he was looking to hail a cab. Actually, he was waiting to be told to grab a shower and jump on an airplane, preferably to L.A.

Despite all the distractions and Gill's inability to make shots, the Hornets played great early, leading the Spurs by 22. San Antonio star center David Robinson missed much of the game with a sprained thumb. So Reid played extensively in the second half, and led the Spurs on a comeback that closed the gap to one with 1:30 left.

Reid loved it... *Show 'em what they gave away! Make 'em think they made a mistake.*

After making an inside basket and drawing a foul, Reid looked up at the crowd that booed him during introductions and swung his fist in anger. "Fuck 'em all!" Reid yelled out.

Dell Curry saved the Hornets with a 20-footer and a three-pointer for the victory, but Reid had made his statement. Maybe he wasn't what the Hornets thought they were getting with the No. 5 overall pick. Maybe he had been immature and needed a change of scenery. But he belonged in the NBA and didn't deserve to be booed at the start of the game, particularly in the state where he played his college ball and started his pro career.

"I expected it. It's just the way Charlotte fans are," Reid said of the booing. "They were on me, and now they're on Kendall. But that's fine. I'm fine. I'm not a part of this organization. To hell with them.

"I just hope they treat these guys well. It's going to be a good team. But (the fans) don't treat them with the respect they deserve."

Bristow was relieved following the game that Gill hadn't been traded. He thought there was still hope Gill would change his mind and sign a long-term contract extension in Charlotte. And even if Gill ended up leaving, the Hornets would pick up a huge salary slot to sign a free agent to replace Gill.

"I can't think of a better situation for a player of Kendall Gill's skills to reach the point he wants to reach," Bristow said. "If he wants a championship, I can't imagine a place better than here. I guess it's confusing to me why anyone would not want to be here."

It was no less confusing to Gill's teammates. Kevin Lynch, the 12th man who hardly ever played, couldn't imagine why Gill was unhappy. He would have walked a path of raised knitting needles to have a team want him the way the Hornets wanted Gill.

Other players thought Gill was just plain nuts not to take what the Hornets were offering. It was no big secret that the Hornets were willing to pay Gill well more than $3 million per season to re-sign. Considering Gill was shooting less than 42 percent at the time of the trade deadline, a $3 million salary sounded awfully generous.

Bristow wanted to save the Gill-Hornets marriage, but he was plenty peeved at the bizarre charade of the past few weeks. When a reporter mentioned Gill looked distracted on the court, Bristow jumped at the chance to say Gill could only blame himself and his handlers if that was the case.

"(Gill has) made a tremendous mistake, put tremendous pressure on himself," Bristow said. "Everything you've seen and heard is coming out from his agent. He has to (blame) his agent for putting him in that situation. It wasn't the club, it was his agent."

Bristow didn't have a problem with Gill pursuing restricted free agency. He didn't have a problem with Gill asking for a trade, though he was convinced Gill would regret the decision if he left Charlotte. Bristow was livid that Gill and his advisors were manipulating the situation through *USA Today* columnist Peter Vecsey and distracting the team from its playoff drive.

Vecsey wasn't done with Bristow, either. Later in the season he speculated that Bristow's job could hang on whether Gill would re-sign with the Hornets.

Apparently Vecsey had information that Gill didn't want to sign with the Hornets if Bristow stayed as coach. Certainly, Vecsey's previous column demonstrated Gill could blame others, like Bogues, for his troubles. But Vecsey's conclusion couldn't have been further from the truth.

First off, Bristow was Gill's biggest supporter among team management. But more important, Stolpen made it clear immediately after Vecsey's column that if owner George Shinn had to choose between Gill and Bristow, then Gill would undoubtedly be the one to leave.

Basically, Shinn distrusted Gill's loyalty from the start, apparently with cause. Whether or not Bristow has major potential as an NBA coach, Shinn believes in him. And Shinn has always trusted his instincts on such decisions.

In other words, when Bristow leaves the bench in Charlotte, probably for a front-office job (his contract is structured that way), it won't be because Kendall Gill ran him off.

WSOC-TV sports director Harold Johnson spent much of the San Antonio game in the stands, talking with Shinn. On his late-night newscast, Johnson promised a big story the next night concerning Kendall Gill.

Johnson had learned of the letter Tellem sent to the Hornets, requesting a trade. Johnson had a scoop, and made sure everyone in Charlotte was watching him the next night.

Team personnel said Shinn told Johnson about the letter, which the Hornets received five weeks earlier. On his early-evening newscast, Johnson wasn't satisfied just to report the letter's existence. He editorialized, urging Hornets fans to boo Gill.

Johnson is the best sports reporter in Charlotte television. He has lots of sources and gets them to talk. But he doesn't play by very strict rules. Immodestly referring to himself as "the big guy," he's as much showman as journalist. He pulls silly stunts (he once got a brush cut to resemble Eric Montross after North Carolina won the national championship), and brags incessantly on the air about his scoops.

This time Johnson tried to embellish a good story into a great story. Johnson reported the letter Tellem sent stated Gill would never re-sign with the Hornets. The letter said no such thing. It was particularly abrupt — one paragraph long — and stated only Gill's desire for a trade. Nowhere in its text did Tellem specifically say Gill's stance was irreversible.

"It's obvious he'd rather be in a larger market," Stolpen said of the letter. "But Charlotte is not out of the realm of possibility."

Johnson heard as much from Stolpen in a telephone conversation between his 6 and 11 p.m. newscasts. Worse yet, some of Johnson's viewers were calling the station, complaining that Johnson had no business telling fans to boo Gill. Johnson knew he'd overplayed his hand. Contritely, he said on his late-night show that he shouldn't have told fans to boo Gill. In fact, Johnson called Gill the next day to apologize.

That's showbiz.

It's amazing how quickly bad news can spread. The team was in Indianapolis' Market Square Arena, preparing for that night's game, when Johnson did his initial sportscast of the day. Gill knew what Johnson had done, from Indianapolis, by the end of the game.

"Tell Harold Johnson I love him, too. I don't feel I've done anything to deserve this," Gill said. "It's over, why pour salt in the wounds? I've been hurting all season, and now this. What did I do to Harold Johnson?"

Gill was glad the Hornets were leaving town, considering all that had happened the past few weeks. As he said months later, "It was true I was unhappy, but who wouldn't be unhappy with all that stuff going around over the top of their heads?"

Starting with the Indiana game, the Hornets would play 13 of the next 17 games away from Charlotte Coliseum, ending the run at Detroit March 26. In that span, the Hornets would barnstorm everywhere from Los Angeles to Boston.

Gill might have been pleased to get away from Charlotte, but the rest of the team dreaded the stretch. Even though the Hornets had been as good on the road as at home, this was the excursion to hell. The Hornets would fly cross-country to play six road games over 10 nights, come home for one game with the Washington Bullets, then fly back out for games at Cleveland, Chicago, and Boston.

The Hornets knew even before the schedule came out that March would be a brutal month on the road. The Atlantic Coast Conference tournament had made Charlotte Coliseum a semi-permanent home, which ate up one five-day weekend of home dates. And the Southeast regional of the NCAA tournament would also be held in the Coliseum, eating up a second weekend.

Since Charlotte is the epicenter of the ACC, and since the Coliseum is so large and modern, it's inevitable college basketball will take up many attractive home dates each March. In 1994, the Final Four will be held in Charlotte, which will eat up 10 home dates in late March and early April.

On top of everything else, the team lost Kenny Gattison for 11 days to a family emergency. Gattison's wife, Wanda, was experiencing serious complications with a pregnancy and would eventually lose the baby.

Bristow knew he was in trouble before the Pacers game ever began. The Hornets were 0-9 all-time in Market Square Arena and 0-3 overall this season against Indiana. And worst of all, Bristow's old adversary, referee Bernie Fryer, showed up along with chief official Darell Garretson and third official Nolan Fine.

Fryer didn't eject Bristow, but he did something even more costly to the Hornets. Fryer threw out center Alonzo Mourning early in the third quarter for allegedly punching Pacers center Rik Smits.

Only one problem with Fryer's decision: Neither Mourning nor Smits thought a punch was thrown. The two became tangled under the basket, Mourning pushed Smits away and grazed Smits's face with the back of his hand.

A punch? Not even close.

"I couldn't even tell," Smits said. "I didn't feel a punch, although he must have gotten me on the lip. I just turned around and pushed him away."

As Mourning said, "If I had swung, it would not be a tap. I definitely would have connected. I wasn't trying to mess around with him. I was trying to get back on defense.

"I'm definitely going to talk to league security. I should not get fined."

An Indianapolis television station videotaped the supposed punch from a perfect angle that confirmed Mourning's description. If what Mourning did justifies an ejection, then league officials should make about 200 more ejections per season. Unfortunately for Mourning, he bumped Smits directly in front of Fryer, who apparently surmised more than what actually occurred.

The game was essentially over before Mourning's ejection. When he left the game, the Hornets already trailed by 23. With Mourning out, things got utterly ridiculous. With Gattison in Charlotte and Sidney Green unavailable due to the flu, the Hornets were short-handed at center. Mike Gminski would score his season high, with 12 points off 6-of-8 shooting. But Smits would score a career-high 37 points and the Pacers would win, 137-105.

Smits is somewhat mechanical and not particularly aggressive against most of the league. Against the Hornets, he is Kareem. Smits would sign a five-year, $17.5 million contract extension with the Pacers later in the season, reconfirming the Jon Koncak/7-footer Rule of Market Forces. At that price, Pacers general manager Donnie Walsh must have evaluated Smits's potential exclusively off games against Charlotte.

Needless to say, this was the widest margin of defeat for the Hornets this season. It was only eight points short of the widest margin in franchise history. For one night, the Hornets of Larry Johnson and Alonzo Mourning were no better than the Hornets of Dave Hoppen and Earl Cureton.

"I'm sort of glad we have one more against them (March 19). This is not a particularly hard place to play," Bristow said.

Bristow was more concerned over Mourning's ejection than the margin of defeat. He was furious three days later, when the league announced it had fined Mourning $3,500 for the incident with Smits. Earlier in the season, Mourning drew a $5,000 fine for fighting Detroit's Bill Laimbeer.

Mourning felt thoroughly picked upon. He said this wouldn't happen if his name were Joe or Tom, but "Alonzo" was apparently in the back of NBA officials' minds. Bristow agreed Mourning was being persecuted.

"I have made that clear to the league — I don't want anything to stymie his career," said Bristow. "Referees, particularly younger officials, can be predisposed. I'm not saying that's happened yet, but they're too quick to judge Zo."

Mourning had been wronged in this case, but there's no question he contributes to a reputation around the league as nasty bordering on dirty. In early January, Mourning elbowed Boston's Alaa Abdelnaby in the back of the head for no apparent reason. The ball wasn't anywhere near Mourning and Abdelnaby at the time. Abdelnaby ended up drawing a technical foul for complaining about it. Boston coach Chris Ford took Abdelnaby out of the game and never reinserted him.

"I know all about him," Abdelnaby said of Mourning, grimacing after the game.

Later in the season, Mourning and New Jersey Nets center Sam Bowie would get into a shoving match. Bowie said the little fight started because Mourning can't take the same punishment he dishes out to others.

"I've never been the type of guy to get into altercations," Bowie said. "I felt I was the recipient of some cheap shots. He doesn't like it when you go down and give it back to him at the other end."

In fairness to Mourning, he was doing little more than what was expected of him to succeed in the most physical position in basketball. He once described just how physical.

"The position I play is a very aggressive position," Mourning said. "Elbows are flying, people pushing, barking. You're up in people's faces, smelling people's breath. It's not too pleasant down there in the hole.

"That's why only a select few play down there. A lot of people get big bucks, but very rarely do you find people that want to go down there and put up with that night in and night out. I'm one of the select few who do."

Put it this way: If you were being threatened in a bar, wouldn't you want Mourning as your buddy on the next stool?

From Indianapolis, the team flew to Denver, the city the entire coaching staff used to call home. T. R. Dunn lasted 14 seasons in the NBA; and Bill Hanzlik lasted 11. In both cases, their defense kept them in the league. Denver coach Doug Moe would stick Hanzlik, about 6-7, on just about anyone, including 7-2 Houston center Ralph Sampson (Sampson and Hanzlik once ended up in a memorable fight).

Hanzlik's nose is the best testament to his defense — it curves about three different ways, due to the various times he's broken it. Hanzlik promised his wife, Mary Beth, that the kids wouldn't inherit his profile. True to Hanzlik's word, they have four beautiful children.

Dunn occasionally scrimmages with the players in practice and is still an excellent defender.

Dunn and Hanzlik have sort of a good cop/bad cop relationship with the younger players. Dunn is the one a Kevin Lynch will go to for advice. In contrast, Hanzlik is the one to get on a player who's not playing hard enough or losing his concentration.

Gill lost his temper with Hanzlik late in the season, screaming at him from the court. Bristow grew upset, telling Gill to shut up and get back into the game. Hanzlik didn't mind the shouting.

"I kind of like it when a player does that. I did that when I played," Hanzlik said. "Let him blow off steam at me."

Hanzlik and Dunn are good with the players and know the passing game Bristow uses, but neither had a minute of coaching experience before signing on with the Hornets. It seems obvious at times that Bristow would benefit from hiring a veteran assistant. He says he wants everyone on his staff to be committed to the passing game. Fine, but he could use some alternative input.

Bristow often consults with Twardzik, a former assistant coach with the Pacers and Clippers, but that is only after games or occasionally at halftime at home. Other young head coaches have seen the value of a veteran assistant. John Bach and Tex Winter convinced Phil Jackson to install the triangle offense in Chicago. Pat Riley often credits Dick Harter with molding the Knicks' defense. Some "old codger" might do Bristow a lot of good on the Hornets' bench.

The Hornets weren't as bad in Denver as they had been in Indianapolis, but they were beaten by a big stiff who makes Rik Smits look like a hall-of-famer. Scott Hastings has made a career out of being 12th man, first in Miami, then Detroit, and now

Denver. Like Tree Rollins and Charles Jones, Hastings is just good enough (and just big enough at 6-11) to earn the last seat on an NBA bench every season. He's far better known for his wisecracks than his ability.

The Hornets thought they had the Nuggets when Denver center Dikembe Mutombo got into foul trouble. Then, Hastings came off the bench and somehow scored the last five points in a 12-2 run that gave the Nuggets a 110-103 victory.

Naturally, since Hastings is quick with a one-liner, the Nuggets' radio network brought him on as a guest after the game. "You hold a guy to 28, man, and you're a star," Hastings joked, referring to Mourning.

Bristow wasn't amused. He got downright steamed when the media suggested Hastings was the difference.

"Everybody looks good when you win," Bristow whined. "(Players like Hastings) are just there to pass the time. You wouldn't have even remembered he was out there if they lost."

Prospects for the road trip looked bleak. The Hornets had lost two straight, and the remaining games — at Utah, Seattle, Portland, and the Los Angeles Lakers — were the tougher part of the trip. The Jazz is traditionally one of the NBA's better home teams. The SuperSonics were chasing the best record in the Western Conference. The Trail Blazers had never lost to the Hornets in 11 meetings. And the Lakers were 5-0 all-time against the Hornets at the Forum.

Few players look forward to the trip to Salt Lake City for a variety of reasons. The thin air makes it hard to catch your breath. The weather changes drastically — the temperature can drop 20 degrees in an hour. Plus the place is overrun with Mormons looking for religious conversions. When ex-Hornets coach Gene Littles coached there, his wife kept a beer and a pack of cigarettes handy around the house so that she could light up and pop a top whenever the missionaries knocked on her door. The sight of alcohol and tobacco helped keep the conversations with the missionaries short.

Of course, the real reason teams hate visiting Utah is that the Jazz is so good. Karl Malone and John Stockton are two of the 10 best players in the league. And the crowd support in Salt Lake City is fantastic. Much like Charlotte, Salt Lake City is a mid-sized market madly in love with its only major league franchise.

The Jazz had moved out of the cozy Salt Palace and into the 19,500-seat Delta Center to meet the demand for tickets. Jazz crowds are raucous and nasty. There is a fellow in the front row, known to everyone around the league as the fat, bald guy, who might be the league's most creative heckler. The fat, bald guy was the one who started calling Armon Gilliam "Gumby" for Gilliam's left-to-right haircut slant.

The Jazz is big, physical, and deliberate, more like the Pistons or Celtics in style than a typical run-and-gun Western Conference team. Utah has Malone, 7-4 Mark Eaton, and 6-10 brawler Mike Brown. And the Hornets were still missing Kenny Gattison to back up Johnson and Mourning inside.

Everything about this matchup suggested a Charlotte loss. Which might be the best reason why the Hornets won, 110-107. Just like in Chicago to end a four-game losing streak, the Hornets knew they had to get their act together in Utah.

"We play better when things aren't going well for us," Mourning said after tying a career-high with 22 rebounds. "A lot of guys on this team have heart and guts. We really know when to play hard. We got blown out in Indiana, then lost a game in Denver we should have won."

In other words, the losses got their attention.

"I think we realize when we've hit the low spot, and we know to fight back," Johnson said.

So this was a must win?

"Not so much a must win as a must effort," Johnson replied.

Bristow sure coached it like a must win. Mourning played 46 of a possible 48 minutes and Johnson played 45. It was apparent that Bristow had lost faith in Mike Gminski as anything more than a spot player. Gattison was not with the team and Green was still recovering from the flu. If there was ever a time when playing Gminski made sense, this was it. But the "G Man," as they used to call him in Philadelphia, never played a minute against the Jazz.

Two games later in Portland, Bristow played Gminski in the second quarter against the Trail Blazers. Portland inserted center-forward Cliff Robinson, who quickly grabbed an offensive rebound over Gminski and dunked it in.

Bristow was so frustrated he momentarily turned his back on the game. "And he wonders why I don't play him," Bristow said, obviously referring to Gminski.

Gminski played one minute in the second half of the Portland game. He played 10 or more only twice the rest of the season, and that was in mop-up time in easy victories over Washington and Minnesota. Gminski wouldn't play at all in 14 of the last 17 regular-season games.

As was their topsy-turvy pattern after so big a victory, the Hornets lost their next game, 138-112, to the Seattle SuperSonics. Despite the final score, Bristow and the Hornets didn't lose their confidence. For some reason that wasn't easily detectable watching the game, Bristow was actually encouraged by his team's performance. Bristow liked that his team hadn't quit just because it was losing badly. The Hornets made a run on the Sonics early in the second half, and Johnson finished with 24 points and 11 rebounds. Seattle was among the NBA's best young teams. Losing to the Sonics was no tragedy.

From Seattle, the Hornets took the short hop south to Portland. If Salt Lake City is among the least liked stops on an NBA road trip, then Portland is among the best liked, at least for the two-thirds of the league who play in Nikes. For Nike-wearers, Portland means it's payola time.

Nike, the world's leading sneaker maker, is based in the Portland suburb of Beaverton. The company's corporate offices are called a campus, and it does look far more like a small college than a corporate center. There are luxurious gymnasiums and cafeterias open to all employees. Nike CEO Phil Knight is very generous to his employees — particularly his celebrity endorsers.

The stories of Nike's endorsement contracts are legend. The company recently bought Duke coach Mike Krzyzewski away from Adidas with a reported $1 million signing bonus and a 15-year, $5 million contract. Nike's NBA endorsers include dream-teamers Michael Jordan, Charles Barkley, David Robinson, Scottie Pippen, and John Stockton.

A $3.4 billion company, Nike controls about 30 percent of the world athletic shoe market and about half of the basketball shoe market. Clearly, Nike designs and manufactures good sneakers. But it's Nike's marketing, its star-studded group of endorsers, that appears to have made this company into a global giant.

Jordan's endorsement has made Nike hundreds of millions of dollars. But Jordan's cross-marketing — in particular, a

commercial for Hanes underwear with a cheeky plot line —
helped convince Nike to seek more control over its endorsers'
marketing.

That's where Nike's sports management arm started.

"We wanted more control over an athlete's image. The
company has really built itself around marketing," said Fred
Schreyer, Nike's director of sports marketing.

So the underwear ad pushed the company into the agent
business?

"That oversimplifies it," said Schreyer. "It may have played
a role. Not any particular decision Michael made changed
things, but there was kind of an awareness."

That "awareness" came straight from the top. According to
a Nike source, the sports management division exists, and will
continue to exist, because Phil Knight believes in it. Nike wants
to manage the entire career of a few elite athletes each year, right
down to negotiating their contracts with the teams drafting them.

"We've always invested money and research time into
developing athletes' images. Now, we're assuming more of a
managerial role in their careers," said Schreyer, a former Los
Angeles lawyer with ties to sports agent Howard Slusher. "We
create a lot of value in the guys we market. We're kind of at the
mercy of athletes and the agents to make good decisions."

So Nike decided to pay the athlete what was necessary to
control that process. If *Forbes* magazine is right — and Schreyer
wouldn't confirm this information — Mourning was guaranteed
$16 million against his contract with the Hornets and various
endorsement deals to let Nike manage his career.

It's only logical Mourning would end up with Nike —
Georgetown coach John Thompson is on the company's board of
directors and former Nike operative Sonny Vaccaro befriended
Mourning early on. Thompson has bragged to friends that he
had Nike over a barrel in the Mourning deal because Nike was
trying something so radical and needed a high-profile guinea pig
like Mourning.

Mourning says it's obvious why he agreed to let Nike
manage his career — just look at the money and fame Nike
brought Jordan and Bo Jackson.

The real question is why Nike would take on the headache
of playing sports agent. Nike is a mass-marketing company,

promoting a feel-good, carefree lifestyle. Agents are about as popular among the general public as tax collectors and loan sharks.

"That's a good question, considering all the negative perceptions—athletes getting paid too much, the holdouts," Schreyer said. "But Nike's never been afraid to kind of take chances. We've always been involved with somewhat controversial people — a John McEnroe, an Andre Agassi, a Charles Barkley.

"We were attracted to Alonzo's fiercely competitive nature. He's a bright, articulate, disciplined kid. And clearly we thought he'd been one hell of a basketball player."

Actually, Mourning's quick success in the NBA surprised Schreyer and Don Coleman, the marketing representative Nike assigned to Mourning. At first, they thought it would be two to three years before Mourning would have the national appeal to do Nike commercials. But by March, they were making plans to have a Mourning commercial on the air by fall. It would serve as a nice counter-measure to Reebok's "All Shaq, all the time" media blitz.

"Given the amount of attention given to Shaquille, Alonzo's been a little ignored," Schreyer said. "But Alonzo's proven he doesn't have to take a backseat to anyone."

Schreyer acknowledged he and Coleman still have some work to do on Mourning's social skills if Mourning is to be a Jordan or a Barkley in the endorsement business.

"He's a little rough around the edges," Schreyer said.

A few hours later, Mourning exposed those rough edges at Nike's factory store. Players who wear Nikes in games get varying amounts of free merchandise from the company as partial compensation. A store employee explained later that there are endorsers and then there are *endorsers*. If Kendall Gill wanted something, he'd request it and an employee would go to the back, get it out of stock if available, and count it against Gill's shoe and apparel allowance. Mourning, thanks to his great status in the company, could walk in, point to something, and have half the store's employees scurrying around to wrap it up for him.

In the eyes of one employee, Mourning was just a little too bossy, particularly for a rookie whom the company had taken so far under its wing.

"He ought to be more grateful," the employee said. "We've been paying him since he was in high school."

Indirectly, that's true. Nike supplied sneakers to Mourning's high school team back at Indian River in Virginia because he was already getting national attention.

Maybe Nike thought it signed up the wrong Georgetown grad that night. Mourning had a rough shooting night — six of 18 from the field, three of nine from the foul line — but fellow Hoya David Wingate grabbed an offensive rebound and hit an eight-footer with five seconds left for a 94-92 victory.

Naturally, Larry Johnson took the opportunity to renew his lobbying campaign through the media to get Wingate a contract extension. It wasn't necessary. First off, league rules barred the Hornets from re-signing Wingate until his original one-year deal expired in July. Also, the Hornets were already leaning toward re-signing Wingate if he would agree to something in the $500,000-per-year range.

With Gattison still out — he would rejoin the team in Charlotte in three days — Bristow continued to treat the starters as marathoners. Johnson, Mourning, Gill, and Muggsy Bogues each played 39 or more minutes against the Trail Blazers.

NBA coaches often say the worst two games of a long road trip are the first and the last. The first game, the players are fighting through jet lag and readjusting their schedules to a week of hotel rooms. The last game, the players are exhausted and their minds are wandering to the impending flight home.

So no one was particularly surprised when the Hornets fell behind the Lakers, 66-55, in the first half at the Forum. The shocking part was the 18-2 run that got the Hornets back the lead in the third quarter. In victories over Utah and Portland, the Hornets had developed a resiliency, a confidence that trailing on the road didn't automatically mean a defeat.

They were growing up.

"It seems like we play better when we're behind," said Mourning, who scored 27 points and grabbed 11 rebounds in the 105-101 victory. "When we get leads, we get complacent."

Complacency isn't part of Mourning's makeup. There's a passion, a will about his game that was foreign to the Hornets before his arrival. Mourning takes losing harder than any other Hornet, and sometimes it comes out in graphic ways.

Mourning lost a ball out of bounds against the Lakers, and found himself beyond the baseline and full of rage. Reporters sit along that baseline at the Forum, behind tables padded to protect the players from possible injury. Mourning grabbed a wad of that padding and crushed it like Silly Putty. The foam rubber, designed for its resiliency, never restored its form.

More than one reporter at that table felt lucky Mourning didn't grab for a lap-top computer instead of that padding.

Another time, Mourning got so upset in Charlotte that he yanked the padding away from one of the basketball supports and flung it to the ground. It was like watching the Incredible Hulk, both in strength and temper.

Of course, Mourning wasn't the center who got himself thrown out of this game. The Lakers' Vlade Divac got so agitated at Mourning's tough defense that he threw the ball at Mourning, drawing an ejection.

Bristow can live with Mourning's rage because he knows it's part of what makes Mourning so good.

"He works so hard, he's so relentless," Bristow said. "Zo makes us respectable defensively."

If Johnson is any example, then Mourning will learn in later years how to pace himself, how to conserve energy while still playing hard.

"I can see where a year's experience has helped me," Johnson said. "I've seen Jordan do it and Barkley do it. I take my time and pick my points. Say, we really need a stop here, you turn it up, then you pick your point to rest. It's not relaxing. You need to pace yourself."

Following the game, Johnson couldn't understand why the beat writers thought it was such a big deal that the Hornets had beaten the Lakers at the Forum. That broke up Dell Curry and Muggsy Bogues, the two players who remain from the Hornets' first season. There was a time, back when Magic Johnson was healthy and James Worthy was young, when the Hornets wondered if they would ever beat the Lakers.

Bristow was subdued following the victory because he learned midway through the game that close friend Doug Moe had been fired as coach of the Philadelphia 76ers. The Lakers had flashed news of Moe's firing on the scoreboards late in the first quarter. Hornets equipment manager Dave Jovanovic ran over to the writers during a timeout to double-check the news. Yes, Moe really had been fired just five months into his first season as Sixers coach. Moe's gruff candor hadn't worn well with his new players and the up-tempo passing game wasn't a good mix with the roster.

Sixers owner Harold Katz planned to turn over half his roster in the off-season. But he wasn't willing to let Moe be part of that rebuilding process. Bristow didn't know what to say. If Moe knew he was about to be fired, he didn't let on to Bristow.

The road trip was a huge success. Particularly considering the Hornets started out 0-2, finishing 3-3 on the longest trip of the season was downright amazing. Most teams, even the elite ones like the Bulls, hope they win a third of their road games in the other conference. The Hornets finished 8-5 on the road against the Western Conference.

The trip was all about efficiency. The Hornets won three games by an average of three points and lost the other three by an average of 22. If the trip had been a tennis match, the Hornets would have won it, 0-6, 0-6, 7-6, 7-6, 7-6.

CHAPTER THIRTEEN

"This is a cocky team, those Charlotte Hornets."

Time and distance were good to Kendall Gill. The long road trip helped clear his head and remind him basketball could be fun. He even started making shots again. Over the last three games of the road trip, he made 24 of 43 attempts. That's 56 percent, or 14 percent better than he was shooting for the season.

"It was mental, psychological," Gill said of the worst slump of his career. "If you go out there and think you won't shoot well, you won't shoot well. Last year, I thought I'd hit everything. This year, I was second-guessing myself."

Bristow didn't know how long Gill would be a Hornet, but he was determined Gill would not act like a lame duck the rest of the season. Gill had gone into a shell, and Bristow told him to start acting like his old self. To be vocal, to be a leader, to be the way Kendall Gill naturally is.

The kid who wasn't afraid as a rookie to tell off veterans was avoiding his teammates.

"He's the first one who really spoke out about shedding expansion. That's the Kendall I know and the one I want to see," said Bristow. "I've said for him to be a little more outspoken. Not in a negative way, but that's the way he is."

Gill saw Bristow's point, but also knew things had changed in his relationship with his teammates. Some resented him, particularly around the trade deadline, for bringing all this controversy down on the locker room. Most of the players agreed with Bristow that Gill and Tellem were to blame for the criticism they received.

"You can't yell at players, when in the press they're saying you don't want to be here," Gill said. "The players would say, 'Who are you? You don't want to be here.'

"It's not my nature to be quiet, but maybe I had to be in that situation. My teammates didn't know where I was coming from."

Truth is, they still didn't know. Gill's leanings seemed to change almost daily. But since Gill was definitely here the rest of the season, they wanted him focused on winning. Finally, that seemed to be the case.

The Hornets were so exhausted following their cross-country flight that there weren't many teams they would have beaten the next night. Fortunately, the Washington Bullets were in town.

If the Hornets couldn't beat the Pacers this season, then they couldn't help but beat the Bullets, a hodgepodge of mediocre players often used out of position. Center Pervis Ellison is really a power forward, power forward Harvey Grant has the game of a small forward. Rex Chapman is a ... uh ... well if he's anything, he's a shooting guard, but he was already chained to the Bullets' bench after just a season in Washington. Coach Wes Unseld had discovered all the reasons the Hornets wanted to jettison Chapman. There probably wasn't a greater fool in the NBA now willing to take on Chapman's contract.

Worse yet, Ellison, Chapman, and several other Bullets were hurt and didn't make the trip. That left rookie forward Tom Gugliotta trying to guard center Mourning, which would have been vintage slapstick if it hadn't been so pathetic. Washington was the one team in the NBA with so little muscle and size that the Hornets could always count on bullying them. And so they did, 124-104.

For once, the schedule makers had been kind to the Hornets in March.

"I was talking to Dell (Curry) before the game, telling him I was tired and weak," Larry Johnson said. "Our systems haven't turned around (from Pacific time). I didn't get to sleep until 5:30 (a.m.)."

The best thing about this game is the Hornets didn't have one of their usual swoons once the lead swelled. That left plenty of time for reserves Mike Gminski and Sidney Green to play, and also gave Kenny Gattison an opportunity to regain his form in garbage time.

Gattison had jogged to keep in shape while helping his wife through their family crisis. But as Gattison and so many others have said, the only way to be in basketball shape is to play basketball. You can't re-create the movements, the sudden stops and turns, the action and reaction, by yourself.

The Hornets were home just long enough to recycle their wardrobes at various Charlotte dry cleaners. The afternoon following the home game with the Bullets, they flew off to play in Cleveland, Chicago and Boston — arenas where their all-time record was a combined 1-25.

Despite that, Bristow was excited and confident leaving for Cleveland. Perhaps overconfident. His team was 32-26, already a victory better than any previous Hornets team had finished. The western travel was completed except for a highly winnable game in Minneapolis. The Hornets would play 10 of their last 11 games back in Charlotte. It would take a collapse of massive proportions for Charlotte to miss its first trip to the NBA playoffs.

Bristow wouldn't grab the bait before the game when a reporter suggested his team had already locked up a playoff spot. There were 24 games left, after all. However, it was easy to see Bristow felt good about his team's chances. He was already discussing the advantages of playing a New Jersey or Boston in the first round, rather than a Cleveland or Chicago or New York.

As if on cue, the Cleveland Cavaliers provided a reality check. They barbecued the Hornets, 118-99. The Cavaliers shot 54 percent from the field, and every Cleveland starter scored in double figures. Worse yet, they did this to the Hornets without point guard Mark Price, their best player, who sat out the game with a sprained right thumb.

Center Brad Daugherty is the Cavaliers' most valuable asset because centers of Daugherty's athleticism number perhaps 10 in the entire league. But Price is Cleveland's best player. When he isn't shredding the other team's defense with his penetration, he is hitting 20-foot jump shots. Price was chosen in the second round of the 1986 draft. That it took so long for Price to be chosen proves whites can also be victims of racial prejudice. Basically, no one around the NBA believed a short, pudgy white kid had the quickness Price displays. That 24 players could be chosen before Price, the NBA's best point guard now that Magic Johnson has retired, proves the fallibility of the NBA scouting process.

The striking thing about the Cavs is they have not only the NBA's best point guard, but also its best backup point guard. Terrell Brandon, just as quick as Price and nearly as cunning after just two seasons in the pros, had 12 assists and no turnovers.

Ten trips to Richfield, Ohio; 10 losses by the Hornets.

"They're not that much better than us," Gattison said. "But somewhere along the way, for four or five minutes, they're a lot better than us."

Mount Bristow erupted after the game, screaming that he and his team have to stop talking about the playoffs and get back to concentrating on each game. Of course, he was as guilty as anyone of thinking too far ahead.

"I'm done talking about the playoffs, guys. . . . Over. . . OVER!" Bristow shouted at the beat writers following that game.

There was a message in Cleveland's victory. The Cavaliers had been watching the standings. They recognized the potential for a Charlotte-Cleveland first-round matchup.

"There's a very real possibility we'll face these guys in the playoffs. It's 10-0 and we plan to keep it that way," said Cleveland guard Gerald Wilkins. "We had to make a statement."

Another team ready to make a statement waited in Chicago. The Hornets were in for a rough pair of nights.

Remember when Gill said it was never wise to talk trash to Michael Jordan because it might motivate Jordan to score 50?

Gill was off, but not by much. Jordan scored 52.

Jordan wasn't slow to remind the Hornets of their bragging after a victory in Chicago January 22. Neither were his teammates, following a 123-108 Bulls victory.

"It was some retaliation for what was said back then," Jordan said of the Bulls' grandstanding late in the game. "There were some comments in the paper last time they beat us. Memories go a long way, you know."

Like Bulls coach Phil Jackson said, "This is a cocky team, those Charlotte Hornets. They beat us here the last time, and that upset us. We remembered that game."

The Bulls treated them like brats. Reserve center Stacey King told Chicago radio in a postgame interview that his team pulled the Hornets' diapers down for a good spanking. With 3:30 left after a tomahawk dunk, Jordan swung his fist in the air and screamed out in an almost primal rage.

"That was my Larry Johnson imitation," Jordan joked later.

The Hornets might have avoided this indignity, at least keeping the game close, had Bristow not been so conservative in his use of Mourning. After picking up his fourth foul, Mourning sat out the last 17 seconds of the third quarter and the first four minutes of the fourth quarter. In that span, a two-point deficit bloated to 11, and the Hornets fell out of the game.

"Hopefully, you think you can tread water until he gets back in," Bristow explained of his decision.

Mourning wasn't about to second-guess his coach, so he deflected questions about his absence with a shrug. However, Jordan said Bristow blew it.

"He carried them in the third quarter," Jordan said of Mourning's 17 points that period. "When he left, they didn't have any offense in the middle."

By leaving Mourning out so long, Bristow had displayed his inexperience, just as his players had by needling the Bulls in their previous trip to Chicago. The callers on the talk shows got all over Bristow for leaving Mourning on the bench. March became the big month to rip Bristow.

Gill wasn't worried. For one thing, all the players were accustomed to the idea that the Hornets could raise their games whenever things looked bleak. That helped explain the January victory in Chicago as well as the March victory in Salt Lake City. So what if they were headed to Boston Garden, another arena where they had never won?

"We're a young team, and we beat (the Bulls) last time. I expected this," Gill said. "I think we'll have a great game against the Celtics. After two losses, we always rebound."

Hmmm. Two losses, then a rebound. By now, the Hornets even had their gyrations down to a formula.

Half the challenge in beating the Celtics in March was getting to Boston. As the players dressed following the Bulls game, team president Spencer Stolpen wished the beat writers luck in flying out the next morning. A winter storm approaching blizzard intensity stomped across the Eastern half of the country. The team charter flying overnight was the only way Stolpen could see for anyone to get from Chicago to Boston this weekend.

When the team plane landed around 3 a.m. in Boston, it was clear and cold, a starkly beautiful winter night straight out of Hallmark cards' Christmas collection. However, by midday, the wind blew 50 miles per hour and several feet of snow were falling on New England. Those few boats still anchored on the bay or on the Charles bounced around like children's bath toys.

Just as Stolpen predicted, no commercial flights traveled between Chicago and Boston for days. In fact, the Eastern Seaboard essentially shut down for three days. Charlotte's Douglas Airport, a hub for USAir, became a gigantic flophouse for thousands of college students stranded between their schools and spring-break resorts. Ice storms all the way south to Florida had been nearly as crippling to travel as snow to the north. Most sporting events north of Washington were postponed Saturday.

The blizzard stopped planes, trains, and automobiles, but not Boston's resilient autograph hounds. Their numbers dwindled, but a hearty few huddled in the lobby of Boston's Long Wharf Marriott, searching for a Kendall Gill or Muggsy Bogues to sign their trading cards. These are people sadly in need of lives.

The game was scheduled for national television on TNT cable, but the network's production trucks couldn't travel from New York to Boston due to closed highways. Despite all that, the Celtics announced late Sunday morning that the game would be played for any ticket holders who could make it to the Garden.

Charlotteans were disappointed twice Sunday. First, top-ranked North Carolina was upset in the finals of the ACC tournament by Georgia Tech. Then, as night fell, they turned on TNT to discover a movie and not their beloved Hornets.

TNT did little to inform the public it couldn't televise the Hornets game. *The Observer* and the five Charlotte television stations were flooded with calls about the game's absence from local television. Based on those calls, WBT's radio audience must have tripled as fans circled their clock radios or switched their stereo receivers to that seldom-used AM setting.

WBT paid heavily to continue as the Hornets' flagship station the previous summer, giving up its affiliation with North Carolina basketball and football. Neither the Hornets nor the Heels would agree to be bumped to WBT's FM sister station on a night when both played, so WBT let the Heels walk off to WWMG, an FM oldies station in need of the exposure the Tar Heels could provide.

The Hornets were true to Gill's prediction. They recovered from an 11-point deficit to beat the Celtics, 96-93. Larry Johnson had 23 points and 16 rebounds, while Mourning had 25 points and 11 rebounds.

The Hornets had no idea how valuable this victory would be two months later. This wasn't the last time they would win at Boston Garden.

CHAPTER FOURTEEN

"If Allan Bristow's an NBA coach, I'm an astronaut."

Allan Bristow once said his big fear with this young, emotional team was that it would burn itself out before the late-season playoff run. "Hopefully, I'm going to look back on this season and say we didn't peak until March," Bristow said.

Clearly, things did not go according to script. The Hornets were awful in late March, losing seven of nine after the victory at Boston. Even those two victories amounted to flukes of the schedule. The Minnesota Timberwolves, by far the worst of the four expansion teams, represented both Charlotte wins between March 14 and April 1. Beating the Timberwolves does not exactly restore a team's confidence. It's like a major-league baseball team knocking off its Triple-A affiliate. Or as Bristow once said of beating the Dallas Mavericks, it's fool's gold.

In the 15-day span, the Hornets dropped from a tie for the fifth-best record in the Eastern Conference to a game better than the ninth-best record. In other words, they flirted with another trip to the draft lottery, the consolation prize for the 11 NBA teams missing the playoffs.

Gallows humor was rampant among the media regularly covering the team. One day at practice, Hornets director of player personnel Dave Twardzik was facetiously asked who he liked for the 11th pick of June's draft.

"Nobody," Twardzik replied, reminding reporters this was the shallowest draft in many years and no time to drop out of the playoff race.

The inexperience of the Hornets and their young head coach was showing up more than at any other time in the season. The players were grumbling that they needed more structured plays called, as an alternative to the freeform passing game Bristow preferred. They wanted more detailed scouting reports to re-familiarize themselves with opponents before games. And they wanted more coaching in what practice time was available during a busy slate of games.

In short, Bristow's less-is-more philosophy of coaching grew stale as the pressure to make the playoffs increased.

A coach needs to be as much a psychologist as a technician. Reality and perception are often hard to distinguish in basketball — if the players believe in the system they are running, it doesn't really matter whether it's the best offense or defense at that moment. The most important thing is they have confidence in the system. The Hornets were losing, and their confidence in the passing game was eroding at least temporarily.

Take the game in Minneapolis, for instance. Larry Johnson grabbed a defensive rebound, looked up and screamed for Bristow to run a play for him. Johnson had watched the Timberwolves repeatedly run plays for Johnson's counterpart, Minnesota rookie Christian Laettner, so Johnson felt the Hornets needed a countermeasure.

"Last game I'm guarding Laettner. Did you see how many plays they ran through him? That's what we need to do," Johnson later said.

Or take the loss at Indiana. The Hornets were beaten repeatedly by a screen-and-roll play that left LaSalle Thompson wide open for a 15-foot jump shot. Mourning wondered at practice shortly after that game why the Hornets couldn't run something similar to get him such open jump shots.

Or take the shootaround before a road loss to the Detroit Pistons. The players felt the pregame scouting report was superficial, failing to give them enough hints as to how the Pistons were playing now that they had climbed back into the playoff race.

Some of the players' complaints were legitimate criticism. Some amounted to the chronic whining that grows out of a losing streak. Regardless of the cause, Bristow didn't handle it well. If his players wanted a longer scouting report on the Pistons, then why not add more information to a blackboard or do a longer walk-through of Detroit's plays at shootaround? Bristow could benefit from what Nets coach Chuck Daly says about coaching — even if you can't give them everything they need, at least make them believe they have everything they need.

One of the best things about Allan Bristow, the person, is his sense of conviction. He doesn't have situational ethics. He's honest and candid and consistent, and he doesn't bend to the latest trend just to look in vogue. He and his wife, Etoila, are the folks you'd want as your kids' godparents.

Unfortunately, those qualities limit Allan Bristow, the coach. He often appears stubborn to his players because he believes so strongly in his Doug Moe-bred theories on basketball. If he is going to grow and prosper as a head coach at the NBA level, Bristow has to become more flexible, more adaptive to his players' needs. If he doesn't, he will become obsolete like Cotton Fitzsimmons did as coach of the Phoenix Suns. Fitzsimmons knows a lot of basketball, but the Suns just stopped listening because they'd heard it all before.

Bristow and his assistants see the more extensive scouting done by some other teams as overkill, and they are probably right. To justify their existence, some coaching staffs throw so much information at players before games that it becomes confusing rather than enlightening. But it was obvious throughout the spring that Charlotte's players wanted more scouting and coaching than they were getting. And even if that information would serve no purpose except make the players more confident, why not offer it? It couldn't hurt, and it could help.

When the coaches did do more teaching in practice late in the season, some players saw it as little more than window dressing. "Don't be fooled by appearances," one player snickered.

The fans sensed something was wrong, and predictably they overreacted. Fans demanding a coaching change follows any losing streak as sure as fall follows summer.

WBT had added a post-game call-in show to its broadcasts of home games. During the losing steak, the post-game show was a marathon of Bristow-bashing. Most fans were at least diplomatic, suggesting Bristow might be of more use back in the front office. A few were downright cruel.

"If Allan Bristow is an NBA coach, I'm an astronaut," one fan barked over WBT following another loss.

Presumably this was not John Glenn on the phone.

The flash point of all this criticism was the end of a game at New Jersey March 24. The Hornets had the ball for the last possession down two. Often in this situation, coaches tell their players to look for a three-pointer, since visiting teams seldom win in overtime.

Bristow went a step further, substituting rookie point guard Tony Bennett for center Alonzo Mourning. It was either incredibly bold or just plain crazy. Bristow wanted Bennett in there for his shooting range — he was 32 percent from three-point range, second-best on the team — but what a spot to place Bennett in. Perhaps Mourning was also a rookie, but he had 50 times Bennett's NBA experience in these situations.

Predictably, the Nets let Bennett get the ball, and he got a wide open shot on the wing. Bennett panicked, much as he did in that game against the Los Angeles Clippers, ignoring the shot and passing back to Muggsy Bogues. Left with no alternative with the clock ticking down, Bogues threw up a 20-footer that never made it to the basket. Nets forward Derrick Coleman came out to block Bogues' attempt.

Of course, if Mourning had been in the lane, along with Larry Johnson, it's hard to imagine that Coleman would have risked running to the perimeter to double-team Bogues.

The fans got all over Bristow, and with cause. The beat writers also asked Bristow about the play several times. Rather than really explaining his thinking, Bristow just chided the reporters for harping on a single play. Management also ducked the question.

"If the play had worked and we had won, nobody would be asking that question," said team president Spencer Stolpen. "No game we've won or lost has been decided on one play."

Even if accurate, Stolpen's response was self-serving. And it wasn't accurate. Had Bennett thrown up some lucky shot to win it, the media and fans would still be asking what possessed Bristow to pull Mourning in such a situation. It simply added to Bristow's reputation among Charlotte fans as a young and sometimes erratic coach. You know — that guy who kicks his coat at officials.

It didn't help any that Bristow got himself ejected again, this time from a home game against the Hawks. It was justified — Bristow was complaining about an awful charging call against Johnny Newman — but getting thrown out added to the legend of the wild man of Charlotte. Both the coach and his players were getting testy. They felt Charlotte fans were all front-runners looking to run them off.

"We're sensitive enough to know people have totally written us off," Bristow said following a loss to the Miami Heat on March 30. "We can only count on our families for support. Certainly, that's the sense from talk radio."

One day, after some particularly probing questions by the beat writers, Bristow moaned, "you guys are just like our fans."

But give Bristow credit for holding his temper in one particularly absurd post-game press conference. After the Portland Trail Blazers beat the Hornets 121-114 in a Sunday afternoon game, Chris Tomasson of the *Spartanburg (S.C.) Herald Journal* asked Bristow if he thought the Blazers had been hurt by the three-hour time difference from the West Coast. Considering the score, and the fact that the Hornets had just lost their fourth straight, it was perhaps the stupidest and strangest question Bristow had ever been asked. Rather than treat Tomasson like Arn Tellem and grab him in a choke-hold, Bristow abruptly asked if any other reporter had something to say.

No doubt Bristow was sleeping in the fetal position again. He became paranoid and short-tempered in ways totally atypical of his personality. Normally among the more open coaches in the league, he started holding separate interview sessions after practice for print and electronic media. Apparently he feared that if he said something off the record to a newspaper reporter, it would end up being recorded for a radio or television broadcast. And he grew increasingly sarcastic when asked for answers about what was wrong.

One day Bristow brought up Kentucky coach Rick Pitino, well known for his know-it-all persona.

"Maybe if I was Rick Pitino I could say exactly how to fix this," Bristow said. "But I'm not going to lie to you, saying, 'Oh, I know what will fix this.'"

Another time, Bristow took a subtle jab at predecessors Gene Littles and Dick Harter.

"We're still in a learning process, but that's not the reason we've lost four in a row," Bristow said. "That sounds like the previous coaches who've been here."

The scary thing is Bristow did sound a little like Harter or Littles — paranoid, short-tempered, out of solutions.

"We've done all the different things," Bristow said. "I've called plays, I've gone to the passing game. I've gone 60-40 plays and 60-40 passing game."

Bristow dismissed the widely held theory that this young team was freezing up from the pressure of a playoff race.

"What's happened is not a result of the end of the (season). It could have happened anytime. We're good enough to be a playoff team, but we're in a growing process," Bristow said.

"This team has got to have room to grow. And maybe we grew too fast."

That was Stolpen's concern, that the team had created false expectations around town by playing so well earlier in the season. When the Hornets reached five games above .500, fans started taking it for granted the team would make the playoffs. They even started talking about reaching the fourth seed and having home-court advantage in the first round.

To season-ticket holders, qualifying for the last of eight playoff spots in the Eastern Conference started sounding like a disappointment rather than a first-time accomplishment.

"I think we all became spoiled by this talk of the four versus the five spots," said Stolpen. "Basically, we've been playing .500 ball all year. If we keep doing that, we'll be happy. It's not time for anybody to panic."

Normally the prince of panic, owner George Shinn held firm in his support of Bristow. The coach would later say Shinn called him almost daily for little pep talks, reminding Bristow "you're my guy."

"During the time that Allan was getting beat-up, it was something new after every game," Shinn later said. "Always something different — TNT, NBC, Peter Vecsey, Bill Walton, all saying Charlotte wasn't going to win because of Charlotte's system. I had to reach down and pick Allan up. If he doesn't have confidence, then the troops won't, either."

Stolpen and Shinn showed up at practice the day after the Miami loss, which amounted to a red flag to the beat writers. They wondered if Shinn might be considering a coaching change.

After all, this was his third coach in five seasons. Asked if he was disappointed by the team's slump, Shinn measured his words carefully.

"That's a loaded question, like asking if I'd be disappointed if my kid flunked out of school or got a 'D' on a subject," said Shinn. "We've got a great group of guys — young and they've got a lot of room to grow."

Panic was the prevailing emotion in the stands at Charlotte Coliseum. North Carolina was chasing a national championship up the road in Chapel Hill. What had the Hornets done lately, besides disappoint?

Hundreds, sometimes thousands of fans regularly left the Coliseum halfway through the fourth quarter, even if the game was still close. The team kept selling out, but the early departures were troubling. The Hornets' marketing department seemed desperate to rouse the crowd to its former enthusiasm. The team resurrected the fat-guy acrobat, a local businessman who was a college gymnast before growing a pot belly. The first few seasons, the guy would do flips across the floor during timeouts, drawing wild applause. His sudden reappearance suggested the franchise was hurting for entertainment.

Also, the Honey Bees sat at courtside throughout the game, rather than just showing up for routines during timeouts. Apparently, the franchise decided keeping 15 striking young women in Spandex along the baselines would help keep at least the male ticketholders happy. Besides, the Hornets were paying each Honey Bee $35 a home game, so why not get full value on the dollar?

It was particularly apparent at the home game against the Heat on March 30 that the team was hurting for support. Public address announcer James K. Flynn, moonlighting from his job as a morning disk jockey, recognizes a section of the house each home game. For the Miami game, Flynn's patter went, "Tonight's special section is. . . the entire arena!"

The call to arms didn't help. In fact, the Hornets would have been better off if the crowd had just stayed home that night. Instead, they booed — loudly and continuously — as the Hornets were outscored 59-38 in the second half of a 116-89 loss to the Heat.

Kenny Gattison would later say it was the worst loss of the season, and offensively he was clearly accurate. The Hornets shot 42 percent from the field and committed 21 turnovers to eight by Miami. Johnson committed four of those turnovers, which was a major factor in the team's problems.

"We're making entirely too many turnovers, and that includes me, too," Johnson said.

Bogues missed one game and played sparingly in another in the span, due to the flu. Bristow asked Johnson to take more ballhandling responsibility in Bogues's absence, and for awhile it was a big plus. Johnson assembled the team's first two regular-season triple-doubles in consecutive games — a home victory over Minnesota and a loss at Indiana. But over the last five games in March, Johnson committed 24 turnovers. He was holding the ball too much and not reacting assertively enough to the double-teams.

"Every time they passed the ball to Larry Johnson, we tried to make it tough for him to catch the ball and also to pass out to his teammates," Miami's Grant Long said after the game.

Gill said Johnson had to pass quicker to scare off the double-team. Bogues told Johnson just to drive to the goal, to split the double-team the way he did as a rookie.

"Muggsy said we can't panic. That was the best thing said all night," Johnson recalled following the Miami game.

Bogues said more, far more. He told Johnson to stop being so self-conscious and just take over. Johnson had taken only one shot in the game's last 11 minutes.

Bogues was primarily upset with the home crowd. The relationship with Charlotte's fans had gone sour. All the players felt it, but Bogues was the most vocal.

"We've got to not worry about the so-called fans booing us," said Bogues, clearly bitter. "We've got to rely on the people in this locker room. A lot of people have gotten off the bandwagon.

"We've got teams behind us, maybe not far behind us, but still they're behind us.

"Maybe we don't feel like this is our home. Before, everything was great, the atmosphere was great. We understand it's not the same atmosphere."

This "us-against-the-world," attitude was rather trite. Bogues had to know the fans would come running back to the team as soon as it started winning again. But at this point anything that drew the players together made a certain sense.

"It might be good for us to look at it that way," said Dell Curry. "The 12 players and the coaches are the only ones who can do it. Maybe we're the only ones who think we can do it."

Bristow was too discouraged to blame the fans for his mood.

"I was surprised it wasn't worse," Bristow said of the home crowd booing. "They're discouraged. They have a right to be. How can we be any more out of sync than we've been?"

Bristow used to say the difference between this team and its predecessors was the current Hornets didn't have to depend on the other team having a bad night to win a game. But after the Miami game, the Hornets gratefully accepted the gift of Shaquille O'Neal's absence.

At just about the time the Heat was wiping the floor with the Hornets, Magic superstar rookie O'Neal was engaging Detroit forward Alvin Robertson in a fateful debate. The Pistons were doing their usual hockey-goon routine, trying to disrupt the concentration of the other team's star.

Robertson, who was traded at midseason from Milwaukee to Detroit, was trying to play peacemaker. Apparently his words weren't quite soothing enough, because O'Neal suddenly became enraged and hit Robertson with a roundhouse punch to the head.

O'Neal would later claim Robertson had butted him in the groin when the two were talking. Robertson said that's ridiculous, and no videotape of the incident revealed any such cheap shot. O'Neal apparently just blew his top, which is unfortunately typical of the men in his family. O'Neal's father, a boorish type who drives Magic management crazy by storming around wherever he chooses, once roughed up a free-lance writer doing a book on O'Neal.

Anyway, it was obvious O'Neal would be suspended for the home game against Charlotte two nights later. Any punch to the head, regardless of the alleged provocation, means a player is automatically suspended for his team's next game. Some around the Hornets fretted the NBA would somehow delay O'Neal's suspension, since the game was scheduled for national television on TNT cable. But league vice president Rod Thorn did the honorable thing, and ruled immediately on O'Neal's punch.

It would be O'Neal's first missed game of the season. Bristow didn't know how to speak of the Hornets' sudden stroke of luck. On the one hand, he had to be turning cartwheels on the inside. But on the surface, he had to insure that his players didn't take the game for granted.

"I'm not saying we don't need all the help we can get," Bristow said. "(But) we've got to worry about our game."

Actually, the Hornets had a track record of losing when the other team lost a key player. Mark Price's absence hadn't helped the Hornets any in Cleveland. And the absence of starting guards Kenny Anderson and Drazen Petrovic in New Jersey hadn't made enough difference for the Hornets to beat the Nets.

But this was different. The Magic had become so dependent on O'Neal for offense that when the Hornets turned up their defense in the fourth quarter, the Magic essentially gave up. Orlando failed to score off five straight possessions in the fourth quarter, giving the Hornets a 102-93 victory.

In every sense it was a relief. Had the Hornets lost in Orlando, they would have dropped out of the top eight in the Eastern Conference because they had already lost the tiebreaker with the Indiana Pacers.

"It's a good thing I don't know those things," Johnson said, admitting he didn't keep close tabs on the standings.

The Hornets broke a five-game losing streak, their longest of the season. They clinched a potential tiebreaker against the Magic by winning the first three of four games with Orlando this season. And they convinced themselves they could still play tough defense.

"There was just more helping out there," said Mourning, who finished with 30 points, nine rebounds and three blocks. "More hand movement, more stepping into screens. We didn't let them run their offense."

O'Neal's absence was more costly to the Magic's playoff chances than Orlando could have guessed April Fool's Day. Eventually, the Magic would lose a tiebreaker to the Pacers for the eighth and final playoff spot in the East. So winning this home game against the then-struggling Hornets would have propelled the Magic to its first appearance in the playoffs.

It was revealing that Mourning talked of getting more help on defense from teammates stepping into screens and knocking down passes. He finally needed that help after showing amazing durability on the defensive end. In late March and early April

Mourning showed subtle signs of wearing down, and it was measurable in shots blocked.

In the 18 games between March 16 and April 17, Mourning averaged 1.4 blocks per game, compared to a 3.5 average for the season. All six of Mourning's games without a block his rookie season were in that span.

It's understandable that Mourning's blocks would drop considerably as fatigue set in. Consistent shotblocking takes exceptional anticipation and quick, springy legs. The physical and mental wear of 70-some games could rob any rookie of those attributes.

What Mourning lost at the defensive end, he was clearly compensating for on offense. What had been a quiet tug-of-war between Johnson and Mourning had evolved into a symphony. They were learning each other's game, when and where each wanted the ball to maximize his scoring ability. And they learned that having someone to share the scoring load in the lane was a luxury both could enjoy for many years.

Mourning often referred to Johnson as "our go-to guy," tipping his hat to what Johnson had already accomplished offensively for the Hornets. Johnson accommodated Mourning early in the season; Mourning was returning the favor now.

"You look at teams like Boston — they all know each other, what the other guy wants," Mourning said. "Those things really count. That's when you reach the level of greatness."

Mourning had earned the unqualified respect and admiration of his teammates. They appreciated his burning desire to excel. Mourning stayed the longest in the weight room, and ran the hardest at the end of games.

Every player in the NBA wants to win, but few are so willing to exert all the energy necessary to win day-in and day-out. Gattison put it best: "Zo never had a home run trot."

Johnson recognized those qualities in Mourning and knew he was lucky to be playing with him. So the two learned to coexist.

"Both guys have made some sacrifices," Johnson said late in the season. "That's what has to happen. Both of us have got to realize the other one's going to be around here for a long time."

Mourning is so preoccupied with team success that sometimes he gets downright ornery when the media brings up individual honors. When Mourning was named rookie of the month for April, he bristled when reporters suggested he might finally be taking some of the spotlight away from O'Neal. "I don't care if I'm not in the spotlight. Spotlights won't win games," Mourning said.

Another time, when asked about he and Johnson sharing the scoring opportunities, Mourning replied, "Hey, if he scored all the points, and we kept winning, that would be fine with me." The look on Mourning's face said he absolutely meant it. Mourning epitomized what Bristow meant when he said, "Stats are for losers. Winning is what matters."

The victory in Orlando must have helped, because the Hornets' momentum carried over to a one-point victory over the Cavaliers in Charlotte. Johnson was great, with 26 points and 16 rebounds, and the crowd actually stuck around for the ending. Gill made a steal with 15 seconds left and drove for the go-ahead basket. Then Mourning blocked Terrell Brandon's shot at the buzzer for the one-point victory.

Once again Mourning's theory on shotblocking — it's not how many shots you block, it's when you block them — proved out.

The Magic came to Charlotte in the Hornets' next game, and apparently Orlando reviewed the videotape of the Heat effectively double-teaming Johnson. The Magic separated Johnson from the ball in the fourth quarter — he shot only three times — and upset the Hornets 109-96.

It was a pitiful performance by the Hornets, who picked an unfortunate night to hand out windshield shades as promotional giveaways. As the game concluded, one disgruntled fan spread his shade at courtside to read, "need assistance — please call police." The Hornets needed assistance, though Charlotte's cops wouldn't have helped this situation. The loss, combined with the Pacers' victory that night over Minnesota, left the Hornets in eighth place, 1 1/2 games ahead of ninth-place Orlando. The Hornets thought they'd left their troubles behind in March, but as Johnson said, this loss "knocked us right on our butts."

The players seemed particularly flustered after this one. Several were huddled in a corner, privately discussing the team's problems. Eventually one or two of the players even suggested Bristow's job might be in imminent jeopardy, considering Shinn's quick-trigger reputation. The players said they had no specific reason to think Bristow might be replaced, just a sense that Shinn could be losing his patience.

One thing was certain. Those 23,000-plus in the stands weren't going to be satisfied with another trip to the draft lottery.

CHAPTER FIFTEEN

"I'll walk out of here with a Honey Bee under each arm."

On the surface, the Hornets had a pretty easy road to the playoffs. With nine games left, Charlotte had a 1 1/2-game lead over the Orlando Magic. Six of those nine games were at home and four were against Philadelphia and Milwaukee, two of the worst three teams in the Eastern Conference.

But as coaches often do, Allan Bristow searched out reasons to fret. He was particularly worried about having been swept by the Indiana Pacers, a potentially critical disadvantage in the tiebreaker system. Obviously, if the Hornets and Pacers finished in a tie for eighth place, Indiana would advance to the playoffs and Charlotte would stay home. But that wasn't the only problem. If the Hornets, Pacers and some other team finished in a three-way tie for seventh, then it was inevitable the Hornets would also miss the playoffs. That's because the NBA breaks a three-way tie by comparing cumulative records between the three teams involved. Obviously, the Hornets stood no chance under such a system with five losses to Indiana against their record.

For that reason, the Hornets paid nearly as much attention to the Pacers' record as their own in April. They didn't know whether to root for or against the Pacers, but whichever way Indiana went, the Hornets wanted them to go far. Either get on a winning streak and jump into sixth place or fall into a massive slump and fall into 10th. One way or the other, just please stay out of seventh, eighth or ninth.

And of course Murphy's Law ruled April. Indiana shadowed eighth place like there was some magnetic attraction between the Pacers and that spot in the standings.

Worse yet, the race was tightening up. Miami and Detroit, left for dead in February, both got hot. Heat point guard Steve Smith finally recovered from his knee injury, and Miami surged. Mercurial Pistons forward Dennis Rodman decided as long as he was stuck in Detroit for the season, why not stop pouting and get his 20 rebounds a game? The Heat and the Pistons were in the race to stay.

Atlanta forward Dominique Wilkins played the role of Lazarus. The season before, Wilkins suffered a severe Achilles tendon injury that many thought would end his career. However, Wilkins played like he was 25 instead of 34. The Hawks had passed the Hornets in the standings in March. Atlanta was playing so well that coach Bob Weiss just might save his job after all.

Add Indiana and Orlando to this muddle, and the Hornets were in a more precarious position than it appeared from the standings. At least two worthy teams in the East would miss the playoffs.

"It's the playoff run. Teams play harder, smarter," said Hornets star Larry Johnson. "We've got to do the same."

Not that Johnson knew anything first-hand about an NBA playoff race. The team's so-called Big Three — Johnson, Alonzo Mourning, and Kendall Gill — had never been in one, unless you count the brief flirtation the Hornets made with eighth place the previous season. That didn't even last until April, when the Hornets knew they were headed for the lottery.

The only Hornets with extensive playoff experience were Johnny Newman, Mike Gminski, and Sidney Green. Of those three, Newman was the only one playing regularly. Newman kept saying his post-season experience would be crucial down the stretch. Bristow appreciated Newman's enthusiasm, but worried that he'd try too hard, get reckless with his shots, and mess the whole thing up.

Bristow had reinserted Newman into the starting lineup starting in the game at Orlando. The offense had broken down so much in the five-game losing streak that Bristow figured Newman's scoring would be a plus. Also, David Wingate was having trouble with his left knee. The more he played the more it hurt, like a pitcher with a sore elbow late in the season. Wingate would need minor surgery in the off season. For now, the only treatment was to sit him out of practice and use him sparingly in games.

The Hornets made much of Gminski's potential leadership value when they traded for him the previous season. Gminski is a leader — articulate, wise, experienced — but not for this team. He hardly played and some of his fellow players wrote him off as downright obsolete. Gminski said he couldn't very well tell his teammates how to react to a playoff race. It wasn't like there were rules that governed this experience. He was right, Gminski couldn't lead from the end of the bench, and that was more the pity. Gminski, the MX missile, was growing rusty in the silo.

The Hornets traveled to Philadelphia to face Gminski's old team, the 76ers. This would be the first time Charlotte played the Sixers since Bristow's mentor, Doug Moe, was fired as Philly's coach. That was fortunate. Bristow didn't need any distractions, and he seemed almost guilty about beating Moe the first two times the teams met this season.

It was a lousy experience, whether you won or lost, to coach against a close friend.

"If you win, you're skipping around the court, and the other guy has to come schlepping over to shake your hand," Moe once said. "You're so happy you don't even notice. You just start dancing in front of the poor bastard, then ask him, 'Hey, want to go for a beer?'"

The game in Philadelphia proved to be the defining moment in the Hornets breaking with expansion. Charlotte fell behind by 11, and Bristow stopped worrying about anything except winning that game. He stopped placating players' egos or building for the future. He just coached.

Primarily, that meant benching Muggsy Bogues early in the game after the Hornets committed six turnovers in the first six minutes. While Bogues moped on the bench, Tony Bennett handed out six assists in 19 minutes.

No one thought Bennett was after Bogues' job. The two weren't even close in ability at that point, and most nights

Bennett barely belonged on the court. But on this night, Bennett was the right choice, and Bristow had the guts to trust his instincts.

"Hey, whatever works is how it's going to be," said Bristow. "Whoever is playing well is going to play."

It's a dynamic the late Jim Valvano used to talk of often in preparing his N.C. State teams for the NCAA tournament. Valvano used to call it "survive and advance" as in use whatever strategy is necessary to win this game, because if you don't, there won't be a next one. The Hornets' situation wasn't quite that dire — there was some margin for error — but Bristow decided just to do what he believed, and clean up the mess later.

The other big move Bristow made was using Sidney Green. Presumed lost since the trade from San Antonio, Green suddenly found himself playing 11 crucial minutes against the Sixers. His numbers — two points, four rebounds, one-of-four shooting — didn't tell the story. Green pushed, shoved and kept the Sixers' Armon Gilliam from having a big second half.

Green was thrilled at contributing more than a slap on the back during timeouts.

"It speaks for itself. There is a change, and I was very startled — and pleased — to do more than cheer for the guys out there," said Green after the 122-113 victory.

Bennett was thrilled to be playing, but worried about upsetting Bogues. "It's not a discredit to anybody else out there," said Bennett.

Typical Tony Bennett — don't sass your elders. Bennett's innocent walk through his first NBA season was a constant source of amusement. One day before a game in Minneapolis, Bennett was chatting with fellow rookie Christian Laettner. Gminski and assistant coach Bill Hanzlik noticed the conversation.

"What do you think they're talking about?" Hanzlik asked Gminski.

"Maybe Tony wants an autograph," Gminski answered. "He can collect a whole set."

Bristow's sense of urgency was apparent after the Sixers game. He knew the Hornets had to win at least three of the four against the Sixers and Bucks to make the playoffs. "We're making our playoff run, and we had to have that one," said Bristow.

The Hornets flew home immediately after the game to face the Hawks the next night. They encountered heavy fog on the return to Charlotte, and the pilot had to abort two landings before finally touching down. Every player was relieved to be on the ground. A commercial airliner might have just diverted to another airport.

The urgency apparent in the Sixers game didn't have much staying power in Charlotte's locker room. The Hornets were awful and the officials were even worse in a 118-105 fall to the Hawks. The referees didn't cost the Hornets the game — the Hawks won it in the third quarter on an 18-0 run — but this might have been the worst-officiated game in franchise history.

Surprise, surprise, the officials included Bernie Fryer.

Fryer couldn't distinguish center Alonzo Mourning from Johnny Newman, which is rather like not distinguishing a string bean from a sledgehammer. Or perhaps, Fryer just couldn't differentiate Mourning's jersey No. 33 from Newman's No. 22. In any case, Newman fouled Hawks center Jon Koncak, but Mourning was charged with the foul. Newman's foul couldn't have been particularly noticeable, because both teams were running downcourt before the officials stopped the game to charge the foul.

Mourning blew his top, which was understandable since he was nowhere near the play. Another official, Jack Madden, whistled Mourning for a technical shortly before Fryer corrected his call to Newman. The technical stood. Apparently, it's all right for officials to make mistakes and correct them, but it's not all right for Mourning to protest those mistakes.

Madden also called a technical foul on Johnson for complaining over a traveling call. If Johnson walked on that play, then there are 400 uncalled walks in every NBA game.

But the call that most perturbed the Hornets was the one never made. After the Hornets cut the Hawks' lead to five in the fourth quarter, Atlanta reserve point guard Steve Henson clearly held Muggsy Bogues to keep him from retrieving a loose ball on a big play.

"One ref said he was out of position," said Bogues. "I thought (Henson) grabbed me, myself."

Many Charlotte fans have this paranoid fear that the NBA is out to get them, or at least to protect more established teams like the Bulls or the Knicks. It's a silly thought, like when a parent thinks a newspaper intentionally misspells his child's name in a story about a high-school football game. But incompetent officiating like what was on display in the game against the Hawks feeds such paranoia.

Bristow's urgency was obvious through two walls during halftime of a home game against the Sixers. Two feet of concrete couldn't contain Bristow's hollering after his team sleep-walked through the first half. In the second half, Bristow applied full-court pressure virtually every Philadelphia possession, a tactic that would be considered heresy by most NBA coaches.

The Hornets shout out "55" as a signal to go full-court pressure, usually just off the other team's free throws. The signal "55" was a virtual chant in this game, as the Hornets came back from 13 down to win 120-101.

"We've never pressed like that. Never!" said Hornets guard Kendall Gill. "We pressed off every timeout, after every turnover, after every missed shot. Everything. I think it really rattled them."

"We didn't overexert ourselves. We weren't just running around gambling, we had a purpose," Bogues added. "If you made a mistake, someone was always there to cover for you."

It was bold, but far short of reckless. Bristow knew from previous games that the Sixers guards were nothing special at breaking pressure. Injuries had robbed Johnny Dawkins of his quickness and made him an easy target for Bogues and Gill.

Finally, nearly two months after the All-Star game, Johnson would have his chance for revenge. The Knicks and Pat Riley were coming to Charlotte.

Johnson had scored 34 against the Sixers, two short of his career high. So he merely had to double that performance, plus 12 points, to make good on his promise to score 80 against the Knicks.

Most athletes try to play down old threats when they actually have to make good on them. To Johnson's credit, he didn't hide his smoldering anger when reminded what he'd said in Salt Lake City.

"There's still a bad taste there," Johnson said following the Sixers game.

Bristow was fanning the controversy, taking snide jabs at Riley. "I don't know if we can afford to give Larry 14 minutes against Riley," Bristow said. "Pat hasn't seen him play more than 14."

Actually, it was 16, but the point was obvious — Bristow also resented Riley forgetting about Johnson in the All-Star game.

"There's got to be a little extra time for the starters," Bristow said. "They're voted in by the fans, and they're the ones with the TVs turned on."

Besides, if Bristow could light a fire under Johnson, it could only help against a team of the Knicks' stature.

"If it were reversed — if we were the Knicks, the team on top — maybe I'd want to calm this down," Bristow said.

In truth, Bristow enjoyed giving Riley heat whenever the opportunity arose. There are two coaches Bristow has little use for — Riley and another former Knicks coach, Rick Pitino. Bristow thinks they are both arrogant know-it-alls. Pitino's autobiography is called "Born to Coach," which says much about the high opinion Pitino has of himself.

Bristow respected Riley for the way he changed his style to match New York's personnel. Riley's Lakers ran in Los Angeles, while the Knicks were better suited to a grind-it-out, methodical game. But Bristow thought Riley went too far, turning the Knicks into a street gang. He once said he was "disgusted" by the brutish way the Knicks approached defense in the previous season's playoffs.

Bristow also resented Riley for comments Riley made years ago about Doug Moe's passing game. Riley looked down on the passing game as striving for mediocrity, a system that would never allow a team to be great.

Needless to say, Bristow took great pleasure in beating the Knicks. He wouldn't experience that pleasure in April. New York won at Charlotte, 111-107.

The Hornets played well — Kendall Gill was correct in saying his team would have beaten two-thirds of the league with this effort — but it was the same old story against the Knicks. First Patrick Ewing got Alonzo Mourning in foul trouble, then he posted up Kenny Gattison for 17 points in the fourth quarter. Riley would complain late in the season that Ewing deserved more consideration for league most valuable player. On nights like these, it was hard to argue with Riley's point.

Johnson scored 22, just 58 short of his goal, which gave the Knicks the opportunity to crow. Charles Oakley, the Knicks' tough-guy power forward, had said before the game, "Eighty? Maybe 80 stitches."

Afterward, Oakley lectured Johnson through the media on the dangers of pre-game promises.

"You've got to know what you're saying and who you're playing," Oakley told a circle of reporters. "He must have been talking about 80 over the four games," against the Knicks.

The loss placed the Hornets' playoff chances back in jeopardy. Orlando and Indiana had both won, so Charlotte's lead over those two teams fell to just a half-game. If the Hornets finished in a three-way tie with the Pacers and Pistons for seventh place, they would miss the playoffs.

The weekend looked decisive. The Hornets would play the Pistons at home Friday night, then play at Atlanta Saturday. If they split those games, they were alive. A sweep would all but lock up a playoff berth. Losing both games would leave the Hornets effectively in ninth place in the East, in grave danger of missing the playoffs.

Mourning's foul troubles against the Knicks showed how quickly the Hornets could fall apart with him on the bench. So Bill Laimbeer's arrival in Charlotte was cause for concern. He had agitated Mourning into one ejection, then tried to re-fracture Mourning's thumb in another game. Even now back as a starter, Laimbeer would gladly sacrifice himself for a game if that also got Mourning ejected.

"We have to remind Zo a little bit — Laimbeer will be trying to do something to get Zo out of the game," Gill said. "I will remind Zo before the game."

Laimbeer and Mourning passed each other the morning of the game. The Pistons were arriving for shootaround just as Mourning was leaving the Coliseum. They stared down each other like heavyweights before a title fight. Laimbeer liked it that way.

"He's still intimidated by me," Laimbeer told Larry Tait, who coordinates traffic and parking behind the Coliseum.

"Everyone in this town hates me," Laimbeer said, drawing quick agreement from Tait.

"I'm gonna come in here and kick Hugo (the Hornets' mascot) into the third row. . . . Then I'll walk out of here with a Honey Bee under each arm."

Promises, promises. Laimbeer's evening wasn't nearly as interesting as he predicted. Mourning totaled 36 points and a career-high 22 rebounds before leaving the game with nearly seven minutes left and the Hornets ahead by 28.

Laimbeer, who had just been fined $12,000 for fighting with Chicago's Scott Williams, looked ancient trying to guard Mourning.

"They had a lot more intensity than we did," Laimbeer admitted before leaving the Coliseum.

No Honey Bees were in sight as Laimbeer boarded the Pistons' bus, and Hugo left the game with no sneaker marks on his stinger. Detroit would miss the NBA playoffs for the first time in 10 years.

The Hornets knew the importance of this victory. Larry Johnson pulled on a baseball cap after the game, labeled "1993 NBA Playoffs." Message received; he didn't have to say a word.

After the Detroit game, Bristow actually talked of the Hornets still chasing the fifth seeding. It sounded wacky — before this victory the Hornets were in real danger of not making the playoffs at all.

However, fifth-place New Jersey was playing its worst basketball of the season. What had been a seven-game gap between the seventh-place Hornets and the Nets had dwindled to two games with four left to play. If the Hornets did end up tying the Nets' record, Charlotte would win the tiebreaker through a superior record against Eastern Conference opponents.

However, the Hawks still led the Hornets by a half-game.

The Atlanta game took care of that. The Hawks lost their third straight overall, 110-107 to the Hornets, allowing Charlotte to jump into sixth place. Muggsy Bogues, who hit four free throws over the last 13 seconds to win it, knew the Nets were catchable.

"That's how close it is," Bogues said. "We gave teams an opportunity to catch us, and now other teams are giving us a chance to catch them."

The difference between the sixth and fifth seeds was a huge one for the Hornets. As a sixth seed, Charlotte would play Cleveland in the first round. They had no realistic chance of beating the Cavaliers. In fact some Hornets thought they would be better off playing higher-seeded Chicago or New York. The fifth seed meant playing the fourth-seeded Boston Celtics. True, the Celtics won three of four against the Hornets, but every Charlotte player knew they had a chance against Boston.

"Boston isn't quite as good as New York or Chicago or Cleveland," said Kenny Gattison. "The five spot would be nice."

To get there, the Hornets needed some help from the Nets' remaining opponents. They nearly got a huge boost from the Washington Bullets, who led the Nets by 23 points the same night the Hornets were beating the Hawks.

The Hawks are owned by Ted Turner, whose cable television empire includes CNN and TNT. So monitors along the scorer's table at the Omni can pick up games from other NBA cities off a satellite dish. Charlotte beat writers watched as the Bullets collapsed, letting the Nets back in the game. Former Hornet Rex Chapman missed consecutive free throws late for the Bullets, and the Nets won 104-103, their first victory in eight games.

Screwed again by Rex, more than one Hornets official thought.

Had the Nets' lead over the Hornets dropped to a game, this was a realistic chase. Now, the Hornets probably had to win all three of their remaining games to catch New Jersey. That would include beating the Bulls in Charlotte, and that seemed far-fetched. After all, the two-time NBA champions were still in a fight with the Knicks for the best record in the Eastern Conference.

The strange thing was that the Nets probably preferred to finish sixth so they could face Cleveland. Though the Cavaliers are a better team than the Celtics, New Jersey matches up better with Cleveland. Other than Petrovic, the Nets were poor shooters. But they were big and tough with Derrick Coleman, Sam Bowie and Chris Dudley. The soft Cavaliers let the Nets push them around.

Meanwhile, the Hornets' quick, young legs exploited the advancing age of Celtics Robert Parish and Kevin McHale. The Hornets wanted the Celtics.

First things first, though. Technically, the Hornets still hadn't clinched a playoff spot. A home victory over the Milwaukee

Bucks, combined with an Orlando loss in Boston, would clinch at least eighth place for Charlotte.

The Hornets were surprisingly subdued approaching this game. Perhaps they still brooded over the fans' reaction when they struggled in March. Or perhaps they were just relieved to stop answering questions about whether they would make the playoffs or spend another off-season in the lottery.

"Our fans are probably more excited than we are," said Kendall Gill. "We just want to get the playoffs started."

Or as Gattison put it, "It will be more a sense of relief than a wild whoop and holler. For a while it was one day in (the top eight), one day out. Now we've pretty much settled things. In our minds, we're in the playoffs."

Of course, neither Gill nor Gattison were there five years ago, when the Hornets were so awful their first season. Muggsy Bogues and Dell Curry were probably the most happy, and they deserved to be. They had survived all five seasons to reach this accomplishment.

"The worst part was going home in May," Bogues said of the four seasons without the playoffs.

For Bristow, this was a relief almost beyond description. *Almost* beyond description.

"I'll probably have my first bowel movement in a month," said Bristow, admitting what the press corps always suspected, that he was as anal-retentive as they come.

The Hornets had to feel good about their chances in this game — they were 14-1 against the teams already eliminated from playoff contention. Of course, their one loss to those league dredges was to the Bucks in Milwaukee.

But this was at home, and the Hornets were playing their best basketball of the season. Johnson had recovered from his slump, and had survived a grueling season. He played the most minutes — 3,328 — in the league the 1992-93 season. Partially, that was because he was so good, but also it was because the Hornets' margin for error was so small.

"Sometimes I want to give Larry a blow, and just can't," Bristow said. "The better the team gets, the more we'll be able to rest these guys."

Johnson knew all about that tiny margin for error. He once said he didn't feel comfortable on this team unless the Hornets were ahead by 30 with two minutes left.

Owner George Shinn took no chances. He wore the lucky teal and purple tie he wore five years ago at the team's first game. Not that the tie had helped much that night, when the Hornets lost by 40 to Cleveland at home.

Initially, the Hornets played tight against the Bucks. Charlotte's first eight possessions amounted to six misses, a turnover and one basket. But the tension didn't last long. The Hornets outscored the Bucks 20-10 in the first six minutes of the second half to build a 19-point lead. Meanwhile, the Celtics were pounding the Magic in Boston, 126-98. It was no longer *if* the Hornets would start the playoffs, but where.

And Johnny Newman made good on his prediction; his experience *was* crucial to the playoff run. When the other Hornets played tight in the first quarter, Newman took charge. He scored a season-high 30 points in the victory. Apparently Newman's "play me or trade me" demand was now ancient history.

All the talk of a sedate reaction to making the playoffs was also forgotten. The players were downright giddy. They all pulled on those playoff baseball caps, like the one Johnson wore after the Detroit game. The team handed out teal and purple T-shirts, commemorating the event, to all the players, who happily changed jerseys. Johnson and Newman ran back out on the court to line-dance with the Honey Bees.

Shinn cried. Long before the franchise's first game, Shinn publicly set a goal of making the playoffs in five seasons. When that guy rode the billboard just looking for two victories in a row midway through the fourth season, Shinn's prediction looked pretty lame. Now just the opposite was true.

"Somebody said I was a prophet. That's B.S.," Shinn said. "I just did a little research. We were modeling ourselves after Dallas. The Mavericks were the latest expansion team and it took them five years to reach the playoffs. I felt like we were as good as Dallas was. So I said five years was the goal."

Perhaps not coincidentally, this was also the last season before the Hornets would likely compete with the NFL for the Charlotte market. The Richardson family was about to launch a season-ticket drive that would determine whether Charlotte would get an expansion team in football. The Richardsons used the Hornets' success to convince the NFL of the Carolinas' potential, and hired Max Muhleman, who engineered Shinn's own expansion campaign, to lobby the NFL.

No one in the current Hornets regime would publicly admit it, but reaching the playoffs this season was important in what could be a future war for ticket and advertising revenue between the Hornets and the Richardsons' proposed team, the Panthers.

The Hornets wanted to be well established in the town's psyche before the NFL showed up. Former Hornets general manager Carl Scheer, who once competed with Bronco-mania in Denver, harped on that point in the team's first two seasons.

There was no competing with the Hornets on this night. As Johnson and Newman danced with the cheerleaders, the players owned the town.

In fact, the team was so much the center of attention that Bristow decided to skip town. Right after the Bucks game, he announced that the team would practice in Boone the following week in preparation for the playoffs. He said he wanted to escape the "hoopla" in Charlotte by traveling two hours into the Blue Ridge Mountains to the campus of Appalachian State. If "hoopla" meant media, Bristow was out of luck, because newspapers and television stations would go wherever the team did. Possibly, though he never admitted it, Bristow wanted to defuse the possibility of Shinn inviting the Chamber of Commerce or some such body to practice every day.

Shinn's excitement gets the best of him this way. Dick Harter used to schedule practices through the noon hour specifically so that Shinn couldn't schedule the players for constant speaking appearances at Rotary Club luncheons.

The players were livid at the thought of busing two hours into the mountains for three days of practice. First off, the players hate the gym at Appalachian State. The team had held training camp there for two years and several players complained one of the two floors was so hard it made their knees and ankles sore. Bristow thought that was ridiculous, but in fact all you had to do was walk on that court to tell it had no give — the wood was laid right on the cement underneath.

Also most players wanted to spend the few days between the season-ender and the playoffs with their families.

One player summed up the team's reaction to Boone as he left the Coliseum following the Bucks game. "Fuck Allan," the player said matter-of-factly.

Actually, Bristow admitted his real agenda the first day in Boone. He wanted to eliminate what Bristow calls the "Honey-dew factor" — as in "Honey, do this... Honey, do that." In other words, Bristow wanted to make sure his players' minds were on basketball, not on their wives and kids.

TNT chose at the last minute to air the Hornets-Bulls game on national cable. It was the last regular-season home game, which is always a big event in Charlotte. The Hornets hold an elaborate fan appreciation night that includes giving a new home to a season-ticket holder. They chose the winner at halftime by blindfolding 10 or so fans and having them search out a large cardboard-and-tin foil key left somewhere on the basketball court. The first one to touch the key with any body part won the house. Finally, one fan started barrel-rolling his body along the court until he touched the key.

The key search was hilarious, and would have been the highlight most nights. Only this wasn't most nights.

On this night, the Hornets beat the Bulls 104-103.

Michael Jordan was great, as expected, scoring 38 points. But Larry Johnson made the difference, scoring five points in the last 48 seconds. Johnson drove past Bulls point guard B.J. Armstrong, picked up a foul, and threw up a shot, as all NBA players do to get to the foul line. The difference was Johnson's off-balance scoop shot fell through, then Johnson made a free throw for a 102-101 lead.

"That was designed in the two seconds I was going up," Johnson said. "As soon as I felt the contact, I put it up."

"Your good players make shots like that," Jordan said. "And I've never doubted he was a good player."

Jordan answered by hitting a 17-footer with 17 seconds left to put the Bulls back ahead by one. Again, the Hornets isolated Johnson, who drove and drew a foul from Darrell Walker with 2.9 seconds left. The shot missed, so Johnson went to the foul line for two free throws.

"For a split-second I said, 'What if I miss these?'"Johnson recalled later.

No way. He swished both, giving the Bulls possession at midcourt.

The Hornets beat the Bulls on national television Charlotte's first season when Kurt Rambis made a miracle tip-in at the buzzer. Would this be the cosmic give-back? Would Jordan make a prayer? Would he draw a shooting foul?

The Hornets had a foul to give before they would enter the penalty situation. Surely the Bulls would get the ball to Jordan. Perhaps the wise move was to foul Jordan before he ever got a shot off. That would kill some clock, and force the Bulls to again inbound the ball.

Bristow decided against that strategy. He had too much respect for Jordan's ability to get off a shot when feeling the foul in order to get to the line.

Instead, Bristow placed Alonzo Mourning on the sideline to defend Scottie Pippen's inbounds pass. Mourning used his 7-foot, 6-inch wingspan to force a lob pass out of Pippen. Dell Curry jumped in front of Jordan, grabbed away the looping pass, and the final buzzer sounded. "It felt like a playoff game," Jordan concluded.

It essentially was, as far as the Hornets were concerned. The victory, combined with a loss by New Jersey and a victory by Atlanta, created a three-way tie for fifth place in the Eastern Conference. The Hornets would win a head-to-head tiebreaker with the Nets, but would finish last in a three-way tiebreaker with the Hawks and the Nets. So the Hornets had to win at Milwaukee and Atlanta had to lose at Orlando the next night for Charlotte to reach the fifth seed.

The way the Hornets' momentum was building, anything seemed possible.

"I think we sent a message to the league that we're a legitimate team by beating the Bulls," said Kendall Gill. "It means we're right there. We're playing the best ball we've ever played. We're peaking at the right time."

The world outside Charlotte took notice. "Sport Reporters," ESPN's Sunday morning talk show with prominent sports columnists, was dominated by talk of the Hornets. Mike Lupica, the *New York Daily News's* normally acerbic voice, said the Hornets-Bulls game was as gripping as any he'd seen this season. Bill Rhoden of the *New York Times* said Charlotte was clearly the most appealing darkhorse of the playoffs.

The trip to Milwaukee was challenging for several reasons. First, the Hornets were exhausted both mentally and physically from the victory the night before over the Bulls. Second, Milwaukee was overrun with middle-aged housewives hawking make-up. A Mary Kay Cosmetics convention had taken over every downtown hotel.

And third, the Bucks had chosen this game to retire the jersey of Kareem Abdul-Jabbar.

Abdul-Jabbar played four seasons in Milwaukee before demanding a trade to a bigger market (maybe Kareem was the one telling Gill to leave Charlotte). Abdul-Jabbar had his best years as a Laker, but the Bucks won their sole NBA title with Kareem, so it was appropriate to retire his jersey. Unfortunately, the Hornets had to wait out the ceremony.

Because Milwaukee is in the Midwest time zone, the game was already scheduled for 9 p.m. EDT. The Bucks had warned the Hornets that the game would probably not start until closer to 9:30. Even that was wishful thinking. The parade of speeches pushed tip-off closer to 9:45.

It was a hurry-up-and-wait scene straight out of army basic training. Both teams warmed up. Then the Hornets returned to the locker room, while the Bucks sat at courtside during the ceremony. Then, both teams warmed up again, trying to keep their minds on a basketball game.

The game's result was of no consequence to the Bucks; they were eliminated from playoff contention weeks ago. But to the Hornets, the wait was akin to the Chinese Water Torture.

The Charlotte media in Milwaukee — three beat reporters, plus the radio and television crews — monitored the Atlanta-Orlando game as best they could. John Delong of the *Winston-Salem Journal* had family in central Florida, so he made several phone calls for score updates. As the players assembled at their benches for introductions, Delong made one final call, learning that the Magic led the Hawks by 16 late in the fourth quarter. The Hawks were cooked; the Hornets needed only to beat the Bucks to reach the fifth seed.

A reporter passed the score on to Bristow, and his reaction was a strange one. He told the beat writers not to tell the players anything about Orlando-Atlanta. Apparently, Bristow didn't want the team distracted, but that was a pipe dream. Every arena in the NBA flashes scores from other games on the message boards. It was only a matter of minutes before the players would see Atlanta had lost.

Bristow was right about one thing — there was a letdown. Charlotte trailed by 13 points in the first half. The fatigue had robbed the Hornets of their rebounding — Milwaukee had 12 offensive rebounds in the first quarter, while the Hornets had one.

As in the Hornets' previous trip to Milwaukee, rookie guard Jon Barry gave Kendall Gill problems. The son of hall-of-famer Rick Barry, Jon had his dad's jump shot and his surly attitude. After hitting a 20-footer in the first half for a 50-38 lead, Barry fouled Gill at the other end. Barry ripped into veteran NBA referee Jess Kersey for the call, and the Hornets coaches lobbied for a technical foul against Barry.

"If it had been his father, he would've gotten one," Kersey later joked with Bristow.

Kersey lost his sense of humor at the end of the first half, when Johnny Newman complained that he'd been fouled but there was no call. After Newman stared him down for several seconds, Kersey screamed at Newman, "Turn your head or you'll start the second half with a T!"

Assistant coach Bill Hanzlik jumped to the rescue. He rushed between Newman and Kersey, and spread his coat wide enough that Kersey and Newman couldn't look at each other. Hanzlik looked like an amateur magician frantically searching for a rabbit in his pocket, but the stunt ended the confrontation.

A 10-3 run early in the second half gave the Hornets a 65-61 lead. But the Bucks came back with a 6-0 run for a 67-65 edge. Maybe the Bucks were loose and carefree. Or maybe they wanted to impress Kareem. In any case, it was obvious Milwaukee wasn't going to give up and hand the Hornets that fifth seeding.

The Hornets seemingly had the thing won with 13 seconds left when Johnson hit two free throws for a three-point lead. But Bucks forward Brad Lohaus hit a three-pointer from the corner to tie it with 9.7 seconds left. The Hornets can't say they weren't warned. Lohaus banked in a three-pointer the previous season to send into overtime a game in which Milwaukee defeated Charlotte.

The Hornets needed a quick basket, and had already lost their best ballhandler, Muggsy Bogues. Bogues pulled a groin muscle while changing direction earlier in the game. The injury was serious enough that the Hornets didn't know initially if Bogues would recover in time for the playoffs.

That left Gill as the point guard, and he wasn't looking to pass. With just under three seconds left, Gill split two defenders for a finger-roll layup and the winning points. Milwaukee didn't have a timeout, and could get only a desperate heave from half-court by Lee Mayberry that fell short.

The Hornets would face the Celtics in a four-versus-five first-round series. They would be in the same side of the bracket with the top-seeded Knicks.

"I'm really glad we're in New York's draw," Bristow said with fire in his eyes.

The meaning was clear; Bristow wanted another shot at Pat Riley.

CHAPTER SIXTEEN

"They've got the slowest front line in the history of the game!"

Fifteen months before his team's first playoff experience, owner George Shinn had daydreamed about a post-season series against the Boston Celtics. "Can you imagine that? This city is going to go zonkers," Shinn had said, and indeed it did.

The Hornets were guaranteed only one home game in the series since it was best of five, and the first two games were in Boston. The 2,000 or so playoff tickets still available for Game 3 after season-ticket holders got their share sold out in 14 minutes. It took that long only because of the time involved in processing orders on Ticketmaster's computers around the Carolinas.

Anticipation matched that for a Springsteen concert. Charlotteans jumped in their cars and drove to Raleigh or Spartanburg in search of deserted ticket outlets so they could be first in line when the doors opened at 10 a.m.. The margin for error was tiny. End up 10th in line at some record store when the tickets went on sale, and you could end up shut out.

It was history. You wanted to tell your grandchildren you were in Charlotte Coliseum the night the Hornets hosted their first home playoff game. And it was salvation, too. Finally, the Hornets were no longer an expansion team. No longer could the Stacey Kings of the world say they took down the Hornets' diapers and spanked them.

And the enthusiasm for the Hornets spread beyond the Carolinas. They were already the second most popular logo in the NBA, based on merchandising. The league wouldn't reveal the figures, but they confirmed the obvious; the Hornets were right behind the Chicago Bulls in sales. Now there were talented young faces — Johnson, Mourning, Gill — to wear the teal and purple pin stripes designed by clothier Alexander Julian. Johnson's No. 2 jersey (he picked the number because college coach Jerry Tarkanian once wore it) was second only to Michael Jordan's in replica sales.

TNT and NBC picked up immediately on the enthusiasm. The two networks announced the first two games of the Boston-Charlotte series would be nationally televised. As it played out, every Hornets playoff game ended up on national television. Including the regular-season victory over the Bulls, 10 of the team's last 11 games could be seen coast to coast.

Normally television networks cringe when a major league's better teams are in smaller markets. A Chicago-Los Angeles final naturally draws better ratings than a Portland-Indiana series would. There's a running joke around the NBA that if the Utah Jazz ever makes the finals, NBC will return to showing the games tape-delayed at 11:30 p.m., as CBS once did more than a decade ago.

But there was a charisma about the Hornets that tran-scended their relatively small market. Walk through any shop-ping mall in the country and you'll see three or four kids dressed in Hornets T-shirts or jackets or caps. The marketers say teal is second only to black as the hot color among kids in the '90s. How else can you explain why the expansion San Jose Sharks, a dreadful hockey team, sell so much teal-and-black merchandise?

"I think we're a team people just get into," Bristow said after the season's conclusion. "It's a new team and people love the colors."

Even Hugo, the Hornets' pudgy insect mascot, has a big following. Dick Harter was amazed the first season when he'd make appearances with the mascot how that fuzzy bug would get mobbed.

By contrast, Bostonians treated a Hornets-Celtics series with a collective yawn. It wasn't overconfidence on display around New England. Quite the opposite. The Celtics were just good, not great, and their fans have become spoiled by those 16 championship banners hanging in Boston Garden. The sense around Boston was that the Hornets had a good chance to beat the Celtics, so the home team wasn't worth following. It was spring, after all, and the Red Sox had briefly flirted with first place in the American League East. The Sox own Boston, though they have done little but disappoint the most loyal baseball fans east of Chicago's Cubs.

In the fall, when the Celtics fell to last place in the Atlantic Division with a 4-8 start, fans often called Boston radio shows suggesting the home team sit down veterans Robert Parish and Kevin McHale, play the young prospects extensively, and essentially tank the rest of the season in search of the lottery.

The Celtics hadn't had a top 10 pick since Len Bias in 1986, and that ended in tragedy. Bias died of cocaine poisoning one day after the Celtics drafted him with the No. 2 overall pick. Bias, a Maryland forward of exceptional strength and grace, had been cast as Larry Bird's heir apparent. Some around the league took private pleasure in the tragedy because for once the Celtics looked like fools for not discovering Bias' drug use before drafting him. To those people, this was an overdue cosmic payback for years of arrogance. The Celtics were, after all, the Notre Dame of the NBA.

Since Bias's death, the Celtics had made over their management team, hiring Big East commissioner and one-time Olympic coach Dave Gavitt as CEO. Considering they were bottom-fishing every draft since '86, the Celtics did a decent job of finding Reggie Lewis and Dee Brown late in two first rounds. Brian Shaw and Rick Fox were just fair picks. Michael Smith, a total bust drafted in 1989, was in part responsible for the shakeup that brought in Gavitt.

Bird had retired the previous summer, and it was the worst-kept secret in the league that McHale would retire at the end of this season. Charlotte and Boston were passing each other in opposite directions — the Hornets on the upswing, the Celtics sliding down.

"We didn't want to see them," Gavitt said of the pairing with the Hornets. "We didn't want to see them at all!"

Despite all the player complaints over packing off to Boone, the mini-camp was a wise move. The coaches had easy access to the players for meetings between two-a-day practices. There was more videotape study than during the regular season,·

and coaches used the light workout in the morning to clean up little things, like inbounds plays, that grew stale through 82 games. The simple change in geography was refreshing. The setting told the players this was a new season. The fresh, brisk mountain air was invigorating. Bristow and Dell Curry, both lovers of the outdoors, even talked of getting up early to go fishing nearby.

Actually, more than half the NBA's playoff teams leave town for similar mini-camps. The Phoenix Suns went to a secluded Arizona mining town to practice at a small college. The Knicks flew to scenic Charleston, South Carolina, where they also hold preseason camp.

The writers, aware of Bristow's dislike of Riley, needled him one day by suggesting the trip to Boone was just stealing a Riley idea. Bristow said the difference was the Hornets trained in the mountains, not the shore.

"We save the beach for the summertime," Bristow said with a smirk.

It wouldn't be the last snide remark Bristow would direct at Riley and his Knicks.

The team bused back to Charlotte Wednesday, just in time for a pep rally at a shopping mall. Bristow said the crowd looked like Woodstock (and what did Bristow know about sex and drugs and rock-and-roll?). Actually, the crowd wasn't nearly that large. About 5,000 showed up, but they were more representative of the team's fans than the collection of yuppies at home games. Black, white, rich, poor, young, old; they all mingled in a parking lot to send the Hornets off on their mission. The rally wasn't for the players, but rather for the fans. It was a celebration of their love for the team.

By the time the Hornets arrived in Boston for Thursday's game, the all-sports radio station there (conveniently owned by the Celtics) was spewing out all sorts of crazy propaganda. Suddenly, the Hornets were just a notch below the Bulls, a basketball machine that threatened the very existence of the beloved, old Celtics. It had been a long time since the Celtics could call themselves underdogs. The locals were enjoying this.

Of course the fact that the Celtics beat the Hornets three of four times this season was never brought up. Finally, a Charlottean on business in Boston called the station with a reality check. He reminded listeners that just three weeks earlier the Hornets were a single game better than ninth place in the Eastern Conference.

The caller was surprised to learn Bostonians assumed the Hornets would win the series. He was downright shocked when told over the air that tickets to playoff games in Boston were still available in all price categories.

Think about that — 23,000-plus tickets sold out in Charlotte 14 minutes after the last 2,000 went on sale. Meanwhile, the Celtics were still hawking some of the 14,890 seats available at Boston Garden on game day.

If comparative fan interest counted for anything, maybe the Celtics really were the underdogs.

It seemed so far-fetched that the Hornets would play the Celtics that by the time the team arranged for rooms, their usual Boston hotel, the Marriott Long Wharf, was sold out. They opted for the Parker House, a quaint old place near Boston Common park and Paul Revere's burial spot. Now owned by the Omni chain, Parker House was built back in 1855 and was a pleasant departure from the cookie-cutter chain hotels where teams usually stay.

"We're wondering when (Thomas) Edison invented the light bulb, whether they had to wire the building after it was built," Hornets president Spencer Stolpen noted.

To the Hornets, Parker House was still far more modern than the Boston Garden — a seedy, antiquated building destined for demolition as soon as its replacement is finished. Six months after the circus leaves town, the Garden still wreaks of elephant waste. The parquet floor, which looks so good on television, is full of dead spots and divots where the boards meet.

Thirteen-year veteran Mike Gminski, the closest thing the Hornets have to a league historian, loves talking about those dead spots. He has seen point guards dribble through them so that the ball stops and the guard keeps right on going — like the Coyote careening off a cliff in some Road Runner cartoon. Gminski also remembers when the visitors' locker room at Boston Garden had a single shower head. It's nicer now, but no more than the league mandates.

The only thing visiting players like about the Garden is the soft, old rims, the most forgiving in the league. They must be made of sponge cake. They make an entirely different sound than rims anywhere else, perhaps because the backboard supports at the Garden are also ancient. Any shots touching those rims have a great chance of falling through.

The Celtics blame the Garden for all the problems visiting teams have. Funny, though, the home team's locker room is comfortable, spacious, and never overheats around playoff time. Windows with a Western exposure bake the visiting locker room at the Garden. There are no such windows in the home locker room.

"It's a sauna in there," Hornets reserve Kevin Lynch said as he passed from the visiting locker room to the hall leading to the court. "And it's freezing out here."

If that sudden change in temperature leads to a pulled muscle for one of the visiting players, well, just chalk it up to homecourt advantage.

There was reason to believe the series would be determined by the Kendall Gill-Reggie Lewis matchup at shooting guard. Superficially, at least, these were similar players. Both were rangy, young, and possessing all-star potential. But their personalities were complete opposites.

Gill is a cocky extrovert who tells anyone willing to listen he aspires to be one of the league's top five players. Lewis was quiet and hesitant to take charge; his talent vastly exceeded his desire to dominate.

When the Celtics made Lewis captain after Bird's retirement, they seemed to be forcing him to take a special status justified only by his ability. Like Danny Manning, Lewis is more comfortable as the second- or third-best player on his team. He wants to blend in, not give orders. But with Bird gone, and McHale and Parish both nearing retirement, Lewis had to be molded as the team's senior statesman by default. No one else among the younger players had the credentials to take charge.

Meanwhile, Gill had no interest in blending in as third wheel behind Johnson or Mourning. It was apparent throughout the organization, all the way up to owner Shinn, that Gill's ego just couldn't tolerate being third in the pecking order.

"I've just always had a feeling that Kendall is more an individual player than a team player," Shinn would say after the season's conclusion. "He just didn't fit in."

Despite that, Shinn tried to set up a lunch with Gill during the Boston series to discuss Gill staying in Charlotte. Some suspected this was Shinn, the master salesman, looking to close a deal. On the contrary, Shinn just wanted a better reading of Gill's intentions. After all, Gill had sent out so many conflicting signals that it was hard to guess what he really wanted.

Bristow talked Shinn out of pressing that meeting, reminding him that Gill didn't need any distractions at so important a juncture. Similarly, Bristow didn't want Stolpen and Twardzik to negotiate a contract extension for Johnny Newman until after the season. He just thought such talk took the players' minds away from basketball.

If Gill was leaving at the end of the season, he wanted Hornets fans to remember him as an elite player. He hit 19 of his last 35 shots in the regular season, including that game-winner in Milwaukee that set up the series with the Celtics.

"I wanted to show the fans. I didn't want them to forget what kind of player I was," said Gill. "I think some of them did."

Actually, his friends thought Gill was the one in need of a reminder. Before that final Charlotte home game, Michael Jordan told a circle of reporters that Gill should stay a Hornet.

"They've got a good trio in Mourning, Johnson and Gill. And that's not even talking about Newman," Jordan said. "It takes some of the pressure off to be on a team with players like this. You could go to a team where you could be the star and the focus, but that's a load to carry."

Jordan couldn't have been much more blunt without flat-out calling Gill a fool if he leaves:

"I've always believed and still believe if the team is successful, everybody is successful. Even though on our team I got a lot of attention early, when we started winning championships, Scottie (Pippen) got endorsements, Horace (Grant) got them and John Paxson got them. If you lose and you're the top dog, sure you'll get it. But which is better?

"The Hornets have a great opportunity to win. This team is going to be known. If you stay here, you will get the recognition you deserve." Here was Jordan, the player and person Gill idolizes, telling him thoughts of leaving made no sense. Gill said that mattered.

"Of course it does; he's a champion," Gill said. "Anytime it's coming from the greatest player in the world, you have to listen to him.

"Everybody thinks I only care about accolades. That's definitely wrong. I do want to be an all-star, but what everybody fails to realize is my main thing is I want to be on a team that wins."

People who knew Gill all three seasons in Charlotte wanted to believe that. But how then did they explain him wanting to be a Los Angeles Clipper over a Charlotte Hornet?

Though the Celtics won the regular-season series, 3-1, Gill clearly outplayed Lewis. Lewis shot 37% and averaged 16 points against the Hornets. Gill shot 47% and averaged 17.3 points.

Gill and Lewis didn't spend long on the court together. Just 5 1/2 minutes into the game, after Lewis had hit four of his first five shots, he staggered, then fell to the parquet floor. It was a scene out of a prize fight. Lewis' step slowed, as if he was suddenly running through waves. He stopped, his legs wobbling, and fell to the floor nearly limp.

"I didn't see it, but I heard a loud thump as he hit the floor," Gill said. "It was scary. He gave no warning signs it was about to happen."

Newman was closest to Lewis when he collapsed. Newman's expression said horror. Players don't just fall in a heap for no particular reason.

"Yeah, I was scared," Lewis told the *Boston Globe's* Jackie MacMullan later that night. "I started having flashbacks to that Hank Gathers thing."

Gathers, a potential lottery pick, collapsed and died of a heart condition while playing for Loyola-Marymount. The dazed look on Lewis's face matched the expression Gathers had when he collapsed.

Timeout was called and Lewis was helped to the bench. This wasn't the first time he became dizzy on a basketball court. He grew lightheaded in a home game against Miami earlier in the season, but blamed it on some grapefruit juice he drank. Lewis decided the juice had spoiled, causing him to become ill.

Initially, the Celtics decided Lewis had taken an elbow to the head, perhaps from Gill, causing the dizziness. In fact, Celtics publicists went from reporter to reporter, saying Lewis had "his bell rung."

Trouble was, videotape of the game showed no such collision. Celtics team physician, Dr. Arnold Scheller, realized

Lewis had fainted. Lewis said he was fine and could play in the second half. Gavitt wasn't so sure. He asked Scheller if he was positive it was safe to play Lewis. Scheller said he was, speculating that either Lewis' blood sugar was low or he was just excited and hyperventilated.

Lewis started in the second half, and lasted six minutes before teammates noticed he was again wobbling. Coach Chris Ford pulled Lewis, this time for the night. Lewis was admitted to New England Baptist Hospital for a full work-up of tests.

Lewis's absence didn't seem to hurt the Celtics in Game One. Boston continually ran a screen-and-roll play — one of the most basic elements of a pro offense — to score easy baskets. A screen-and-roll is pretty simple. A big man sets a screen to free up a teammate, usually a guard. When the opposing big man comes out to double-team that guard, the screener darts away from the play to catch a pass. If someone else doesn't guard the screener, he has an open jump shot or a route to drive to the basket.

Though every team in the NBA runs some form of the screen-and-roll, the Hornets often looked baffled trying to defend the play. The Indiana Pacers and Atlanta Hawks had made the Hornets look particularly foolish against the screen-and-roll.

The Celtics are well suited for the play. Point guard Sherman Douglas's forte is the look-away pass. Center Robert Parish and power forward Alaa Abdelnaby are both agile enough to score off those passes.

But this was ridiculous. Abdelnaby or Parish would catch the pass, turn and find no teal jerseys blocking off the basket. The Hornets' defensive rotation was pathetic.

"Usually, when you turn around, you have to get by someone," said Abdelnaby. "I'd turn around, and I was wide open."

So many Celtics were wide open that Boston won the first game of the five-game series 112-101.

"Tomorrow, we're going to go back out and relearn how to defend that," said Gill.

Actually, the Hornets were nothing special offensively, either. Larry Johnson was limited to 13 shots — four in the second half — as the Celtics double-teamed him constantly in the lane. That should have opened up the perimeter, but Dell Curry and

Johnny Newman were a combined five of 20 shooting. Shooting 25 percent from the outside is no way to scare the opposition out of a double-team in the lane.

Johnson didn't accept that his offensive limitations were all the Celtics' doing. Once again, he reminded himself to be more assertive in demanding the ball.

"My thing is I mostly tell Muggsy (who had recovered from his groin pull) to get me the ball because he's the point guard. Shoot, like Muggsy told me, I've got to start talking to everybody else, too," Johnson said. "I've got to stop being so polite, saying 'Yeah, let the ball go there. That's OK.' I need to say, 'Hey, fellas, bring the ball here!'

"The burden is on me. I've got to be more aggressive."

Johnson was badly outplayed in the first game by Xavier McDaniel, the Celtics' burly sixth man and the most natural counterpart to Johnson for Boston. McDaniel was making a fuss from the start of the week over Gill's and Gattison's comments that the Hornets were better off playing the Celtics than the alternatives.

"Those guys overlooked us from the start, saying they would rather play us than New York, Chicago, or Cleveland," said McDaniel, who grew up in Columbia, S.C., and apparently had friends who read *The Charlotte Observer*.

"If we beat them, what are they going to say then? They said they wanted us. Now they have us."

McDaniel was playing a silly but effective mind game that has gone on since newspapers started covering sports. Take a quote out of the paper, embellish it into an insult, and use it as incentive. North Carolina coach Dean Smith is a master of this gambit. He once had Tar Heels point guard Jeff Lebo believing a preseason magazine picked North Carolina fifth in the Atlantic Coast Conference. Of course, Smith never said which magazine, because it didn't exist. No preseason publication would stay in business picking the Tar Heels fifth in the ACC because it's preposterous even in the Heels' worst season.

For McDaniel, thinking the Hornets disrespected the Celtics got his engine started. That's his business — more power to him if it helped him perform — but that just wasn't true. The Hornets never said, nor implied, that the Celtics would be easy to beat. They simply stated the obvious — that the Knicks, Bulls or Cavaliers would be far tougher for the Hornets to beat than Boston.

The Hornets' troubles preparing for Game 2 on Saturday afternoon were minor compared to the Celtics' worries over Lewis. There was no easy explanation for his continued dizziness. It was obvious that Lewis would miss Saturday's game. Boston media quickly started wondering whether he would ever play again.

WEEI, the all-sports station owned by the Celtics, has a nighttime host named Jimmy Meyers. He is somewhat of a maverick and a close friend of Lewis's. Friday night, Meyers quoted an unnamed source as saying Lewis' condition appeared to be heart-related. The Celtics would neither confirm nor deny Meyers's reporting. Gavitt emerged from the hospital Friday night around 8 p.m., declining all comment to a Charlotte reporter he'd known for a decade from Gavitt's Big East days. The Celtics were determined to avoid leaks on Lewis's condition.

The Celtics' relationship with the Boston media is not a good one. The Celtics feel the Boston newspapers — the broadsheet *Globe* and the tabloid *Herald* — are overzealous in their efforts to scoop each other. Boston reporters think the Celtics have been unnecessarily evasive in their relations with the media, particularly during Larry Bird's back and foot injuries.

Actually, both perceptions are true, and the situation is occasionally tense. It didn't help any when the Celtics erroneously announced that Lewis suffered a blow to the head to induce his dizziness. It was an honest mistake, but it added to a sense of paranoia among the press.

Gavitt made a brief announcement just before Game 2 that doctors had not yet discovered a cause of Lewis's dizziness and he would remain at New England Baptist Hospital. Dee Brown, a 6-1 guard who could leap like a human slinky, would replace Lewis in the starting lineup.

Though Muggsy Bogues and David Wingate both played high school ball with Lewis at Baltimore Dunbar, Gill might have been the most shaken Hornet. Gill regularly suffered from migraine headaches, and once passed out while sitting in a whirlpool bath. The memory of that experience terrified Gill when he thought of Lewis collapsing.

"I don't think I'd go back out there until I knew what was wrong," said Gill. "Would you?"

Questions such as this were circulating and would grow in volume. Was it appropriate for Scheller to clear Lewis to play in the second half of Game 1 without a complete cardiovascular examination? Upon reflection, the answer was clearly that he should not have.

Kevin McHale is 35, old for a professional basketball player. On that bum ankle, McHale often looked more like 45 this season. For one game, the second of the playoff series against the Hornets, McHale was 25 again.

The fadeaway jumper swished. The jump hook swished. The pump fake baffled whoever guarded him. McHale would end the game with 30 points on 13-of-18 shooting, plus 10 rebounds.

McHale is just six years younger than Bristow. If McHale was dominating, then the younger, quicker Hornets were not running the Celtics hard enough.

"They've got the slowest front line in the history of the game!" Bristow screamed at the Hornets during a timeout. "So run 'em hard.

"We've got to run them! Run 'em and we change the game!"

The Hornets followed Bristow's directions in a 10-0 run to lead 67-61. But instead of wearing down, McHale just grew stronger. He scored 17 of the Celtics' last 30 points in regulation.

Johnson had reversed McDaniel's dominance in Game One, as if the two were engaged in some judo match. McDaniel missed 10 straight shots until finally hitting a 12-footer from the baseline with 25 seconds left in the fourth quarter. Unfortunately, his only made shot tied the game.

The Hornets went to "Dallas" on their last possession (that play was as predictable as rain minutes after you wash your car), and Johnson missed a 12-footer.

That gave the Celtics one last chance at victory in regulation. Boston set up an alley-oop play where McDaniel would throw the inbounds pass above the rim, and Dee Brown would leap to tap it in. McHale's screen to free Brown was excellent and McDaniel's pass was good enough to make the play. But Brown couldn't quite redirect it into the basket, throwing the game into overtime.

This wouldn't be Brown's last chance to win a game with that play.

The last possession of the first overtime was eerily similar to the Hornets' last possession of regulation. Again, Johnson found an open jump shot 12 feet from the basket. Again there were seconds left (2.6, to be precise). Again, Johnson would miss, throwing the game into a second overtime.

Fatigue affects shooting percentages more than any other statistical gauge of basketball. When players lose their speed, they no longer score easily off runaway layups. Also, as legs lose their spring, jump shooters lose their aim. Instead of brushing the back of the rim then nestling in the net, shots start hitting the front of the rim with a sickening "clang."

The second overtime was definitive tired basketball. The Hornets won the tap, and Johnson found himself wide open 20 feet from the basket five seconds later. Why would anyone guard him? First off, he'd missed those two big shots eight feet closer to the basket. Second, McHale had been burned by Johnson in the first overtime, when Johnson drove past him for a reverse layup. So McHale dared Johnson to shoot from the top of the key.

Surprise! Johnson's attempt swished.

They were the Hornets' last points. It was the game's last field goal. It was the difference in a 99-98 Charlotte victory that turned around the series.

The Celtics scored one point off seven possessions in the second overtime, that when McHale made one of two free throws off a foul by Kendall Gill. Boston's other possessions in the second overtime amounted to seven missed shots and a turnover. The Hornets accomplished all this defense with their best defensive player, Mourning, sitting out the last 3:06 of the game.

Mourning fouled out trying to break up one of those screen-and-roll plays that so frustrated the Hornets in Game One. Robert Parish set a screen high in the lane on Muggsy Bogues, and Mourning was determined not to let Sherman Douglas drive by. Unfortunately for Mourning, that meant reaching across Douglas and slapping him in the eyes with his left forearm. Douglas looked like a tailback being clotheslined by a middle linebacker. The referees had to blow their whistles, which gave Mourning his sixth and final foul.

Bogues pleaded with the official to take back his call (Why do players do this? Have you ever seen a referee say, "OK, you didn't really mean to do that. Never mind that last whistle.").

The officials' only response to Bogues was to remind him that if Mourning had five fouls, he should have known better than to do something so blatant. Bogues knew the referees were right, shrugged and prepared to win this game with Gattison instead of Mourning.

"I was on the sideline praying. Praying for a win," Mourning said. "We had worked so hard."

The Hornets didn't score for more than 4 1/2 minutes, but they did accomplish something offensively — they managed to hold the ball for all but six seconds of the last minute. Brown missed a wide-open 20-footer with 54 seconds left to give the Hornets possession. Charlotte didn't score, but it did grab two offensive rebounds to extend the possession to the last three seconds.

The Celtics called timeout, then Rick Fox inbounded the ball. Again Brown ended up with possession, this time outside the three-point line. Again he was wide open. Again he missed. This time the buzzer following Brown's shot gave the Hornets a 1-1 tie of the series.

The Hornets entered the second game with two priorities — stop the screen-and-roll and double-team off Dee Brown. He is a decent player with some versatility and exceptional leaping ability, but Brown is no Reggie Lewis. It certainly showed in Game 2. Brown missed nine of his last 10 shots from the field.

"I got good looks," said Brown. "If I get those looks in Charlotte, I'll take them and I guarantee I'll make them."

Actually, McHale making both his free throws would have been enough to at least give the Celtics another five minutes of overtime.

"I guess if I'd made it, we'd probably have gone 0-0 in the third overtime," McHale said with a laugh.

McHale had nearly retired at the beginning of the season because his body was wearing down so badly. He chose to play through the pain one more season, he said, because his son so enjoyed being one of the Celtics' ballboys. More than an hour after the game, McHale walked his son over to the Hornets' locker room to ask for Johnson's autograph. Johnson barely had enough energy left to scrawl the kid a signature.

"Hey, kid, did you see me educate your dad out there?" Johnson joked, winking at McHale.

Of course, it was McHale who taught the lesson, even if the Hornets had come out on top.

"I've seen him do what he did today since I was a kid," Johnson said. "His game is so ugly. I used to watch him on TV when I was in high school and college, and say, 'Man, they can't stop that? He's big, old, slow. Somebody stop that stuff!'

"But who can stop it? Ain't nobody stopped it yet, so there ain't no reason to think we would today."

No reason at all. Only Kevin McHale's battered legs could stop Kevin McHale.

"It looked like the '80s, didn't it?" Bristow marveled. "If the guy had a new set of knees, he'd still be one of the best big men in the game."

Actually, it was McHale's ankle that was the real problem, but the point was still valid.

The Hornets said goodbye to the Boston Garden, they hoped for the last time this season. No Hornet looked forward to the possibility of a fifth and deciding game back in the Garden. Then again, after beating the Celtics on the parquet floor two out of the past three times, no Hornet feared the Garden mystique, either.

"We're not in awe of that Boston mystique," said Gattison, who broke his nose when McHale hit him with a forearm in Game 1. "We weren't around when Boston was winning championships. Those banners look nice up there, but they don't mean anything to us."

Whichever god watches over the Boston Garden must have heard Gattison's heresy, because the Hornets weren't getting out of there so easily. The charter bus rented to take the team from the Garden to Boston's Logan Airport wouldn't start. The battery was dead, and the bus was wedged into a space in the Garden's bowels where it couldn't be jump-started. Eventually the bus would have to be towed out, and that would take hours.

Exhausted and starving basketball players are not particularly patient in such situations. Stolpen tried to buy a shipping box full of candy from the vendors who were packing up. The vendor wouldn't sell, giving Stolpen some bureaucratic gibberish about taking inventory.

One of the blue-collar types who keep the Garden from crumbling put the entire experience in perspective for Stolpen: "Beat our team here and we fuck up your bus," the laborer joked.

Finally, Stolpen managed to hire two bright-red tourist trolleys to take the players to the airport. Picture it — a $14 million payroll of basketball players touring through the streets of Boston like Gladys and her bridge club up from Cranston, Rhode Island. Stolpen even rang the bell, then had to do some fast talking to convince the airport to allow the trolleys to drive onto the runway and meet the charter flight.

The Celtics had far more serious troubles than a stalled bus, and there was no comic relief in sight. Sunday night, upon arrival in Charlotte, Celtics CEO Dave Gavitt confirmed that doctors had diagnosed a serious heart problem in Lewis. At best, Lewis was done for the season.

Gavitt said the Celtics had assembled a "dream team" of Boston's best cardiologists to determine what was wrong with Lewis. Before Game 3 on Monday, team physician Scheller confirmed that Lewis had a serious heart condition similar to the one that killed Hank Gathers. Scheller acknowledged that Lewis's chances of playing again were not good. He also said the spell that made Lewis collapse had been potentially life-threatening.

It sounded almost like a confession. Scheller was the one who had sent Lewis back out on the court after he initially collapsed. His decision to do so brought to light a long-running, if usually hypothetical debate over the loyalties of a team doctor. Does being employed by the team, rather than the players, in any way influence the judgment of such a physician? And is a man trained primarily in the treatment of joints and bones qualified to make judgments about cardiovascular fitness, as Scheller did when he cleared Lewis to play in the second half of Game 1?

Clearly, Lewis should not have played. And clearly Scheller would not have sent Lewis out there if he thought Lewis' life was in danger. But shouldn't the NBA and all other major leagues take the gray area out of such situations with a simple rule that no player returns to a game after fainting without a complete cardiovascular work-up?

This would not have happened to a Hornet in the Coliseum, because team physician Dr. Glenn Perry is so thorough and conservative in his treatment. That was illustrated when Perry told Mourning and the coaches he would order Mourning to sit out games if his thumb didn't heal quickly in February. The Hornets' agreement with Perry is to keep the players healthy first and foremost, regardless of whether that means they sit. Unfortunately, as the Lewis incident illustrated, not every team doctor is as vigilant.

Lewis was so upset with his treatment that he checked himself out of New England Baptist Hospital, and into another Boston facility, Brigham and Women's. Lewis and his wife complained publicly that they weren't included in meetings to discuss the initial diagnosis. Eventually, doctors at the second hospital made an alternative diagnosis that was dramatically more optimistic. Lewis' new doctor diagnosed that Lewis had a benign nerve problem that would probably allow him to play basketball again.

That diagnosis now appears gravely incorrect. Lewis collapsed and died of cardiac arrest in July while shooting baskets at the Celtics' training facility. An autopsy determined that Lewis' heart was enlarged and badly scarred, both signs of serious heart disease.

Brown demonstrated in Game 2 that he wasn't ready to take over in Lewis's absence. That meant McHale would once again be asked to rediscover his youth for the Celtics to have any chance in two games in Charlotte.

WBT's Matt Pinto asked McHale if he was still up to such a task physically. Little did Pinto know he was about to become straight man for the last great one-liner of McHale's playing career.

"What, did they not have TVs down here in the '80s?" McHale asked, reminding Pinto of McHale's seven all-star game appearances.

Actually, Pinto, who grew up in Boston, knew all about McHale's career. He just doubted McHale could hold up physically. And Pinto was right.

McHale wasn't the only one enjoying a joust with the media. Peter Vecsey had arrived in Charlotte Sunday to interview Bristow for NBC-TV. Bristow had refused to do some phone interviews with Vecsey in the past. This was different. Bristow had to try to be accommodating this time, since NBC had the NBA's primary television contract.

Bristow granting Vecsey an interview amounted to Nixon visiting China. If Bristow doesn't hate Vecsey, then at least there's a profound dislike. And Vecsey's columns suggested he placed Bristow on his short list of league buffoons. Whenever Vecsey grew tired of making Frank Layden fat jokes, he poked a stick at Bristow.

Local reporters and Hornets personnel snickered as Vecsey and Bristow had their little chat. There was talk of a pool to guess how long it would take for one to swing at the other. The interview concluded before the kitty of dollars could be collected.

This wouldn't be the last the Hornets would see of Vecsey. He popped up later in the week to interview Mourning in Charlotte, and held up a team bus. That exhausted whatever diplomacy Bristow could muster. Bristow told NBC's Steve Jones that if Vecsey and Bill Walton continued to take constant cheap shots at coaches on the network's "Insiders" segment, there wouldn't be a coach left willing to grant the network an interview.

In fact, the "Insiders" had become a hatchet factory. The original idea, a good one stolen from the network's NFL coverage, is to have a journalist and an out-of-work player or coach dig up gossipy items — trade rumors, job shakeups and the like — for the pre-game show. *Boston Globe* columnist Will McDonough is ideal in this role on NBC's football coverage.

Vecsey and Walton have stepped beyond that role of mere rumormongers. Now, they fancy themselves as king makers and king breakers. They continuously pass judgment on who can and can't play or coach, and sometimes it gets downright cruel. Of course neither one has coached, but apparently that's immaterial. Their act sells beer and car batteries for NBC's advertisers. Or at least the network believes that.

Charlotte's renewed love affair with the Hornets nearly reached the passion of the first season. Hornets playoff games not on NBC were telecast locally on WJZY, an independent station. The last hour of the station's broadcast of Game 4 would attract 51 percent of the televisions in use in the Charlotte market. That's more than what the Super Bowl draws in Charlotte.

Game 2 — the double-overtime marathon in Boston — essentially shut down the town on a Saturday afternoon. You could drive for a mile down a Charlotte road during the game and see perhaps one other moving car. And you could be confident the driver of that other car was also listening to the game on the radio.

Larry Tait of the Coliseum was one of those few Charlotteans in his car during part of the game. Tait could compare the loneliness to only one other occasion.

"Neil Armstrong — the night Neil Armstrong walked on the moon," Tait said. "That's the only time the roads have been this empty."

The momentum generated by such support magnified the difference in the two teams' ages. The Hornets aspired to wear out the aging, and now short-handed, Celtics. Their younger, quicker bodies were the difference in a shockingly one-sided Game 3.

The Hornets won 119-89. It was probably the most dominant performance in franchise history against a quality opponent. The Hornets continuously stripped the Celtics of the ball, then beat their older counterparts downcourt for breakaway dunks.

"The stat that sums it up is they scored 33 points off 17 (Boston) turnovers. That's pretty efficient," said Celtics forward Alaa Abdelnaby. "I didn't think we were strong with the ball. In the last two games, our turnovers weren't nearly that high."

Only one Celtic, small forward Kevin Gamble, played well, hitting eight of 16 shots for 19 points. But Gamble taking all those shots suggested the Hornets did their job on defense. The three Celtics equipped to beat the Hornets — McHale, Parish, and McDaniel — had 15, 10 and seven points, respectively. The Hornets could live with Gamble as the other team's best player.

The game became so one-sided that the Charlotte crowd mocked Boston's traditional chant. They shouted "Larry! Larry! Larry!" but that wasn't Larry Bird on their lips.

"That wasn't Larry Bird they were chanting for, that was the L-ster!" said Johnson, who hit 10 of 13 shots and went to the foul line 12 times, for 29 points.

Bristow even had the luxury of emptying his bench. All except center Mike Gminski. When the crowd chanted for Gminski to be inserted late in the game, Bristow told the public address announcer to pass on that Gminski was injured.

"Injured" wasn't the precise term.

"I wasn't injured. I was stiff from sitting," Gminski corrected after the game.

If fatigue is the curse of age, then overconfidence is the sin of youth. Victories such as this one over the Celtics traditionally made the Hornets lazy and arrogant. The home loss to Indiana, following the victory at Chicago, was the best example, but there were several others, and Bristow was vigilant in changing his team's approach.

Before the media ever got to the players, Bristow reminded his team how deceiving its 2-1 lead was. Let the Celtics win Game 4, and the series would conclude back in Boston, where momentum would swing dramatically back to the Celtics.

When a television interviewer gushed over the Hornets' dominance during an interview, Larry Johnson refused to take the bait.

"Coach said y'all do this. . . . Coach, they're doing it!' Johnson screamed out in mock horror.

The following day at practice, Bristow trotted out some simple arithmetic to illustrate his point.

"It can't be any closer than it is right now. Somebody has to be up 2-1 or it's over," said Bristow, proving he actually did get some math out of Virginia Tech.

The players digested Bristow's reasoning that there was a real danger in a false sense of security.

"When you beat a team by 30 points, you tend to take them lightly the next time. But not when they're the Boston Celtics and not in the playoffs," said Kenny Gattison.

Bristow wasn't the only coach preaching the dangers of overconfidence. Mourning took a call from his college coach, Georgetown's John Thompson.

"I told Alonzo the Celtics didn't come down here to do but one thing — win one ball game and get back to Boston," Thompson told *The Observer's* Charles Chandler. "I told him that series was far from over."

The town was divided on what would happen. Well, not exactly divided — every fan seemed confident the Hornets would win Game 4 because no Charlottean wanted to face the possibility of a return to Boston. Most thought the Hornets would pull out a close game. A few thought the Hornets just might duplicate the blowout of Game 3. Amazingly enough, both descriptions proved partially accurate.

NBA teams have this little competition for the most excessive pre-game show. The Bulls introduce the players with a swirling strobe light. The Knicks use a laser to project the players' signatures and jersey numbers on the court. The Hornets have Neal and the Rockets.

That isn't a rock group. It's Neal Zarrelli, a local restaurant owner, singing the national anthem, while the Hornets reproduce the rockets' red glare. To traditionalists who come just for the basketball (gee, what a novel idea), the flash pots are abusively loud and amazingly trite. But the show somehow amuses the fans, like those dot races on the overhead scoreboard during timeouts at Chicago Stadium.

Zarrelli, an immigrant from Italy, has a passionate voice made for opera and a love of the Hornets. He started sending them pizzas early in the franchise's history, then got his chance to sing. Zarrelli's track record as a Hornets' luck charm is astounding. Entering Game 4, the team was 11-1 all-time when Zarrelli sang. Like they said in Bull Durham, don't ever mess with a streak. Zarrelli would sing at every home game during the playoffs.

As his voice would rise for "rockets' red glare!" game operations would set off theatrical blasts around the ceiling. Every person in the building knew it was coming, but that didn't matter. The noise and flash were still a little startling. And Stolpen confessed before one game that the staff tried to make the explosions a little louder each game.

Zarrelli's track record looked safe when the Hornets assembled an 11-2 run early in the first quarter for a 31-20 lead. The Hornets had even turned the screen-and-roll trick on the Celtics. Boston overplayed Dell Curry on such a play, and Gattison drove for an easy dunk and a 12-point edge with 10 minutes left in the first half.

Clearly, the Celtics were growing frustrated. Boston point guard Sherman Douglas was charged with a flagrant foul for butting Kendall Gill from behind on a drive to the basket. But the play nearly ended up worse for Charlotte than Boston. Gill ran after Douglas ready to fight, but was intercepted by Mourning, acting in the unlikely role of peacemaker.

Charlotte's lead swelled all the way to 18 late in the third quarter on a three-pointer by Tony Bennett. Yes, rookie Tony Bennett was toying with the Boston Celtics. This had to be too easy.

And it was. No matter how hard the Hornets fought overconfidence entering this game, the ease with which they built an 18-point lead lulled them. With 7 1/2 minutes left, Charlotte led by 14. Reporters started writing about McHale's last game in their "running" stories for early editions. The Hornets' radio network started discussing the matchup with either the Knicks or Pacers in the next round. Only the Celtics thought they could still win this game.

The Hornets shut down offensively, scoring only seven points over seven minutes, and Boston actually led 103-102 with 42 seconds left on Douglas' breakaway layup.

The Hornets ran "Dallas," Johnson's isolation play, on Charlotte's last possession. Johnson missed a 12-footer over McDaniel, but the ball bounced out of bounds off Boston center Robert Parish. That gave Charlotte back possession with 3.3 seconds left.

This time, Bristow set up a play for Dell Curry, who had hit 12 of 17 shots in Game 3. Curry would inbound the ball, then get it back behind a series of screens for an open jump shot. But Parish anticipated the strategy and jumped out at Curry. Left alone, Mourning had the presence to improvise, fading to the top of the key to catch an open pass. Mourning also had the poise to not rush the shot, dribbling once to gather himself before launching the 17-footer that would likely determine the series.

The shot swished with just four-tenths of a second left in the game. Mourning fell backward, spread out on the court, and raised his arms in glorious celebration.

You didn't need a radio receiver to hear Matt Pinto's call of the game, as long as you were within 20 paces of Pinto's voice.

"Good!. . . Good!. . . Good!" Pinto shouted. "Hornets win! Hornets win!"

Of course they hadn't yet, though the game clock showed no time and every Hornet had piled on Mourning at midcourt.

The referees correctly put four-tenths of a second back on the clock. The Celtics had the right to one last possession.

Dee Brown would get his chance at atoning for missing that alley-oop in Game 2. The Celtics ran the same alley-oop play, with the back screen springing Brown to tip in a winning shot. It was Boston's best chance to get off a decent attempt before time expired. All Brown had to do was jump high, and that was his greatest gift.

Again the pass reached Brown's fingertips. Again Brown tipped it toward the basket. But this time Kendall Gill jumped just as high, swatting the ball from its path to the basket. The final horn sounded and no official called a violation or foul on Gill's play. The Hornets were headed to the second round.

And the Celtics were flat-out robbed.

Videotape replay showed Gill flagrantly goal-tended on the play, that the ball was above the rim and on its downward flight when Gill tipped it. Also, Gill hit the rim with his right wrist on the play. And finally, Brown felt contact on the play, suggesting Gill probably also fouled in the process.

"Goal-tending. That's it," said Brown, who later called the officials gutless. "There's no way he could have gotten that shot without goal-tending."

Gill just smirked like a kid who emptied the family cookie jar without being caught. "I can't help it if I can jump just like he can," Gill shrugged.

"That wasn't goal-tending. There's no way that was goal-tending," Bristow argued.

Even when videotape evidence piled up to the contrary (WSOC had a view of the play that clearly showed Gill goal-tended) Bristow wouldn't acknowledge the obvious. Which was rather humorous since there was nothing the league could do after the fact anyway. It was a judgment call, nothing the Celtics could protest. Besides, the league couldn't very well publicly criticize the game's officiating crew, which included chief of officials Darell Garretson.

Celtics management was perplexed. Gavitt and the coaches circled around a television after the game to view a videotape replay of the last sequence. "We'll look at the film, and then we'll agonize over it," Celtics coach Chris Ford said immediately following the game.

The Celtics luck had run out after decades of seemingly getting every close call and robbing other teams in trades. Now, they were approaching the down cycle that every major-league team must experience. Even the legendary Celtics.

Perhaps now all the belly-achers among Charlotte fans would stop whining the Hornets never got a close call at the end of a game.

CHAPTER SEVENTEEN

"Now it's a team you can almost root for."

It should have been obvious, but it still came as a surprise — Bristow was packing the players off to Boone for another mini-camp. All coaches retrace their steps when they have succeeded. It's human nature—not that coaches always act human.

Naturally, the beat writers immediately asked Bristow if he planned to stage junkets to Boone all the way to the Finals if the Hornets kept advancing.

"I don't know how many more times I can trick them onto the bus," Bristow admitted.

These journeys to the mountains were particularly annoying to the players' wives, who hardly saw their husbands this time of year. The wives would package whatever family activities they could into the days they thought their husbands would be in town. Dell Curry coaches his son's tee-ball team, and the league had arranged the schedule so that Curry could be there the night after the Hornets eliminated the Celtics. Instead, Curry was back on a team bus to Boone.

The rewards —million-dollar contracts, four months off in the summer, free sneakers for the kids — are massive. But during the season, being a player with a family can be a real hardship.

Again, the trip to Boone was an unpopular but correct decision. There's no question the players were better focused on the Knicks by staying together in a hotel, studying videotapes and scouting reports, than they would have been back in Charlotte.

The Knicks eliminated the Pacers the night after the Hornets knocked off the Celtics. The Hornets would have enjoyed seeing the Pacers extend that series to the full five games, but a Hornets-Pacers second-round series would have been a logistical nightmare for the Hornets. Time trials for the Indy 500 take over Indianapolis that time of year. There is not a vacant hotel room within a hundred miles of downtown Indianapolis the third week of May.

Hornets trainer Terry Kofler had planned ahead, just in case. Kofler used to be an assistant athletic director at Xavier in Cincinnati, and arranged for the team to lodge and practice there during a possible playoff series with Indiana. The Hornets would have just commuted by plane between Cincy and Indy, flying into Indianapolis for the games, then flying back out for the off days.

In situations such as this, leasing that charter jet was looking like an excellent decision.

Needless to say, Bristow was nearly as pleased about meeting the Knicks in the second round as he was to have eliminated the Celtics. Bristow had contracted coach's disease, that unquenchable thirst for more victories. At the start of the season, Bristow just wanted to make the playoffs as a tangible sign of improvement. He even said a couple of times that if he had a choice between the team growing and not making the playoffs, or not growing but backing into the playoffs, he'd prefer the growth.

But a taste of success made him hunger for more gratification. He wanted to beat that arrogant Riley, or at least give the Knicks a good scare before New York went on to face the Bulls.

It wasn't just Riley that Bristow disliked, it was the Knicks' thug persona. Bristow wasn't a softy (as a player he once had a memorable fight with Larry Bird) but he worried that in recent years the NBA had changed for the worse. For teams such as the current Knicks and their recent predecessors, the Detroit Pistons, defense wasn't so much anticipation and quickness as bullying and intimidation. Flagrant fouls — fouling with intent to injure, to "send a message" to the player driving the lane — was just part of the business to such teams.

This troubled Bristow deeply. He didn't want his sport becoming hockey in short pants. He didn't want the league's image defined by Bill Laimbeer's cheap shots or John Starks's crazed fits of rage. Starks, the Knicks' easily excitable shooting guard, had gotten himself thrown out of a playoff game in Indiana for head-butting Pacers guard Reggie Miller. Miller spent the whole series trash-talking — he is a self-indulgent loudmouth of the first order — but that didn't justify Starks playing caveman. Even Riley agreed with that.

"The fact that I'm sitting here talking about this in a playoff game is ridiculous," Riley had said of Starks' head butt. "That's not what this time is about."

It was a different incident involving the Knicks that set off Bristow. A January brawl between New York and Phoenix, ignited when then-injured New York point guard Greg Anthony jumped off the bench to attack Kevin Johnson, drew the highest total fines in NBA history. After those fines were levied, Bristow lit into what the Knicks had become.

He said he'd been "disgusted" by the brutal way the Knicks played defense against the Bulls in the previous season's play-offs. He added that he thought the league was "sending out a message" to the Knicks with the fines and a five-game suspension of Anthony.

If there was a message sent, it wasn't fully received. Entering the playoff series with Charlotte, Starks had already received three heavy fines — $5,000 for a flagrant foul that broke New Jersey point guard Kenny Anderson's wrist, $7,500 for Starks's part in the Phoenix brawl and $5,000 for head-butting Miller.

The head butt was the Knicks' 21st flagrant foul of the season, easily the most in the league. But Starks wasn't New York's enforcer. Charles Oakley, the one who said "Eighty? Maybe 80 stitches," was the Knicks' nastiest, tough guy.

"They're saying, 'Hey, those guys are fresh meat. Let's rough 'em up a little bit,' " Bristow said of the Knicks' approach to the Hornets. "Anytime a team plays that much half-court offense, it has to be rough. It's like the line of scrimmage in football."

Bristow wasn't alone in his distaste for the Knicks' tactics. New York's most vocal critic was Chicago coach Phil Jackson, who found it particularly ironic that the league scheduled a Knicks-Bulls game for Christmas Day.

"This is a team that wants to decapitate and quarter us," Jackson had said before that game. "Christmas is a family day, a day of peace and love. To mar that day in a game where you have to fight. . . . "

Of course the Knicks claimed their style meant they took more punishment than they dished out. That might have been true in the case of point guard Doc Rivers, who lost a tooth and broke his nose from various collisions this season. "We step in front of people when they drive the lane," Rivers said. "We take charges other people won't."

Rivers would add to his battle scars by the end of this series. Muggsy Bogues would give Rivers a forearm to the brow that would take several stitches to close.

The Hornets didn't seem all that concerned about the Knicks' reputation. Bristow had a theory that his players' quickness made it harder for the Knicks to beat on them. Using Bristow's football analogy, this made considerable sense. The really fleet wide receivers almost never get hit hard because they're darting so fast every blow is a glancing one.

Also, the Hornets believed they had outgrown their previous wimp reputation. Mourning said the Knicks aren't thugs, just tough guys. "We have some tough guys, too," Gattison added. "It's up to them. We can play a nice, clean game or we can get in the trenches and play dirty."

No matter how hard he tried, Mourning couldn't avoid being the center of attention in this series. Contrary to what Mourning told that radio reporter back in Milwaukee, his matchup with Patrick Ewing was Godzilla versus the X-monster — an encounter that made NBC-TV programmers froth at the mouth.

If Georgetown's John Thompson wasn't the best-known college basketball coach in the country, then he was in the top three. To have Thompson's prize pupils matched in the playoffs in Mourning's rookie season was pure Hollywood. Thompson couldn't keep up with all the phone calls from reporters working that angle to advance the series.

Those who did reach Thompson were entertained with tales of summertime wars between Mourning and Ewing at Georgetown's McDonough Gym. How Thompson would have to walk in just to quiet down the hollering. Thompson would attend several games in the series and dine with Mourning and

Ewing on off nights if all three were in the same town. He was clearly enjoying this, as he said, "like an old grandfather." And he had a rooting interest. He said it was Ewing's time, that Mourning was young enough to have many chances at a championship.

With or without Thompson in the teal corner, most Hornets thought they had a fighting chance against the Knicks. Hey, they had won eight of their last nine games and were playing the best basketball in franchise history.

However, the 3-1 series victory over the Celtics was deceiving. Sure, the Hornets won one of those games by 30 points. But they won the other two by one point each with the Celtics' best player, captain Reggie Lewis, out. The Hornets were a better team than the Celtics right now, but only slightly better. The Knicks were on a different plane from both the Hornets and the Celtics this season. That would become apparent quickly.

The various major leagues, plus the NCAA, sell their souls to television networks offering millions in rights fees. NBC and TNT dictate the schedule during the playoffs. They can speed up or slow down the pace of each playoff series to fit their programming needs. That obligation to the networks, combined with some poor communications among league personnel, meant Bristow didn't learn the date for Game 2 until the morning of Game 1.

Sunday morning, just hours before his team opened the series against the Knicks, Bristow was told Game 2 would be Wednesday night. The Hornets would have three off nights to kill in Manhattan, too many for Bristow's liking. There was nothing to be gained in a basketball sense from sticking around New York that long. So Bristow decided to fly the team back to Charlotte immediately following the first game, then fly back to New York Tuesday evening.

It took the Knicks only 68 seconds to knock a Hornets starter out of the game. But this wasn't thuggery at work. Just a simple case of clumsiness.

Larry Johnson and Knicks forward Charles Smith both scrambled for a loose ball about 15 feet from the Knicks' basket. Johnson reached the ball first, stepping in Smith's path, and

Smith's momentum carried him about five feet further than he wished. Smith stumbled, falling heavily on the back of Larry Johnson's right leg just as Johnson started sprinting up-court.

It was obvious immediately that something was very wrong. Johnson curled into a ball on the floor for several seconds until timeout could be called. His leg felt like it was aflame. He feared the shin or ankle had been fractured by the force of Smith's weight and the awkward fall.

"I said a thousand prayers," Johnson later recalled.

Johnson had to be carried off the floor by reserves Mike Gminski and Sidney Green, and was immediately rushed to Beth Israel Hospital. It was the ride of team physician Dr. Glenn Perry's life.

Maneuvering around Manhattan is a chore, even on Sunday afternoon. The ambulance driver, James DeJesus, was a veteran who wasn't hesitant to speed through streets at 50 mph and turn into oncoming traffic.

"You should see what we do in a cardiac arrest situation, Doc," DeJesus told Perry.

"You have one — me!" Perry joked as he watched DeJesus' fly down Manhattan's streets.

Perry told DeJesus that with those driving skills, he belonged in a stock car. DeJesus wondered if Perry had any connections with NASCAR. Sadly, Perry's clout didn't extend to Charlotte Motor Speedway. Imagine the potential sponsorship tie-ins — "James DeJesus, driving the No. 54 Band-Aid/Blue Cross Pontiac."

"Doc told me to be glad I couldn't see," said Johnson, who was strapped to a stretcher.

The X-rays showed no fracture, so Perry asked DeJesus to again use the siren and flashers to get Johnson back to Madison Square Garden quickly. There was a chance that, taped up, Johnson could still play a portion of this game.

Johnson's absence had all sorts of potential ramifications. First off, Bristow had said Johnson had to play well for the Hornets to beat the Knicks. You didn't have to be Columbo to deduce that if Johnson couldn't play, he couldn't play well. But there were tumble-down effects as well. With Kenny Gattison replacing Johnson, Bristow's options off the bench were severely limited. He could no longer "go big" with Gattison, Johnson and Mourning together in the front line, and that was the best countermeasure to the Knicks' tall front line of 7-0 Ewing, 6-10 Smith and 6-9 Oakley.

Smith's size made it difficult for Bristow to play 6-7 Johnny Newman against the Knicks. Newman had played just two minutes as a starter in the last regular-season game against New York because Smith was scoring so easily.

Just the opposite happened in Game 1 — Smith had far more trouble with Newman's quickness than Newman had with giving up three inches in height. In fact, Newman finished with 18 points, six assists and three steals.

Newman recognized the offensive opportunities in Johnson's absence, and scored six points early in the third quarter to give the Hornets a 73-63 lead. The Knicks couldn't win at this quick pace, and had to shut down Charlotte's offense. They did so with the thoroughness of a tidal wave attacking a sand castle.

The Hornets scored only 22 points over the last 18 minutes and lost 111-95. Immediately after building the 10-point lead, the Hornets went scoreless for seven possessions. The Knicks badgered Charlotte's outside shooters, and never allowed Johnson to regain his rhythm after returning to the game with five minutes left in the third quarter.

It was the best defense the Hornets faced all season. Yet Bristow wouldn't give the Knicks a single compliment. Not one.

"It was us totally," said Bristow. "We can get the pace the way we want it. Basically, we stopped moving offensively."

The Knicks thought Bristow was downright crazy.

"That's typical Allan Bristow," said Doc Rivers. "First Reggie Miller, now Allan Bristow." Miller had talked trash through the entire first round. Now Bristow refused to acknowledge the obvious.

"He's got to say what he wants to make it look good for him back home," said Knicks reserve Anthony Mason. "What makes a team bad offensively? If they were out there on offense by themselves, I'm sure they wouldn't have lost the ball, thrown it away or missed shots. Look at it on face value."

Exclusively on face value, Bristow sounded like a nut or a fool, perhaps both. But in fact he was playing mind games with both the Knicks and his own players. First off, Bristow wasn't going to give the Knicks the satisfaction of confirming their self-opinion. That would serve only to strengthen New York's confidence, the last thing Bristow wanted. Also, Bristow didn't want anyone thinking in the Hornets' locker room that they were being outclassed. Bristow fell back on the season's themes— focus on your strengths, not the opponents'; run hard and good things will happen.

In fact, there were positives in this game for the Hornets. Minus their leading scorer, the Hornets had built a 10-point lead on the other team's floor. They had done so by luring the Knicks into a tempo faster than they could handle.

It's much easier to speed up a deliberate team than slow down a team that prefers to run. Given the chance to run, players revert to their playground instincts and break for the basket. Riley knew that, and so did his players.

"We can't get random, there has to be some kind of system," said Knicks point guard Greg Anthony. "In the first half, we just ran them. It's a lot easier to score points like that. But then we get caught up in their game. We've done it in spurts."

As Bogues put it, "I loved that game. If we continue to play like that, we win the series."

Even Riley agreed: "They've played that game for 82 nights. They're better than anybody else in the league at it, because they're all conditioned to it."

Indeed, the Hornets felt good about their chances still. The Celtics series had taught them all they needed was a split in New York to take control of the series. Gill was so brimming with confidence that he told New York reporters on a conference call that the Hornets clearly had more talent than the Knicks; the Knicks' only advantage was their comparative experience.

Actually, that wasn't a boast, it was the truth. After Ewing, there was nothing special about New York's roster. John Starks was emerging as a top 50 player, but he had to spend a year in the minor-league CBA before making New York's roster. Charles Oakley and Charles Smith were OK, but the Hornets would never trade Larry Johnson and Kendall Gill for those two. And Doc Rivers was a journeyman nearing the end of his career.

However, Gill missed the importance of the Knicks' greatest strength, chemistry. Pat Riley wove them into a team that achieved more than their combined talents would suggest. They mugged other teams because that was the only way they could beat the Chicago Bulls or Phoenix Suns. They have two scorers, Ewing and Starks, and several tough, disciplined guys like Oakley and Rivers willing to do whatever Riley said would make them win.

If talent alone always prevailed, then Andre Agassi would be the No. 1 tennis player in the world and Jim Courier would be some unknown qualifier. Courier understands the discipline needed to be the best tennis player in the world. Agassi would rather do "Image is everything" commercials. Courier would appreciate how the Knicks won 60 of 82 regular-season games.

Actually, the only Knick who didn't realize his potential, and who appeared grossly out of place, was Smith. He'd used impending free agency to leverage the Los Angeles Clippers into trading him to New York. The Knicks needed his apparent scoring skills and versatility to play all three frontcourt positions. Unfortunately, Smith excelled at none of those positions. He has the height of a center, but the instincts of a soft small forward.

Strangely enough, the Knicks signed Smith just after the season to a six-year, $21 million guaranteed contract. He certainly didn't deserve it, based on his season. One league executive speculated that either the Knicks promised him that deal when the trade was made or the Knicks just ran scared that Smith would go elsewhere and they'd get no compensation. New York general manager Dave Checketts took considerable heat the previous summer for losing Xavier McDaniel to the Celtics because Checketts dragged his feet on re-signing McDaniel.

If there was an unhappy camper among the Hornets entering Game 2, it had to be Mike Gminski. With Johnson hurt, G-man started the second quarter and immediately hit a hook over Ewing. For two minutes, he set screens, grabbed a rebound and knocked down a pass in the trap. Then, Bristow called a timeout, and Gminski was back out, as Mourning returned to the game.

Reinserting Mourning was never a bad move, but Gminski had done nothing wrong. Untypically, Gminski blew up at the end of the bench, throwing his warm-up pants to the floor and pacing off his rage during a timeout.

Gminski figured to see even less time the rest of the series, because Johnson had recovered by Game 2 from his leg injury. There was a bit of a scare in practice Tuesday, when Johnson's leg stiffened up. But a second set of X-rays confirmed he was fine. Johnson just needed to stretch more before playing on Wednesday.

Game 1 taught the Hornets that the only way to beat the Knicks was to become more like them. Match them shove for shove, sneer for sneer. And for 9 1/2 minutes of the second half of Game 2, the Hornets were as nasty as anything the Knicks had seen this season. From down 65-58 with 6 1/2 minutes left in the third quarter, the Hornets led 83-71. The Hornets held the Knicks to a single field goal in that span by fouling constantly and daring the Knicks to beat them with free throws.

One play with 9:43 left in the fourth quarter epitomized the Hornets' approach. Sidney Green knocked Charles Oakley to the floor rather than give up a reverse layup. A nine-year veteran, Green knew instantly he was flirting with a flagrant foul that would have given the Knicks two free throws plus another possession. So he quickly reached down to help Oakley to his feet, a goodwill gesture meant for the referees' notice.

But Bogues noticed the gesture first, and got in Green's face. Actually, it was Green's chest, considering Green is 6-9 and Bogues 5-3, but Bogues lit into Green.

"Fuck him! Don't pick him up!" Bogues screamed at Green.

The meaning was obvious — if playoff basketball was about mayhem, then the Hornets could deal out as many bruises as the Knicks.

Oakley made one of two free throws, then David Wingate scored at the other end to give the Hornets a 13-point lead with 8 1/2 minutes left. Pat Riley's team was being slaughtered by a team that had appropriated its persona, and Riley was out of ideas. Essentially out of desperation, he inserted rookie Hubert Davis, a decent shooting guard from North Carolina.

Davis is better known for his altar-boy personality than his skills. Originally, North Carolina offered him a scholarship not because he was a great prospect, but because he was a hard worker and the nephew of former Tar Heels great Walter Davis. Davis's desire and Dean Smith's tutoring had turned him into a late first-round pick. But his presence in the game at this point looked like a sign of surrender.

Instead, it was the Knicks' salvation.

With 3:30 left, the Hornets led 91-83 on Larry Johnson's dunk. All they had to do was tread water the rest of the game to tie the series. But the Knicks scored off their next four possessions, and the Hornets scored off only one of four. Bogues missed a wide-open 15-footer, David Wingate missed two free throws and the Hornets were charged with a 24-second violation just before Kendall Gill threw in a layup. Had any one of those possessions resulted in a point, the Hornets would have won.

Instead, Davis scored the fourth quarter's last five points on a drive, then a marvelous three-pointer with 43 seconds left that eventually threw the game to overtime.

"I've been in 150, 200 playoff games, and I've never been in one like this," Riley said afterward. "To be so dead in the water . . . things started to happen and then the kid came in."

Patrick Ewing won it with a 15-footer with 35 seconds left in overtime. Ewing's shot just beat the 24-second clock. But the winning shot was almost anticlimactic. The Hornets' collapse in the fourth quarter — four points in the last 4:45 — was the dominant topic of conversation.

"Each turnover, each missed shot had to make them tighter," said Rivers. "It's an eight-point lead. . . it's a six-point lead. . . oh, no!"   And Rivers couldn't resist needling Bristow for his ongoing refusal to credit the Knicks' defense for the Hornets' troubles.

"Oh, no. We're terrible defensively," Rivers mocked.

Bristow was testy when asked by a reporter if the Knicks' defense in both fourth quarters might be playing on the Hornets' minds.

"I think it plays on your minds!" Bristow snapped at a room full of media. The series was slipping away. Now it was essential for the Hornets to win both games in Charlotte to have any realistic chance of advancing.

"This is a playoff. You're supposed to be able to bounce back," Johnson said. "We are professionals."

Professionals, yes, but they were still kids. They had played two of their best games of the year without winning either one. How many more times could this happen before the Hornets would just give up?

Green had managed to work his way off the bench into steady minutes late in the season. He'd become what Mike Gminski was supposed to be — the fourth big man, a tough veteran who wasn't hesitant to use up his fouls wrestling with a Patrick Ewing. Gminski still had the will to be such a player, but Bristow just didn't have faith in Gminski's body anymore.

"Sidney gives us a toughness we need," Bristow said between the second and third games of the series.

Green wasn't quite so complimentary toward Bristow, saying he thought the deciding difference in the series had been Pat Riley.

Certainly, it's no insult to suggest a particular coach is not yet a Pat Riley. But the New York media saw this as controversy, as they did Green's public suggestion to Mourning that he stop socializing with Ewing until after the series had concluded.

Mourning, Ewing, and Georgetown coach John Thompson were dining together throughout the playoff series. Both the Knicks coaches and some Hornets players thought this a little strange. The Hornets' concern was that by playing big brother on off days, Ewing was subconsciously softening Mourning up.

Thompson said this was a ridiculous theory, that in fact he had to regularly shut up their dinner-time trash talking just to finish eating. Thompson was particularly sarcastic when told Green had questioned whether these Georgetown reunions were appropriate during the playoffs.

"Who?" Thompson asked.

Sidney Green, a reporter repeated.

"Enough said," Thompson cracked, suggesting Sidney Green did not have the status to advise Mourning on his social schedule.

Dinner with Ewing couldn't have hurt before Game 3. For the first time in their seven meetings, Mourning dramatically outplayed Ewing in a 110-106 Charlotte victory. Mourning outscored Ewing 34-26. More importantly, he held Ewing to 13-of-31 shooting. Any time Ewing shoots that badly, the Knicks have virtually no chance of winning.

Ewing camouflages the Knicks' severe lack of scoring because he is so versatile. Play him to drive, and he swished 15-foot jump shots like a small forward. Stray out of the lane to defend that jump shot, and he drives by for a jump hook.

"We have the same type of moves, but he's more developed at this point. He's a more skillful player than I am, so I have to outthink him," Mourning said.

In this case, that meant pushing Ewing far enough from the lane that when he finally catches the ball, he's already out of position. Mourning was so effective at pushing Ewing out of his favorite spots in Game 3 that the Knicks gushed afterward. This wasn't some psychological game — Rivers and Riley had the experience to appreciate the emergence of a star.

"I've never seen a man play like that at such heights, so relentless," said Rivers. "He comes at you and comes at you and comes at you. He has a Charles Barkley attitude at 6-11.

"He's a throwback to Nate Thurmond."

It was clear Riley had monitored Mourning's evolution throughout the season.

"Early in the year, when he was really trying to find his way, there was a rawness there," Riley said. "But he has dramatically improved. Now he has put the polish on."

Actually, it wasn't Mourning who was most challenged in this series, it was Johnson. He played well, but the Knicks are uniquely equipped to defend him. With two stocky, quick forwards in Charles Oakley and Anthony Mason, New York could run a tag team at Johnson throughout the series. At just the point Johnson thought he'd worn out one, the other would come in to give Johnson new trouble.

It was frustrating, but Johnson retained his sense of humor. At one point, he told his teammates, "I have 1,000-and-one moves, and Oakley knows them all."

Game 4 had Bristow so flustered that he ran over to lead official Joey Crawford to ask what was taking so long to tip off. Bristow was so preoccupied that he failed to notice the lights were still turned down from the national anthem.

"We like to see the players when we officiate," Crawford said, pointing to his eyes. Bristow responded with only a blank stare.

"That's a joke, Allan," Crawford said, suspecting Bristow might be catatonic.

The game turned not on the Ewing-Mourning matchup or on Oakley and Mason's defense, but rather on the shooting skills of a forgotten veteran.

Rolando Blackman, brought in from the Dallas Mavericks to give the Knicks another scoring option, hit a 20-footer to effectively end the Hornets' season. The shot, with 5.4 seconds left, gave the Knicks the winning points, 94-92, and a commanding 3-1 lead in the series.

The Hornets had defended the play well. John Starks started out with the ball, but Muggsy Bogues forced him to give it up to Davis. The Hornets effectively separated Davis from

Ewing, so Davis drove, then kicked the ball out to Blackman at the top of the key.

From there, instinct took over. Blackman had spent most of the season on the bench, constantly injured. This one shot would earn his salary for the season. Shooting was the gift that kept Blackman in the NBA 12 seasons.

"My hand was right there," David Wingate recalled, stretching to a point near what would have been Blackman's head. Not close enough. The shot fell through, giving the Knicks their lead.

The Hornets had squandered all their full timeouts, so they couldn't just stop the game and inbound the ball from halfcourt. Getting the ball across the midcourt line, then calling a 20-second timeout left the Hornets with 3.9 seconds. Assistant coach Bill Hanzlik took his troubles out on the Charlotte Coliseum timekeeper, running to midcourt and slamming his fist on the padded table. The implication was transparent — to Hanzlik, the timekeeper had an unstated obligation to the home team to dawdle in turning the clock back on after the basket.

Integrity is so inconvenient when you're trying to win a game. This wasn't the first time Hanzlik had made a fool of himself trying to influence the Coliseum timer's judgment.

With so little time left to create a shot, Bogues ended up with the ball in the lane trying to drive. He zigged. The ball he was dribbling zagged. The final horn sounded, and the Hornets trailed 3-1.

"I was headed to the hole," Bogues said. "I had a clear path."

Riley was generous, saying his team had assembled the "great escape" to take that lead. But in fact, this series was settled. The Hornets said all the right things about fighting on, but their eyes said they knew they were beaten. At practice the next day, those who refused to fib just said nothing to Charlotte reporters. Mourning joked his way out of an interview — "make it up, y'all do anyway," he said as he jumped into his Range Rover.

Gminski did a little standup routine in the style of comedian Steve Martin: "OK, how about every cliche in 30 seconds — back against the wall. . . do or die. . . one game and out. . . ."

The gallows humor said the Hornets were ready for the beach or the golf course or wherever else they blew off steam over the summer. Riley, of all people, provided some consolation and perspective.

"They're a team on the climb. They're making a nice, innocent climb," Riley had said the previous Saturday. "But it isn't about what they do this year. It's about them growing from it and coming back next year more mature and experienced.

"It isn't a one-year deal."

Bogues appreciated Riley's compliments, but he didn't want to think about next season, not yet anyway. This one had been too much fun to imagine it ending.

"If a bounce here or there had gone the other way, right now we'd be talking about being up 3-1," Bogues said.

Bristow tried his best to keep the players from treating another trip to New York as the truck ride to the slaughterhouse. "Hey, what's the worst thing that could happen? You think they'll keep us up there for the summer?" Bristow asked.

"I don't think so."

Johnson picked up three quick fouls in the first half of Game 5, eliminating the Hornets' last chance at extending the series. The final score, 105-101, was respectable, but Charlotte's season was over. The Knicks would advance to face Chicago.

"I think we got the respect, not only of the country, but of the NBA," Bristow said. "We leapfrogged a bunch of teams at the end after people said we'd fold, counted us for dead.

"We're at the point where we're building so much. Our graph keeps going upward."

Bristow felt so good, he finally paid the Knicks a compliment. . . sort of.

"I was expecting a more physical series," Bristow said. "They've taken . . . what would you call it, the *criminal element* out of the Knicks. Now it's a team you can almost root for."

Almost, huh? Well, like Doc Rivers said, that's just typical Allan Bristow.

Doug Collins, the former Chicago Bulls coach who does analysis for TNT cable, put the Hornets' post-season in excellent perspective.

"The greatest thing that ever happened to Charlotte was beating Chicago and Milwaukee the last two games of the regular season," Collins said. "If they hadn't, the playoffs would have been three and out. By positioning themselves against Boston and then getting the opportunity when Reggie Lewis went down, although I'm not saying they wouldn't have won the series anyway, really helped.

"Now they're seeing what playoff basketball is really all about, against the Knicks. This team will grow from that."

The players assembled at Grady Cole the next morning to clean out their lockers and leave for a small parade the Chamber of Commerce had arranged uptown. Gattison lingered the longest in the locker room, his hand poised over an ice chest. Did he need an ice pack for his aching back, a Gatorade to quench his thirst?

Neither. The off-season had officially begun.

"Wanna beer?" Gattison asked, pulling Budweiser from the chest.

No thanks, Gatt, you keep it. You earned it.

CHAPTER EIGHTEEN

"If he's here the first day of camp, one of you won't be."

Hornets owner George Shinn wanted Kendall Gill off his team at any cost — even if that meant releasing him and getting nothing in return. Proud and easily hurt, Shinn had taken Gill's posturing so personally that he privately compared Gill to a cancer on a regular basis.

That position drove a wedge through the four-year relationship of Shinn and coach Allan Bristow. Bristow wanted to retain Gill if at all possible, and Shinn just couldn't stomach paying Gill even a minimum contract.

Finally, Shinn laid down the law in a midsummer meeting with Bristow, team president Spencer Stolpen, and director of player personnel Dave Twardzik.

"If he's here the first day of camp, one of you won't be," Stolpen recalls Shinn saying. Stolpen was quick to add that Shinn was joking. Still, the message was clear — trading Gill wasn't an option or a suggestion. It was an order: *Get the best deal you can, but get it quick.*

The Hornets had finally gotten a face-to-face reading on Gill's position in a Chicago meeting in early June. Stolpen and Twardzik met with Gill and agent Arn Tellem before the Chicago pre-draft camp. Stolpen's agenda at the meeting was a simple one.

"I didn't want a confrontation. I'd just never talked to him before about what he wanted," Stolpen said. "I told him, 'You don't have to justify your position. I'm going to ask you what you want and a couple of times during the conversation I'm going to ask why. Not to debate you, but to know what I need to know as this team's president.'"

Stolpen doesn't discuss the details of Gill's reply, except to acknowledge that Gill wanted out of Charlotte. But others with knowledge of the meeting say Gill claimed he couldn't reach his basketball potential with Bristow as coach. Gill said Bristow was a good person, but that his passing-game offense didn't sufficiently highlight Gill.

Bristow was even willing to resign as coach and move into the front office (an option previously structured into his contract), if that was the issue that would keep Gill in Charlotte. However, Stolpen made it clear that replacing Bristow as coach wasn't an option, that no one player would dictate such a decision.

Essentially, Hornets management thought Gill's argument was a transparent rationalization. Passing game or no passing game, they believed the real problems were that Gill couldn't get along with his teammates, and his ego couldn't handle being upstaged by Larry Johnson and Alonzo Mourning.

Twardzik: "Three years ago, he was No. 1. Two years ago, he was No. 2. This year, he was No. 3, maybe not that. He didn't like it. He felt underappreciated."

Shinn: "He didn't like the front office, his coaches, his teammates, or the town. He wanted out. It got to the point like in some marriages where divorce is unavoidable."

Actually, Shinn questioned this marriage even before he walked down the aisle. He saw various warning signs during the negotiation of Gill's initial contract, after the Hornets drafted Gill No. 5 overall in 1990.

"From the very beginning (dealing with Gill) was a very trying experience," Shinn said. "From Allan throwing his agent up against the wall, it was an uncomfortable situation, a strain. It's never been a good relationship."

Stolpen says Shinn was offended when Gill and his father declined his invitation to fly to Charlotte and participate in the 1990 negotiations. Shinn meeting with Rex Chapman and his father in 1988 had broken the team's first big contract impasse, and Shinn thought that personal touch was important to the way he preferred doing business.

Shinn always thought Gill would bolt Charlotte at his first opportunity, and Shinn's instincts appear to be accurate. A college administrator was dining near Gill in a Charlotte restaurant the night before Gill signed with the Hornets in 1990. That administrator told *Observer* columnist Ron Green that he overheard Tellem promising Gill he'd have him out of Charlotte in a couple of years.

Stolpen says Tellem's trade request in January 1993 wasn't the first such letter the team received. According to Stolpen, Tellem sent a "play him or trade him" letter to the Hornets during Gill's rookie season, because Gill wasn't satisfied with how then-coach Gene Littles used Gill.

Stolpen says the clearest warning sign that Gill wanted out came before the 1992-93 season, as Stolpen searched for salary-cap room to sign Mourning. Gill was vocal in demanding that the Hornets hurry up and sign the center the team so badly needed. So Stolpen approached Tellem, asking that Gill set aside $50,000 of his salary for that season to clear cap room.

Stolpen says he promised Tellem to make good on the $50,000, with plenty of interest, as part of Gill's next contract with the Hornets. Tellem called back to say Gill wouldn't do it because such a move would lower his one-year qualifying offer before he'd reach unrestricted free agency. In other words, Stolpen deduced, Gill never intended to sign long-term in Charlotte.

Shinn's discomfort with Gill grew considerably during the 1992-93 season. Shinn tends to be protective of Muggsy Bogues, so the Peter Vecsey column speculating that Bogues was slighting Gill disturbed Shinn greatly. Gill told Bogues he wasn't the source of Vecsey's information. However, two Hornets administrators say Vecsey told them Gill was the source of those comments.

"I know there were some things in the press, but he pretty much did it to himself," Shinn said of Gill's reputation in Charlotte. "I don't think anyone put words in his mouth. That goes back to being a learning experience for everybody. I know he'll be smarter in the future, a better spokesman for he and his teammates."

While no one thought Gill would be ostracized if he returned to the Hornets, there was little affection remaining for him around the Hornets' locker room. The general tone among the players was that if Gill wanted to leave, hurry up and move him out. Some teammates nicknamed him "Solo" behind his back for the way he isolated himself.

Larry Johnson says he has no hard feelings toward Gill. However, Johnson clearly feels Gill mishandled the whole situation.

"Kendall was trying to get what he's worth, and I have no problem with that, but going around saying he doesn't want to be here—his teammates, this, his teammates, that—that causes friction," said Johnson.

"We spoke when we spoke, but clearly our relation wasn't the same as the first year."

"Kendall was more of a loner," Shinn said. "He could be disappointed if his teammates didn't pursue him as a friend. But it was just as important that he go out and make friends. When somebody you work with is upset, disgruntled, it affects you. It has to. (In basketball) it makes their legs a little bit slower, the hoop a little bit smaller."

Gill and Tellem did not accept an invitation in September to be interviewed for this book.

Once Shinn made his feelings clear, the question was not whether to trade Gill but how. The Hornets went back to the Los Angeles Clippers before the draft and worked toward a deal. Shinn was nearly as motivated to acquire Greensboro's Danny Manning as he was to rid himself of Gill.

The Clippers would give up Manning, plus overweight forward John Williams, in exchange for Gill, Kenny Gattison, and two first-round picks. The deal fell through because the Hornets wouldn't give up Gattison. Charlotte thought it was already offering plenty, considering Manning had repeatedly said he would leave the Clippers the minute he becomes an unrestricted free agent July 1, 1994.

However, Stolpen said a Clippers official told him, "(owner) Donald Sterling honestly believes Danny Manning will stay in Los Angeles."

That seemed even less likely when Manning immediately signed his one-year qualifying offer the first day of July, 1993.

That was a problem not only for the Clippers, but also for the Hornets, because it meant Manning couldn't sign a long-term contract extension until July 1994, even if he was traded.

The Hornets made their obligatory qualifying offer to Gill — 125% of his $1.9 million salary for 1992-93 — to retain the option of matching any offer sheet another NBA team might sign with Gill. Then Gill went off on job interviews, first with the New York Knicks, then with the two Los Angeles teams, then finally with the Seattle SuperSonics.

The job interviews, which were covered extensively by the Charlotte media, rankled Hornets fans, who weren't used to their stars negotiating with the competition. Gill compared it to an IBM employee talking to Apple. However, to average Charlotteans, Gill wasn't just looking for more money, he was running from his troubles and turning his back on their town.

At the start of the summer, Gill was perceived to have great leverage over the situation. Because he was just a season away from unrestricted free agency, he could effectively void any trade to a city where he didn't want to play. For instance, the Pistons called, but the conversation ended quickly when the Hornets said Gill simply wouldn't sign a long-term contract to play in Detroit.

Stolpen said the other problem was that many NBA teams treated Gill as damaged goods. Those teams understandably wondered how Gill would be happy somewhere else if he couldn't be happy with an emerging power like the Hornets. Stolpen said the typical reaction around the league was, "What the hell do I need Kendall Gill for?" Particularly so at an asking price of about $4 million per season, plus whatever the Hornets would receive in trade.

However, Stolpen knew time was on his side. He correctly predicted that the longer Gill sat without a contract, the more flexible he would become. "To some extent, Kendall didn't know how to control the bluff," Stolpen said. "I wasn't as impatient as everybody else. My whole goal was to take control of the situation as the summer went on. To put up with all the shit and smile."

The Knicks, Lakers, and Clippers balked at the thought of paying Gill all that money, plus barter away plenty in trade to acquire him. Seattle emerged as the only team Gill was interested in that would pay him what he wanted. Faced with eroding marketability, Gill started sending out various signals in late August that he might want to return to Charlotte after all. However, Stolpen doubts that represented a sincere change of heart by Gill.

"They told us that between Charlotte and Seattle, he'd rather stay here. But he won't stay for less money," Stolpen recalled. "I don't think Kendall really changed his mind about Charlotte. It was not because he wanted to be here, but because he saw the grass wasn't greener in Seattle."

To be traded to Seattle or anywhere else, Gill had to be resigned. The NBA does not allow a team to trade the rights to its unsigned veterans. In fact, teams technically aren't supposed to discuss trades of their unsigned veterans, but the NBA regularly looks the other way because trading an unhappy player is in everyone's best interest.

Seattle was prepared to pay Gill a first-year salary of $2.185 million, which could have projected to a $4 million average over seven years.

Despite the fact that Seattle would ultimately pay Gill his salary, Stolpen wouldn't agree to that contract. He worried that the deal with Seattle could fall through somehow after Gill resigned, leaving the Hornets with a huge contract for a player the owner wouldn't tolerate.

Seizing the shifted momentum, Stolpen said he'd pay Gill no more than $2 million the first season, which projected out to $3.8 million per season over seven years. More importantly, Stolpen demanded that Gill's contract include a clause that the Hornets could cut Gill before September 15, 1993, and not have to pay Gill a cent.

"Those numbers were not out of line (with the market) and there were no outs (escape clauses benefiting Gill). I knew I could trade that contract," Stolpen said.

And if he couldn't, Stolpen had the option of cutting Gill outright without pay, which placated Shinn. Actually, Stolpen acknowledged, if the Hornets had cut Gill "for skill" as the contract read, Tellem probably could have won an arbitration hearing with the Hornets, and restored the contract guarantee.

That Gill and Tellem agreed to such a clause favoring the Hornets shows how their leverage slipped as the summer passed. Stolpen played tough guy, telling Gill and Tellem that Gill's only other option was the one-year qualifying offer. He added that if Gill signed that one-year deal, the Hornets would exile him to the bench his last season in Charlotte.

The Hornets wanted Seattle forward Derrick McKey, a versatile player who would have fit well in a passing game. But McKey was off-limits, and the Sonics instead offered Philadelphia's first-round pick in 1994, which Seattle controlled in a complex series of trades. The Sixers were bad, and figured to be worse in 1993-94 as they rebuilt, so there was a good chance Philadelphia's pick would be a top five selection.

Still, a lottery pick was not the perfect fit with the Hornets' needs. Shinn had lost his patience with signing top picks after the Mourning impasse. And the way the lottery worked, there was no guarantee the Sixers' pick would be top three, even if they were the worst team in the league.

Ultimately, though, Seattle was the only viable deal out there. So the Hornets traded Gill to the Sonics for the Sixers' pick (technically it was the best first-rounder between Philadelphia, Phoenix, Seattle and Charlotte), plus veterans Dana Barros and Eddie Johnson to balance the two teams' salary caps. Then, Twardzik immediately set out to barter that draft pick for a veteran with a stable, long-term contract.

Twardzik immediately called Philadelphia.

It made so much sense. Who needed Philly's first-rounder more than Philly? Besides, the Sixers were overloaded at shooting guard with two former all-stars in Hersey Hawkins and Jeff Hornacek. Earlier in the summer, the Hornets had talked deal with the Knicks and Sixers about a swap of Gill to New York, Charles Oakley to Philly and Hawkins to Charlotte. But New York wouldn't give up Oakley to acquire Gill.

Neither Hawkins nor Hornacek figured to be around by the time the Sixers were again contenders. Superficially, Hornacek looked like the better choice for Charlotte because he could swing between shooting guard and the point. But at 30, Hornacek was two years older than Hawkins. The last thing Bristow needed was another high-priced, 30-something player of decaying skills on the bench. So when the Sixers offered either guard, Bristow picked Hawkins.

The price Philadelphia demanded in return was steep. In addition to the pick and journeymen Sidney Green and Barros, the Sixers had to have the rights to rookie guard Greg Graham, who the Hornets had drafted 17th overall. Sixers owner Harold Katz said losing Graham would be an absolute deal-breaker.

The Hornets gave in, igniting weeks of criticism from their followers. To the fans, the Hornets had once again been stripped bare in a trade, giving up four assets for one. Never mind that the Hornets had 16 players for 12 roster spots before the trade. Never mind that Hawkins could be counted on for 18 points a game, or that he shot better than 40% from three-point range. To the average Charlotte fan, this was robbery.

The Hornets have to take some blame for that exaggerated perception. The Hornets had never drafted as low as 17th before, so the team tried a little too hard between late June and August to hype Graham's potential. After the trade, the Hornets were bitten by their own spin control.

Actually, according to Stolpen, the team had a harder time giving up Barros than Graham. Bristow had seen with Bogues in Charlotte and Michael Adams in Denver that quick, little point guards thrive on the passing game. Though 5-11, Barros had the quickness and three-point range to stabilize the point-guard position behind Bogues. Tony Bennett would have sat and watched.

But to Bristow, the most important goal — perhaps the only goal — was to find a talented and mature replacement for Gill. Bristow felt blessed that the Hornets could find a player as skilled as Hawkins, whose ego could still tolerate being third-best player in Charlotte.

Based on his comments, it was clear Hawkins had been briefed about the controversy surrounding Gill's departure.

"It's not my job to come in and rule over guys," said Hawkins. "I'm not trying to take away the limelight from Alonzo or Larry. They can have it. I've never had a problem with ego. The bottom line is that everybody is happy and you're winning basketball games."

Bristow clearly loved Hawkins' approach. "There's no question Kendall can jump higher or is more explosive. Maybe Kendall has a talent edge," Bristow said. "But as far as chemistry — blending — the team will be better off with Hawkins."

Within days of the trade, several framed prints of Gill as a Hornet had been stripped from the walls of the team's office complex and stacked in a corner room. It looked like one of those purgings in China, where murals of past leaders now in disfavor are destroyed to further the cause.

The pictures were gone, but the bitterness remained.

"It was nothing that we did," Stolpen concluded. "He found a market that wanted him, a team that paid him what he wanted. But I don't think he'll be happy there.

"I blame it on the parents and the people around him."

Strangely enough, the Hornets' greatest short-term loss from the two trades might be Green, who had worked his way off the bench for 10 steady minutes per game in the playoffs. Green wasn't worth the $1.4 million the Hornets would have had to pay him in 1993-94, but at least he was contributing. Gminski was supposed to be that fourth big man, but Bristow didn't seem to have confidence in him over the last third of the season.

With Green gone and Gminski fighting Bristow's perceptions, Kenny Gattison takes on even greater responsibility in 1993-94.

"We've got to get 30 minutes a game from him — productive minutes, not just bricking up free throws. The key is Gatt," Bristow said. "Gatt struggled last season. He's got to play well, and he did at the end of the season. He's got to relieve Larry and Zo for 82 games."

Bristow's point was illustrated by a second straight off-season injury to Johnson. The previous summer, it was worn knee cartilage. This time it was a herniated disc. Both ailments were dangerous signs of wear and tear. Johnson's body showed far too much mileage for a pro entering his third season. He played 6,370 minutes over two seasons, and his 3,323 minutes last season were the most in the NBA.

That Johnson played so long was a compliment, yet also a curse, particularly during that trying, six-game trip, when he played 244 of a possible 288 minutes. Bristow appeared to regret over the summer playing Johnson so much on that trip.

"It didn't hurt us then, but two weeks later, *boom!* It hurt us," Bristow recalled. "You could see it in Larry's play."

Bristow's other superstar, Mourning, had no such problems with playing time. The challenge with Mourning is not using him up, but rather reining him in. The magnificent rage with which Mourning plays is the catalyst to his success. But it is also potentially his handicap. Somewhere along the line, Mourning has to learn the difference between constructive intensity and destructive anger.

Twardzik took Mourning aside last season to pass on a message from a friendly referee. The official had warned Twardzik that Mourning was quickly gaining a reputation as a complainer and a trash-talker. Twardzik wisely told Mourning that such a reputation, if widespread, meant Mourning would never get a judgment call in his favor, that referees would subconsciously be predisposed against him. Twardzik said Mourning took the advice to heart.

Somewhat like Bristow, Mourning has a highly personalized sense of right and wrong, combined with a stubborn streak. It's admirable how he places his values above personal gain. For instance, over the summer he passed up a guest appearance on a television series because the taping would have meant postponing a scheduled visit to a home for troubled children. Mourning sticks by his commitments, and that's downright noble.

However, his refusal to compromise over sometimes trivial inconveniences is not. The confrontation over a woman reporter in the locker room is as good an example as any. For Mourning to reach his full potential, he has to stop sweating the little things, and pick his battles more carefully.

Mourning's emotions still need some work, as Stolpen illustrated with two stories over the summer. First off, Mourning did so much trash-talking after blocking one or two of Shaquille O'Neal's shots during Magic Johnson's summer all-star game, that Magic asked him to tone it down. That is not in the spirit of a summer all-star game, but it is classic Mourning, never able to downshift in a game.

The other example was of greater concern to Stolpen. Mourning and his fiance were driving through Washington in a new Mercedes over the summer when some kids in another car recognized him and asked him for money. Mourning declined and drove off, but the kids followed him, tail-ending his car with theirs. Mourning unbuckled his seat belt, intending to confront the youths over his fiance's objection.

The other car sped off before Mourning reached the punks. But in an age when Michael Jordan's father could be gunned down in his Lexus at a North Carolina rest stop, this story shocked Hornets management. They surmise one of those youths could easily have pulled out a gun and shot Charlotte's franchise center. Again, it's just Mourning's way — never back down.

Shinn was downright bubbly at the news conference introducing Hawkins to Charlotte. He'd ridded himself of Gill, he had a new star to show off to the fans, and plans to make the team even stronger the summer of 1994.

"Hopefully, there's another deal, which I can't talk about," Shinn said, tipping his hat to the NBA's tampering rule. "But everybody knows (it's Danny Manning)."

Shinn might have been bound by a gag order, but Manning's agent, Ron Grinker, told everyone with ears that Manning's first choice upon becoming an unrestricted free agent next summer is Charlotte. Adding Manning at small forward could be the move that pushes Charlotte into an NBA final, assuming Bristow can blend all that scoring into a cohesive unit.

Of course, the Hornets would first have to assemble the salary-cap room to make Manning a competitive offer. One team official figures the cap will reach about $17.5 million after the coming season. By renouncing the rights to Johnny Newman, Kevin Lynch, Eddie Johnson and Mike Gminski in July 1994, the Hornets predict they could be about $2 million under that cap. With a first-year salary of $2 million, the Hornets could build a seven-year offer for Manning of $3.8 million.

If Manning wouldn't sign for that, then he probably wouldn't end up a Hornet.

"We're going to take a run at him," Twardzik concluded. "That's for sure."

Two days before the start of training camp, the Hornets rounded up local media for what they promised would be a "major announcement."

That was no exaggeration.

The Hornets had signed Johnson to the richest contract in U.S. team sports history—an eight-year extension of his previous deal that would pay him $84 million over the next 12 years.

Shinn, the man whose pen used to shake at signing any check, had just agreed to pay a single player more than twice the $32.5 million he originally was charged by the NBA to start the team six years earlier.

"Not only my pen, everything I had quivered," Shinn joked.

Shinn had just one reservation about locking up Johnson to this career-ending contract.

"I told him 'The only thing I ask is that after you sign that long-term contract, you don't sit back on your laurels,'" Shinn said. "I told him to be that much more of a force, that much more committed."

Johnson said the deal could only change him for the better, to be more assertive, more of a leader.

"Hey I'm still the same guy as that $10 million fella yesterday," Johnson joked.

Which is just what Shin hoped to hear.

"He is the leader of this team and he will be the leader," Shinn said. "He's going to bring an NBA championship to Charlotte."

"We might be called crazy tomorrow, but we might be called geniuses in three years."